D1229062

Debates in Economic History

Edited by Peter Mathias

Great Britain
and the Colonies
1815–1865

Great Britain and the Colonies 1815–1865

edited with an introduction by
A. G. L. SHAW

METHUEN & CO LTD
11 NEW FETTER LANE LONDON EC4

First published 1970 by Methuen & Co Ltd
Introduction © 1970 by A. G. L. Shaw
Printed in Great Britain by
Richard Clay (The Chaucer Press), Ltd.,
Bungay, Suffolk

HB *416 14240 0*
UP *416 29940 7*

This title is available in both hard and paperback editions.
The paperback edition is sold subject to the condition that it
shall not, by way of trade or otherwise, be lent, re-sold, hired
out, or otherwise circulated without the publisher's prior
consent in any form of binding or cover other than that in
which it is published and without a similar condition including
this condition being imposed on the subsequent purchaser.

Distributed in the U.S.A.
by Barnes & Noble Inc.

LIBRARY
ALMA COLLEGE
ALMA, MICHIGAN

Contents

Preface

The fate of any historical interpretation about a problem or a period is to become itself re-interpreted. Not infrequently when a reigning hypothesis gets unseated, clarity and simplicity give place to complexity, conflicting evidence, a *mélange* of contributory causes. And, as the inexact science which history will undoubtedly remain, introducing 'multi-variables' is to lose at once that sense of certainty and intellectual satisfaction given by the clean-cutting edge of a single-cause explanation. Major themes in the explanation of nineteenth-century British history are currently in process of re-examination. Not accidentally among the most important of these are some which particularly concern issues involving the relationship between a conceptual position (in contemporary economic thought or philosophy), economic policy (assumptions and intentions embodied in legislation) and the empirical record of what actually happened. When ideas are checked against policy, policy intentions judged against results, general theories tested against the operations of the actual institutions through which they had to be implemented within specific local contexts, the gaps between theory and practice, the incompatibilities between aims and results are exposed. The objective significance of the ideas and the policy in producing the results which occurred are likely to suffer more attrition in this process – however important the theories may have been in influencing changes in policy. Historians (and politicians) know that the influence of an argument *ex ante* has little necessary connection with its truth *ex post facto* – provided that enough people believe it at the time.

One such area of re-interpretation is the debate about the role of government in the Victorian economy – whether acting internally or with intervention overseas. The incompatibilities between a supposedly *laissez-faire*, classical-economics inspired,

Benthamite-promoted theoretical orthodoxy and the progressive intervention encouraged by industrialization and
urbanization, now known as the 'administrative revolution'
in government, is paralleled by the debate about anti-imperialism and the growth of empire. Subsequent volumes will be
addressed to the internal issues. This book demonstrates how
complex were the theoretical arguments about the utility of
colonies and empire which also characterized these decades.
It may help to restore a balance which has recently been
dominated by the controversy conflating the post-1870 thesis
concerning imperialism advanced by Hobson and the post-1896
trends interpreted by Hilferding and Lenin. The main burden
of the challenge to Hobson and Lenin was the assertion that
the facts do not square with the assumptions for the period in
question nor for the reverse of the position implied in the
thesis in the pre-1870 period. Many facets of the later theorizing
were argued out in sophisticated terms by contemporaries
in the first half of the nineteenth century. Assumptions of an
anticipated falling rate of profit from overabundant capital
(at a time when other latter-day assumptions presumed that the
transcendent claims of increasing investment made falling
levels of consumption virtually inevitable); diminishing returns
in agriculture; a Malthusian population crisis; strategic
considerations; as well as the maximization of trade through
international specialization were all used to support colonization and foreign investment in the years when 'free-trade'
theorizing was said to have triumphed.

Professor Shaw shows how *both* these divergent currents of
free trade and colonization – sometimes conflicting but often
complementary – were firmly rooted in the empirical basis of
British economic development *and* in contemporary theoretical
debate. The picture is much more complicated than the older
simplicites allowed. But truth is often complex – and was it not
Lenin who remarked that history is more cunning than any
of us?

PETER MATHIAS

Acknowledgements

The editor and publishers wish to thank the following for permission to reproduce the articles listed below:

Professor John S. Galbraith for 'Myths of the "Little England" Era' (*American Historical Review*, October 1961); Cambridge University Press for 'The Application and Significance of Theories of the Effect of Economic Progress on the Rate of Profit, 1800–1850', by Professor G. S. L. Tucker (*Progress and Profit in British Economic Thought*, 1960); the Economic History Association for 'The Philosophic Radicals and Colonialism', by Professor B. Semmel (*Journal of Modern History*, 1961); Professor J. A. Gallagher for 'The Imperialism of Free Trade', by Professor Gallagher and Dr R. Robinson (*Economic History Review*, August 1953); Dr R. N. Ghosh for 'The Colonization Controversy: R. J. Wilmot-Horton and the Classical Economists' (*Economica*, November 1964); Professor Oliver Mac-Donagh for 'The Anti-Imperialism and Free Trade' (*Economic History Review*, 1962); Dr R. J. Moore for 'Imperialism and Free Trade Policy in India, 1853–1854' (*Economic History Review*, 1964); Dr H. O. Pappé for 'Wakefield and Marx' (*Economic History Review*, 1951); the Southern Economic Association and the University of North Carolina for 'The Development of the Theory of Colonization in English Classical Political Economy' by Professor E. R. Kittrell (*Southern Economic Journal*, 1965); Professor Donald Winch for 'Classical Economists and the Case for Colonization' (*Economica*, November 1963).

Editor's Introduction

The year 1776 remains the date of the publication of Adam Smith's *Wealth of Nations* and of the Declaration of Independence by Britain's revolting colonies in North America, but historians now seem less convinced than they used to be that the theoretical reasonings of the one backed up by the practical lessons of the other ushered in a period of 'anti-imperialism' in Great Britain. 'In his classic attack on the mercantile system, Adam Smith denounced the old colonial system root and branch and went so far as to assert that it would be beneficial to the people of Great Britain if the colonies were given up,' wrote Professor Schuyler in 1945.[1] Many historians have shared this opinion, arguing that after the time lag necessary for their education most nineteenth-century British politicians and publicists came to a similar conclusion, namely that the empire was not worth much, that its expansion should cease, and the public should look forward to, and prepare for, its gradual and peaceful break-up.[2]

Though widespread, this view of English opinion is probably wrong. England had recognized American independence only perforce, and whatever may have been the views of the non-political majority, the government was assuredly representing politically minded opinion in trying to rebuild the empire on lines already laid down. Between 1783 and 1786 the reformed Committee on Trade and Plantations proceeded to renew the old navigation system to suit the new conditions,

[1] R. L. Schuyler, *The Fall of the Old Colonial System* (O.U.P., N.Y., 1945), p. 38; cf. Adam Smith, *The Wealth of Nations* (World's Classics edn., O.U.P., 1904), II, pp. 224–5.

[2] Examples of such writings are C. A. Bodelsen, *Studies in Mid-Victorian Imperialism* (1924. Reprinted, Heinemann, 1960, Kingswood Books on Social History); K. E. Knorr, *British Colonial Theories, 1750–1850* (Univ. of Toronto Press, 1944); Schuyler, op. cit.

and though the 'rising school of Political Economy', basing
their theories on the twin foundations of the *Wealth of Nations*
and the political ideas of Jeremy Bentham, opposed both the
commercial and political restrictions of the colonial system,
and though, according to Professor Knorr, the 'colonial
theories brought forward by the classical economists and the
Philosophic Radicals were never refuted on an intellectually
creditable level of reasoning', yet as he admitted, 'the attachment of large influential groups to the symbols of empire
remained impervious to intellectual arguments', and there remained 'a dogged determination to hold fast to the possession
and exploitation of the remnants of the old Empire'.[1]

Between 1783 and 1815 Britain acquired (despite her much
vaunted renunciation of the Netherlands' Indies to bolster the
power assigned as a barrier against French aggression) Eastern
Australia, Penang and the province Wellesley, vast tracts of
southern and eastern India, Ceylon, the Seychelles, Mauritius,
the Cape Colony in South Africa, Sierra Leone, Trinidad,
Tobago, St Lucia, and parts of Guiana – apart from Malta and
Heligoland in Europe. After the peace, the process went on in
India, Burma, Malaya, Australia, on the Gold Coast, and in
Canada, and although the late nineteenth century is often
looked on as the period in which Empire building reached a
climax – and this may be true of many of the powers – in the
fifty years after 1815, the area of the British Empire expanded
by an average of about 100,000 square miles per year, very little
less than the average annual expansion between 1865 and 1914.[2]
In 1793 Bentham might cry *Emancipate Your Colonies*, and
denounce these as economically worthless, as seeds of war,
expensive to maintain and to defend, and with special reference
to New South Wales, as most inefficient penal institutions; in

[1] Knorr, op. cit., pp. 210–11; cf. Schuyler, op. cit., pp. 67–70. For the re-
furbishing of the Navigation Acts, see V. Harlow, *The Founding of the Second
British Empire, 1763–1793* (2 vols., Longmans, London, 1952 and 1964).

[2] P. Knaplund, *The British Empire, 1815–1939* (London, 1942), *passim*. On this
point I disagree with D. K. Fieldhouse, *The Theory of Capitalist Imperialism*
(London, 1967), pp. xiii–xiv, at least as far as the British Empire is concerned.
Its size in 1914 was rather more than 13,000,000 square miles, of which about
5,000,000 were added in each half of the nineteenth century.

1821 and 1823 James Mill might repeat his arguments, and in 1825 McCulloch might 'defy anybody to point out a single benefit of any sort whatever derived from the possession of Canada',[1] yet the 'practical statesmen' did not agree.

Perhaps, as Bentham and Mill would have argued, this was because of the interests of the 'few', the ruling class, who were looking for jobs and

> places . . . Governorships and judgeships and a long train of et ceteras . . . and above all . . . an additional number of troops and additional portion of the navy . . . generalships and colonelships and captainships and lieutenantships; and in the equipping and supplying of additional portions of army and navy . . . gains, which may be thrown in the way of a friend.

But there were other reasons for imperialism too. If, as Professor Knorr asserts, the 'colonial theories' of Smith and James Mill were not refuted, other justifications for holding colonies were put forward to which these theories were irrelevant; and if he is astonished 'in view of this current of separatism and indifference and the much stronger one of not wanting to augment the encumbrance of empire by extending its boundaries that even the period from 1815 to 1850 produced imperial . . . expansion',[2] it is perhaps because he has not appreciated how strongly the 'counter current' of imperialism (as Dicey might have called it) still ran in political and intellectual circles, as Dr Semmel shows in his article printed below. The idea of a 'climax of anti-imperialism' has been based on a concentration on the opinions expressed by an eloquent few about colonial trade and colonial expenses, and on a superficial identification of the movement for free trade and for the repeal

---

[1] Jeremy Bentham, *Emancipate Your Colonies* (1793), in his *Works* (ed. J. Bowring, Edinburgh, 1837), IV, p. 411; James Mill, *Elements of Political Economy* (1821), and 'Colonies', *Supp. to Encyclopaedia Britannica* (1823); J. R. McCulloch, 'Colonial Policy', *Edinburgh Rev.*, XLII (1825), p. 291, and cf. Knorr, op. cit., p. 262. The article by E. R. Kittrell, 'The Development of the Theory of Colonization in English Classical Political Economy', *Southern Economic Journal*, XXXI (1965) comments on these views (below, p. 46).

[2] Knorr, op. cit., p. 411.

of the Navigation Acts (which, in any case, was not successful until the middle of the century) with an alleged anti-imperialism seemingly effective thirty years earlier, while all other ideas about the colonies have been ignored. Thus insecurely founded, the myth has been buttressed by the ready acceptance of partisan political assertions, such as Disraeli's famous Crystal Palace Speech in 1872:

> If you look to the history of this country since the advent of Liberalism – forty years ago – you will find there has been no effort so continuous, so subtle, supported by so much energy, and carried on with so much ability and acumen, as the efforts of Liberalism to effect the disintegration of the Empire of England.[1]

Of course, though good party propaganda, this is nonsense if applied to more than a sprinkling of the anti-imperialist radicals, and although, as Professor Galbraith has said in the article printed below, such a 'conception of British policy in the mid-nineteenth century, like all distortions, contains an element of truth', yet no 'responsible statesman' held it, and one must agree with Dr Semmel when he declares that the 'reputed mid-Victorian policy of anti-colonialism is a myth'.[2]

In addition Gallagher and Robinson in their now famous article, 'The Imperialism of Free Trade', which caused so many scholars to have further thoughts on the nature of British imperialism in the nineteenth century, have reminded us of what

> ought to be a commonplace, that Great Britain during the so-called anti-imperialist period in the middle of the nineteenth century 'expanded overseas by means of informal

[1] 24 June 1872, quoted W. F. Monypenny and G. E. Buckle, *The Life of Benjamin Disraeli, Earl of Beaconsfield* (in 2 vol. edn., Murray, London, 1929), II, Book V, Chapter 5, pp. 534–5; cf. B. Semmel, 'The Philosophic Radicals and Colonialism', *Journal of Economic History*, XXI (1961), p. 523 (below, p. 77).

[2] John S. Galbraith, 'Myths of the "Little England" Era', *American Historical Review*, LXVII (1961–2), p. 35 (below, p. 27); Semmel, op. cit., p. 513 (below, p. 77). On the question of Parliamentary interest in colonies – see my article, 'British Attitudes to the Colonies, 1820–1850', *Journal of British Studies*, IX (1969), pp. 76–81.

empire' as much as by acquiring dominions in the strict constitutional sense. For purposes of economic analysis it would
clearly be unreal to define imperial history exclusively as the
history of those colonies coloured red on the map. . . . The
common assumption that British governments in the free-
trade era considered empire superfluous arises from over-
estimating the significance of changes in legalistic forms.[1]

As they rightly argue, this is only one side of the coin.
Economic and even political aggression was continuous, but at
certain times and in certain places, opening the door to trade
and investment, or procuring and preserving strategic influence, did not demand large-scale annexation. Hence, while
British expansion was 'vigorous and uninterrupted', it combined 'commercial penetration and political influence' as
required. 'Formal and informal empire' were thus 'essentially
interconnected and to some extent interchangeable', and
British policy might be summed up as 'trade with informal
control of possible trade with rule where necessary'.[2]

This is not to say that such a policy was unchallenged, and
the degree of the 'informal control' imposed certainly varied.
At times this was minimal, for example on occasions in
Argentina and Peru. On other cases it was significant, whether
in Lagos, where changing economic circumstances eventually
led to annexation, or in the Persian Gulf or the Far East.[3] In
his rejoinder to Gallagher and Robinson, Professor Mac-
Donagh rightly emphasizes that some anti-imperialists in their

[1] J. Gallagher and R. Robinson, 'The Imperialism of Free Trade', *Economic
History Review*, 2nd ser., VI (1953), p. 1, (below p. 142); cf. Galbraith, op. cit.,
p. 39 (below p. 34); L. H. Jenks, *The Migration of British Capital* (1927. Reprinted,
Nelson, London, 1963), p. 197; C. R. Fay in *Cambridge History of British Empire*,
II (C.U.P., 1940), p. 399.

[2] J. Gallagher and R. Robinson, op. cit., pp. 11–13 (below pp. 157–8).

[3] W. M. Mathew, 'The Imperialism of Free Trade: Peru, 1820–1870', *Economic
History Review*, 2nd ser., XXI (1968), pp. 562–79; D. C. M. Platt, 'The Imperialism
of Free Trade: some reservations', ibid., pp. 296–306; A. S. Hopkins, 'Economic
Imperialism in West Africa: Lagos 1880–1892', ibid., pp. 580–606; J. B. Kelly,
Britain and the Persian Gulf, 1795–1880 (O.U.P., 1968). Cf. C. K. Webster, *The
Foreign Policy of Palmerston, 1830–1841* (London, 1951), II, p. 750; Gerald G.
Graham, *Great Britain in the Indian Ocean: a Study in Maritime Enterprise 1810–1850*
(O.U.P., 1967).

'implacable opposition to imperialism' criticized the informal empire as much as they did the formal one, and deplored the government's 'loan-mongering and debt-collecting operations'.[1] But though it is proper to notice the existence of such critics, who may not have been *completely* unsuccessful in their activities, their repetitive stridency suggests their ineffectiveness rather than the reverse.

Of course there were many non-economic factors involved in the controversy in addition to questions of trade, investment, and public expenditure. Patriotism, prestige, the conversion of the heathen, the suppression of slavery – these and many other considerations played a part in the unending struggle between the imperialists and their opponents. MacDonagh himself agreed that between 1845 and 1860, for all the continued argument, the character of British policy and public sentiment was essentially imperialistic, and he praised Robinson and Gallagher for helping '*to dissipate the contrary myth*', while Galbraith would go further, asserting that there is 'no evidence to support the assumption that doctrinaire "Little Englandism" was ever influential in either Parliament or Cabinet'.[2]

II

Several articles have been selected for this volume to show that despite the criticisms of Adam Smith, Bentham, James Mill, Ricardo, and McCulloch, English intellectuals and economists were not as 'anti-colonial' as many have implied, nor were Edward Gibbon Wakefield and the other Colonial Reformers, when they came to the fore in the 1830s, running so counter to an established current of opinion as their self-glorification would have us believe.[3] During the Napoleonic

[1] O. MacDonagh, 'The Anti-Imperialism of Free Trade', *Economic History Review*, 2nd ser., XIV (1962), pp. 489–90, 493 and 495 (below, pp. 166, 171).

[2] MacDonagh, op. cit., p. 500 (below, p. 181). The italics are mine. Galbraith, op. cit., p. 39 (below, p. 34).

[3] In addition to Semmel and Kittrell, already referred to, see D. N. Winch, 'Classical Economics and the Case for Colonization', *Economica*, XXX (1963), p. 387 (below, p. 93); R. N. Ghosh, 'The Colonization Controversy: R. J. Wilmot-Horton and the Classical Economists', *Economica*, XXXI (1964), p. 385 (below, p. 110). Cf. L. Robbins, *Robert Torrens and the Evolution of Classical Economics* (Macmillan, London, 1958).

wars, Tory spokesmen had lauded the connection between colonies and commerce, ships, seamen, wealth, and strength, and Whigs like Brougham (though in the debates on Canada in 1837–8 he was to express different views) agreed with them.[1] Colonies, argued the latter, were more valuable markets and outlets for surplus population and surplus capital than 'the territories of hostile and rival neighbours'. In them 'speculations can . . . be undertaken with greater safety and capital invested in a colonial trade with much less danger'; they were of value, not a burden, in defence, and the colonial trade was a nursery for the navy. The general run of Whigs did not share the critical feelings of the radicals, and though after the war they showed themselves anxious for freer trade and economy, with this the government came to agree.[2]

After 1821 there was 'a great change' in the colonial system, but outright anti-imperialists were few. In 1828 Huskisson had emphasized the value of the colonies when he declared 'England cannot afford to be little'.[3] By 1831 Bentham and many of his disciples had been converted, and so had most of the political economists, whether or not it is right to call them 'classical', in the 1830s.[4] In 1838 not only did Lord John Russell, for the Whigs, insist that 'the possession of our colonies materially adds to the prosperity of the Empire', but his radical critic Villiers somewhat regretfully admitted that this was the general opinion.[5] If in some quarters enthusiasm for trade preferences was slowly weakening before the onset

[1] *Quarterly Review*, v (1810), 416–17, and vi (1811), 496–7; Henry Brougham, *An Inquiry into the Colonial Policy of the European Powers* (1803), from which passages are quoted in George Bennett, *The Concept of Empire from Burke to Attlee, 1774–1947* (British Political Tradition Series, A. & C. Black, London 1953), pp. 80–4.

[2] Cf. *Parl. Debs.*, 17 March 1818 and 26 May 1820, and the legislation of the 1820s.

[3] W. Huskisson, *Speeches* (1831), II, p. 287; see George Bennett, op. cit., pp. 87–90, for extracts from his speeches on 21 March 1825 and 2 May 1828.

[4] Semmel, op. cit., p. 513 (below, pp. 77–8); D. Winch, op. cit., p. 396 (below, p. 106). Robbins, op. cit., pp. 166–7, notes that though James Mill and McCulloch remained hostile, Grote, J. S. Mill and 'a number of distinguished Benthamites' were converted.

[5] *Parl. Debs.*, 16 and 25 January 1838, 3rd ser., XL, pp. 34 and 518; cf. my article, *Journal of British Studies*, IX (1969), p. 83.

of free-trade opinions, emigration and colonial investment were coming to receive more attention, especially in the light of the apparent over-population in Ireland, and the considerable economic difficulties which, despite the apparent triumphs of the Industrial Revolution, kept causing periodical unemployment and depressions in trade in England for about thirty years after the end of the Napoleonic wars.

As early as 1817 Robert Torrens had argued that 'a well-regulated system of colonization' would act 'as a safety-valve to the political machine', and although his views did not at first evoke much response, they were later to be repeated with force by Wakefield and by Buller in arguing that colonization was a weapon against the spread of 'Chartism and Socialism' and 'wild visions of political and social change'.[1]

Wilmot-Horton, Under-Secretary for the Colonies, advocated emigration from Ireland in the twenties to relieve the great distress prevailing there. He wanted to gain the support of the 'scientific men who from their writings were admitted as authorities' on the subject, and the answers they gave to his queries show the prevailing 'expert' opinions.[2] Malthus, Ricardo, and James Mill approved, though rather doubtfully. The first feared that emigration would provide only temporary relief, for it would be followed by more marriages and more births, so that the population would soon rise again.[3] The other two argued that the capital employed on financing emigration *might* be more profitably employed at home, and that as a result of its removal the population that remained behind might 'suffer more by the loss of capital, than it gains by the diminu-

---

[1] Edward Gibbon Wakefield, *A View of the Art of Colonization* (1849. Reprinted, ed. James Collier, O.U.P., 1914), p. 74; Charles Buller, speech in House of Commons, 6 April 1843, printed in Wakefield, op. cit., Appendix 1, p. 469; cf. Semmel, op. cit., p. 516 (below, p. 81).

[2] Wilmot-Horton, *Causes and Remedies of Pauperism* (1830), quoted Donald Winch, *Classical Political Economy and Colonies* (Bell, London, 1965), p. 52; cf. R. N. Ghosh, 'Malthus on Emigration and Colonization – Letters to Wilmot-Horton', *Economica*, xxx (1963), p. 47, and 'The Colonization Controversy . . .', ibid., p. 393 (below, p. 121); Kittrell, op. cit., p. 192 (below, p. 145); R. D. C. Black, *Economic Thought and the Irish Question* (Cambridge, 1960), Chapter 7, pp. 203–25.

[3] Winch, op. cit., p. 57; Ghosh, 'Malthus on Emigration . . .', ibid., pp. 46 ff., and 'The Colonization Controversy . . .', ibid., p. 394 (below, p. 122); Kittrell, op. cit., pp. 195 ff. (below, p. 57).

tion of numbers'.[1] But if these three were hardly enthusiastic, Nassau Senior (with some reservations), Whately and even McCulloch were more encouraging, and Torrens of course supported him strongly. Senior recognized that the people's standard of living depended not simply on their stock of capital but on the revenue it produced. Whately had already tried to meet Mill's argument about the effects of the loss of capital, and McCulloch argued that at least as far as Ireland was concerned domestic investment would be less beneficial than investment on financing emigration.[2]

Of course, if the money required for this purpose came from some other source, and neither from the 'wages-fund' nor from capital employed at home, the gain would be all the greater. This, as John Stuart Mill later emphasized, was what the suggestions of Edward Gibbon Wakefield involved,[3] and though his idea of selling crown land in the colonies was not original, his ceaseless propaganda was valuable in influencing public opinion. Certainly if the cost of emigration was to be borne by the colonies, financed by the proceeds of selling land there, one could expect colonial complaints that the land sales there involved an export of capital; however, this met English complaints about the cost of migration, while showing how the colonies might benefit the mother country by relieving it of some of its redundant population.

III

Allied to the emigration of people was overseas investment, and particularly investment in the colonies. As with emigration, some thought this involved loss to the mother country,

---

[1] Winch, op. cit., pp. 61–3, and 'Classical Economics and the Case for Colonization', *Economica*, ibid., p. 390 (below, p. 98).

[2] Winch, *Classical Political Economy and Colonies*, pp. 65–9; Ghosh, op. cit., pp. 395–8 (below, pp. 124 ff.), though he is incorrect in saying that McCulloch 'never supported Horton openly' (p. 394); cf. R. Whately, 'Emigration to Canada', *Quarterly Review*, XXIII (1820), p. 388; Senior, *Remarks on Emigration* (1831) and McCulloch, 'Emigration', *Edinburgh Review*, XLV (1826), p. 57; 'Sadler on Ireland', ibid., XLIX (1829), and 'Emigration', LIII (1831), p. 53.

[3] John Stuart Mill, *Principles of Political Economy*, Book V, Chapter 11, Section 14 (ed. W. J. Ashley, Longmans, London, 1909), p. 972. For Wakefield's ideas see *England and America* (1833) and *The Art of Colonization* (1849).

but as time went on these became fewer. As early as 1801
Bentham had recognized that 'emigration of capital' (foreign
investment) was a possible remedy for falling profits, as it was
for a surplus population, and in 1831 he was converted by
Wakefield to the cause of systematic colonization.[1] Many other
economists came to view the subject in the same light, as it
seemed to them that in post-war England the average or normal
rate of profit was tending to decline, owing, in part at least,
to so much capital seeking investment that its returns were
diminishing. But although all agreed that increasing investment in any particular industry might lead to reduced profits,
the 'classical' economists seemed to deny that general over-
production, or a 'general glut', was possible, because, they
argued, since all profits were spent either on consumption or
investment goods, there could be no shortage of total demand;
this would necessarily increase in the same proportion as the
total supply of commodities, though certainly it might change
its character from consumer goods to raw materials and
equipment.[2]

If this principle is primarily associated with Jean-Baptiste
Say and James Mill, it was the orthodox 'classical' position,
also held by Ricardo and McCulloch. Certainly the former
admitted that it was theoretically *possible* for effective demand
to be insufficient to provide full employment, but he thought
this would be *unlikely*.[3] But Malthus went further, and pointed
out to Ricardo that he himself had admitted

> that a great temporary saving, commencing when profits
> were sufficient to encourage it, might occasion such a divi-
> sion of the produce as to leave no motive to a further
> increase of production. And if a state of things in which for
> a time there is no motive to a further increase in production

[1] Bentham, 'The True Alarm', and 'Defence of a Maximum' in *Economic Writings* (ed. W. Stark, 1952), III, pp. 68 and 299, quoted Winch, *Classical Political Economy and Colonies*, pp. 33–4; Semmel, op. cit., p. 518 (below, p. 83).

[2] Cf. D. Winch, in *Economica*, op. cit., pp. 388 ff. (below, p. 95 ff.) and G. S. L. Tucker, *Progress and Profits in British Economic Thought, 1650–1850* (C.U.P., 1960), p. 123.

[3] A. K. Skinner, 'Say's Law', *Economica*, XXXIV (1967), p. 163; cf. Ricardo, *Works* (ed. P. Sraffa, C.U.P.), VI, pp. 131–3.

be not properly denominated stagnation, I do not know what can be so called, particularly as this stagnation must inevitably throw the rising generation out of employment.[1]

Thus while both Ricardo and Malthus agreed that effectual demand consisted 'of two elements – the *power* and the *will* to purchase', the former believed that 'the will was very seldom wanting', and the latter insisted that this would be the case often.[2] Thus he contended that 'gluts', which would effectively reduce investment, production, and employment, would almost certainly recur, contrary to the views of Ricardo and his followers, who contended that they would be unlikely, except in a 'crisis of confidence' which they assumed would be short-lived.[3] Once this possibility was admitted, it followed that one should consider how it should be avoided, and possibly promoting colonization (as well as overseas investment) would be an effective means of accomplishing this.

Like Ricardo, John Stuart Mill admitted that during 'what is termed a commercial crisis . . . there really is an excess of all commodities above the money demand . . . an under-supply of money . . . and . . . while the crisis lasts an extreme depression of general prices'.[4] He admitted too that 'capital may be temporarily unemployed, as in the case of funds that have not yet found an investment: during the interval it does not set in

---

[1] Malthus to Ricardo, 16 July 1821, quoted J. M. Keynes, *Essays in Biography* (Hart-Davis, London, 1951), p. 120; cf. Keynes, *General Theory of Employment, Interest and Money* (Macmillan, London, 1936), pp. 362–4.

[2] A. K. Skinner, loc. cit. Ricardo admitted, of course, that saving would 'change the objects on which the demand will exercise itself', following Adam Smith's view that 'what is annually saved is as regularly consumed as what is annually spent, and nearly in the same time too, but it is consumed by a different set of people'. *Wealth of Nations* (World's Classics edn.), I, pp. 377–8.

[3] Malthus, *Quarterly Review*, XXIX (1823), pp. 230–1. From this he argued that 'unproductive consumption' was needed to maintain production at a maximum. Notice the 'underconsumption' element in the 'Birmingham' school of economists; S. G. Checkland, 'The Birmingham Economists, 1815–1850', *Economic History Review*, 2nd ser., (1948), pp. 1–18, and Kittrell, op. cit., p. 198, (below, p. 68). Cf. Tucker, op. cit., p. 135; Skinner, op. cit., p. 161; J. S. Mill, *Principles*, Book III, Chapter 14, pp. 551 ff.; B. J. Gordon, 'Say's Law and Effective Demand and Contemporary British Periodicals', *Economica*, XXII (1965), p. 438; L. Robbins, op. cit., p. 248.

[4] J. S. Mill, *Principles*, Book III, p. 561.

motion any industry'; but arguing that this was only temporary
he insisted that 'every increase of capital gives, or is capable
of giving, additional employment to industry; and this without assignable limit', and he criticized Malthus among others
for denying this.[1] However, his further argument that the
capital funds required for colonization can be drawn from 'that
surplus which cannot find employment at such profit as con-
stitutes an adequate remuneration for the abstinence of the
possessor' seems to imply that a surplus was possible if not
'wasted in reckless speculation', and to suggest that if capital
was not so wasted, it would become unprofitable.[2] Though
he still denied that this would produce 'a general glut', he
thought 'it would require but a short time to reduce profits to
the minimum, if capital continued to increase at its present
rate, and no circumstances having a tendency to raise the rate
of profit occurred in the meantime'; there would be 'great
difficulty in finding remunerative employment every year' for
the new capital, and employing it would lead to 'a rapid
reduction of the rate of profit'.[3] It seems then that though Mill
still denied the over-production, he could agree with Wakefield's account of the declining rate of profit. Implicitly at least,
he was denying Say's Law, for when production was unprofitable it would be reduced and there would be idle capital; since
this would not be replaced, what had been produced was not
creating its own demand.[4]

The fear of a declining rate of profit was of course perfectly

---

[1] J. S. Mill, *Principles,* Book III, pp. 65–7. Notice the proviso 'is capable of
giving', but he does not elaborate this. The same qualification is implied by 'nor
even necessarily' in his further statement (p. 70) that 'saving does not imply that
what is saved is not consumed, nor even, necessarily, that its consumption is
deferred; but only that, if consumed immediately, it is not consumed by the
person who saved it'.

[2] Ibid., p. 328. A great deal was wasted in unprofitable investment and in
repudiated loans in Central and South America and in the United States crash
in the 1830s.

[3] Ibid., pp. 731–2.

[4] Of course 'Say's Law' may be being misinterpreted, by Keynes as by many
others. Say had said that 'the act of saving would not cause a loss of effective
demand *provided* the thing saved be re-invested' – but most commentators have
overlooked the proviso. Say, *Treatise on Political Economy* (trans. 1821), I, p. 115.
Quoted Skinner, op. cit., p. 161.

Ricardian and perfectly orthodox, for such a decline followed the application of a law of diminishing return, and as Professor Tucker has said in the extract from his book printed below, 'the question of the effect of economic progress' on this rate of profit 'attained a position of primary importance in English political economy'.[1] The Ricardians thought it would stop accumulation, and therefore economic progress, but Wakefield feared it because he thought that accumulation would not lead to investment because of the limited 'field' of profitable employment. Progress would be retarded, argued Torrens, 'not by the difficulty of accumulating capital, but by the difficulty of employing it beneficially'. Therefore, to Wakefield and Torrens, as to Malthus, excessive accumulation was likely to lead 'to a general slackness in the economic system', and while Malthus agreed with what Keynes could later say about a deficiency in aggregate demand, Wakefield and Torrens did *not exclude* the further explanation of depression 'in terms of savings running to waste'. Here was, says Robbins, an 'anticipation of modern stagnation theory'.[2]

IV

One could justify colonization by developing an argument from the law of diminishing returns. As investment in agriculture at the margin became unprofitable, accumulation would not immediately cease, but as the rate of profit dropped general stagnation would follow, with a 'glut of capital'. For this, colonization would provide a remedy by giving an outlet to capital abroad. John Stuart Mill went further, arguing that just as investment in machinery might initially reduce the demand for labour, the higher profits that would be earned would soon restore and probably increase it, so the export of capital would open up new territories, reduce the cost of producing food, improve Britain's terms of trade, and so raise the rate of profit at home, thereby increasing domestic investment beyond its former level. 'Thus the exportation of capital is an agent of great efficacy in extending the field of employment for that

[1] Tucker, op. cit., p. 157 (below, p. 132).
[2] Robbins, op. cit., pp. 151 and 248–9.

which remains: and it may be said that up to a certain point the more capital we send away, the more we shall possess.'[1]

Resting on diminishing returns in agriculture, here is one explanation of the value of overseas investment. On this basis, says Winch, it 'would have been possible to construct a case for colonization on Ricardian lines'.[2] But Wakefield went further still and included a non-Ricardian element in his position. Britain was suffering from a shortage of investment opportunities. Export of capital provided for the employment of what was *idle*. The profits it earned might ultimately lead to an increase of domestic demand, as Mill had argued, but temporarily it would create a demand for the goods which it was used to buy. According to Wakefield:

> In every kind of trade, from the banker's to the coster-monger's, the complaint is there are too many dealers; but in truth there is too much capital, as is manifested in the banker's trade by the low rate of interest occasioned by the competition of capital with capital in the money market. . . . The competition of capital with capital appears to be the immediate cause of all other competitions. Our power of increasing capital seems to be unlimited. If the continually increasing capital of Great Britain could be continually invested so as to yield high profits, the labourers' competition would cease because there would be ample employment at good wages. Trade of every kind would present an un-limited field of employment for classes above the common people; the professional field of employment would be equally large in proportion to the cultivators. . . . The one thing needful for all society is more room for the profitable employment of capital.[3]

[1] Mill, *Principles*, pp. 382 and 739–41; Winch, *Classical Political Economy*, pp. 179–80.

[2] Winch, *Economica*, pp. 387–8 (below, p. 93).

[3] Wakefield, *Art of Colonization*, pp. 74–6; Kittrell, op. cit., pp. 190–1, (below p. 49); Winch, *Economica*, pp. 398 ff. (below, p. 107); Semmel, op. cit., p. 517 (below, p. 85); Tucker, op. cit., p. 164 (below, p. 133). Cf. Buller's speech, 6 April 1843, in Wakefield, op. cit., pp. 463 and 474–5, and Adam Smith's view that 'as capitals increase in any country, the profits which can be made by employing them necessarily diminish' – but 'the acquisition of new territory . . . may raise the

The 'excess of capital above the means of profitable investment' was the cause of England's 'social ills'; the remedy was colonization, which would also prevent 'the occasional destruction of capital on the grandest scale' due to the foolish speculation in unsafe securities which followed the low rate of return on sound ones. When capital increased without providing employment, it could be exported without reducing employment; in fact 'effective division of labour' between the colony and the mother country would lead to more efficient production in both.

Thus the 'real point at issue' between Wakefield and the Ricardians, says Winch, 'concerned the theoretical possibility and actual existence of secular stagnation in Britain'. Though Wakefield was not a thorough-going under-consumptionist, he denied, says Winch, 'the assumptions of Say's Law by arguing that the demand or "field of employment" for capital was not co-extensive with its supply; that capital accumulation could take place in the absence of profitable investment opportunities, and bring about the simultaneous existence of redundant capital and labour', or as Wakefield put it himself: 'it does not follow that because labour is employed by capital, capital always finds a field in which to employ labour. This is a *non sequitur* always taken for granted by Bentham, Ricardo, [James] Mill, McCulloch and others.'[1]

Malthus had agreed. It was untrue that accumulation ensured effectual demand.[2] So did Torrens. Capital did not possess any 'occult influence or property by which it creates for itself the field in which it is employed, and renders demand co-extensive with supply', and since colonization only entailed loss to the wages fund on 'the *assumed* principle that the increase of capital is in itself sufficient to increase the field of employment and the demand for labour', such colonization was an excellent

profits of stock.... Part of what had been employed in other trades is necessarily withdrawn from them and turned into some of the new and more profitable ones.' *Wealth of Nations* (World's Classics edn.), I, pp. 103–4 and 395.

[1] Winch, *Classical Political Economy*, pp. 79–80, where Wakefield is quoted.

[2] B. A. Corry, *Money Savings and Investment in English Economics, 1800–1850* (Macmillan, London, 1962), pp. 123–4 and 138–42; cf. his review article on Tucker's book, 'Progress and Profits', *Economica*, XXVIII (1961), p. 210.

means of enlarging the field of employment and reducing the pressure on profits. Malthus agreed with this too: 'this country, from the extent of its lands and its rich colonial possessions, has a large arena for the employment of increasing capital'.[1] Thus, it was argued, colonization would solve British problems, and although up to about 1825 there had been in economic thought 'a general feeling against colonization', thereafter it was 'replaced by a movement pressing the economic case for colonies', largely because of the 'fear of the effect of a decreasing rate of profit on the prosperity of the home economy'.[2]

John Stuart Mill seems to have agreed with this analysis, and to have become appreciative of the importance of expanding investment opportunities; but when he accepted Wakefield's ideas, he somewhat muffled their impact when he insisted that there was little theoretically new in Wakefield's explanation of the fall in profits, and overlooked the stagnationist position in the theory on which they were based.[3] This, as we have seen, was not entirely new, and Mill could justly criticize Wakefield for 'supposing his doctrines to be in contradiction to the best school of preceding political economists, instead of being, as they are, corollaries from those principles'.[4] However, it was also true that they were corollaries 'which perhaps would not always have been admitted by those political economists themselves', and though it was perhaps this aspect of the colonizers' theories which, if not entirely original, most needed to be stressed, it was unfortunately almost ignored. Though Ricardo and his first orthodox followers like James Mill and McCulloch were dubious about the advantages of Empire, and all politicians and publicists at all times wanted to keep down its expense, it has been rightly said that after 1830 'no prominent economist ventured to attack colonization in principle', and that McCulloch, though accepting the case

---

[1] Winch, *Classical Political Economy*, pp. 81 and 88.

[2] Corry, op. cit., p. 37.

[3] Tucker, op. cit., pp. 164 and 178 ff. (below, p. 133 ff.); Winch, *Economica*, op. cit., pp. 396–8 (below, p. 107 ff.).

[4] Mill, *Principles*, p. 728.

for emigration, was 'the only reputable classical economist to make systematic efforts to oppose the new doctrines' about colonization generally.[1] The fact that McCulloch was until the mid-1830s the principal writer on economic subjects in the *Edinburgh Review* and closely associated with Powlett Thompson, President of the Board of Trade in successive Whig ministries after 1830 (though not in the Cabinet until 1834), has perhaps caused his importance to be exaggerated, but even McCulloch declared later that he objected not to colonization itself but to 'the trammels' laid on the colonies' industry.[2] On the other side, as well as Torrens, Merivale, lecturing at Oxford as Professor of Political Economy from 1839 to 1841, though opposed, as a good free trader, to the commercial restrictions that appealed to Torrens, gave whole-hearted support to the new doctrine about colonial investment and emigration, as his predecessors, Senior and Whately, had done.[3]

After Mill's enthusiastic backing, it would appear that accusations that the early Victorian economists opposed imperial development could be made only by those who had never read the *Principles*. This would be more surprising if such a neglect of sources was not so common among those who confidently pronounce on what is (or is not) contained in them. Like many such myths, this seems to have had a long life in popular belief, although one could argue that Mill's tone is slightly less enthusiastic in the sixties, when English domestic industry was extremely prosperous, when there was an apparent lack of surplus capital seeking investment, and when the rate of profit seemed to have ceased to decline.[4]

---

[1] D. O. Wagner, 'British Economists and the Empire', *Political Science Quarterly*, XLVI (1931), p. 267; Winch, *Classical Political Economy*, pp. 125–7. On colonial expenditure, see e.g. P. Burroughs, 'Parliamentary Radicals and the Reduction of Imperial Expenditure . . .', *Historical Journal*, XI (1968), p. 446.

[2] Lucy Brown, *The Board of Trade and the Free Trade Movement, 1830–1842* (O.U.P., 1958), pp. 17–19, and B. J. Gordon, op. cit., p. 443; J. R. McCulloch, *Dictionary of Commerce* (1840 edn.), quoted Knorr, op. cit., p. 374.

[3] H. Merivale, *Lectures on Colonization and Colonies, delivered in 1839, 1840* and *1841* (reprinted, O.U.P. 1928), pp. 178 ff. and 230; Robbins, op. cit., pp. 227 ff.; Winch, *Classical Political Economy*, pp. 130 ff.

[4] Mill, *Principles*, p. 385 addendum to 6th edn., and *Representative Government* (1861. Everyman's edn., 1940), p. 379; Kittrell, op. cit., pp. 203–5 (below, p. 74 ff.)

Two other points remain. As both Mill and Wakefield agree, systematic colonization demanded positive state action, of which the economists were often wary. But though Wakefield was certainly a 'planner', both he and Mill seem to have thought that once the basic principle of selling colonial land at a 'sufficient price' had been accepted, the working out of colonization could be left largely to private initiative and private enterprise.[1] Moreover, since the traditional belief that the first half of the nineteenth century was a period of un-inhibited *laissez-faire* is now recognized as a gross exaggeration, this type of objection carries less weight than it would have a generation ago. More important is the incessant demand for economy and retrenchment. This was a constant obstacle to colonial as to all other expenditure. But it neither destroyed the navy nor prevented, for example, the establishment of a factory inspectorate – though it may have impeded both. In the same way, though it led to regular attempts by the government to induce the colonies themselves to contribute towards some items of imperial expenditure, it certainly did not put a stop to all expenditure by the mother country for colonial purposes.

The idea of exporting capital for colonization to keep up the rate of profit on domestic investment, and so saving capitalist society in the old world by stimulating its development in the new, puts at least Wakefield, Torrens, and Mill in line with Hobson and other later critics of 'capitalist imperialism', who looked on colonial expansion as a remedy for 'under-consumption' and for a declining rate of profit. Many of these looked forward to the break-down of capitalism, but their predecessors did not. Mill perhaps thought the diseases of the economy not yet very severe; Wakefield and Torrens certainly thought them curable, and had a cure to offer. 'Foreshadowing later theories of economic imperialism', says Semmel, the Philosophic Radicals 'were convinced that the processes of the new capitalism made it essential for Great

---

[1] Mill, *Principles*, pp. 965–6 and 970–5; Winch, *Economica*, pp. 398–9 (below, pp. 108–9); Ghosh, loc. cit., pp. 392–3 (below, p. 121). Cf. O. Pappé, 'Wakefield and Marx', *Economic History Review*, 2nd ser., IV (1951), p. 94 (below, p. 208).

Britain to have ready access to lands to which it could send people and invest capital'.[1] Mill argued that as a result of a falling rate of profit the economy would become 'stationary', and 'the expansion of capital would soon reach its ultimate boundary if the boundary itself did not continually open'.[2] Of the 'counter-tendencies' to this, foreign (including colonial) investment was 'one of the principal causes by which the decline in profits in England has been arrested'. It carried off 'part of the increase of capital from which the reduction of profit proceeds', and it helped to cheapen food and raw materials sent from overseas, thus 'enabling an increasing capital to find employment in this country, without reduction of profit'.[3] Though a more valuable process than that envisaged by Hobson or Lenin, it seems rooted in the same soil.

V

At times even the theoretically radical anti-imperialists seemed to agree that the Empire was valuable. Ricardo might be as doubtful of the desirability of British rule in India as he was of British colonization generally. McCulloch might think that 'popular opinion in regard to the vast advantages derived by England from the Government of India are as fallacious as can be imagined'. Cobden might deplore the addition in 1852 of the whole of Lower Burma to the provinces on the Bay of Bengal which Britain had annexed in 1826, and he might write in *How Wars are got up in India* (1853) 'the fullest and most consecutive' of his 'condemnations of contemporary imperialism',[4] but these were minority views. Far more Mancunians supported the 'imperialism of free trade' in China by ceaselessly memorializing the Foreign Office to take strong action

---

[1] Semmel, op. cit., p. 514 (below, p. 78).

[2] J. S. Mill, *Principles*, pp. 730–1.

[3] Ibid., pp. 738–9; Semmel, op. cit., p. 522 (below, p. 88).

[4] Ricardo, *Works*, VII, p. 293, quoted Winch, op. cit., pp. 161–3; McCulloch, *Dictionary of Commerce* (edn. 1859), p. 565, quoted L. O'Brien, 'McCulloch and India', *Manchester School*, XXXIII (1965), p. 316; O. MacDonagh, op. cit., p. 495, n. 3 (below, p. 174, n. 1), and cf. John Morley, *Life of Richard Cobden* (Macmillan, London, 1908), II, p. 354.

there than backed Cobden and Bright in opposing it.[1] They found British rule in India to their liking, which perhaps explains, if it scarcely justifies, the 'paucity of references to India in recent works which analyse anti-imperialist . . . thought, between 1832 and 1867'.[2] There, supported even by Bright, as Dr Robin Moore shows in his discussion of this aspect of British rule in India, the Manchester men pushed a 'policy of internal development through the promotion of communications and public works . . . inspired by the motive of obtaining Indian cotton'. Their investments were 'secured against the [Indian] public revenue' so that, in the terms of the later 'anti-imperialists', they were 'associated with the exploitation of India as a source of raw material, and as a field for the guaranteed investment of "finance capital".'[3]

Bright's agitation was doubtless largely humanitarian, for imperialism can mean development as well as exploitation; but if investment was likely to improve the colony, it would also profit the mother country, and, as *The Economist* declared, 'the well-being of India will promote the well-being of England'.[4] Such an expectation of imperial and economic benefits for Britain helped to originate plans for material progress in India, and though no one can deny the immense benefits the railway brought to that part of the undeveloped world, it was Manchester, that alleged centre of 'Little Englandism', which

> underwrote the Government's heavy investment of borrowed funds in public works, and its pledge of the security of the returns on the capital invested in private railways. . . . Just as the costs of the earlier wars and annexations were met from the revenues of India, so now the interest charges

[1] A. Radford et al., *Manchester Merchants and Foreign Trade 1794–1858* (Manchester Univ. Press, 1934), I, p. 116.

[2] H. Furber, 'The Theme of Imperialism and Colonialism in Modern Historical Writing on India', in C. H. Philips (ed.), *Historians of India, Pakistan and Ceylon* (London, O.U.P., 1961), p. 338.

[3] R. J. Moore, 'Imperialism and Free Trade Policy in India, 1853–1854', *Economic History Review*, 2nd ser., XVII (1964), pp. 135–6 (see below, p. 185); cf. Radford, op. cit., II, pp. 21 ff.

[4] *Economist*, 15 July 1854, quoted G. D. Bearce, *British Attitude to India, 1784–1858* (O.U.P., 1961), p. 224.

which arose from the Reformers' policy of internal development increased the dependency's financial burden . . . [and] contributed to the existence of a class of investors with a fixed interest in the permanence of the imperial connexion. Manchester's India policy helped to create a class of rentiers or finance capitalists which Hobson later described as the 'taproot of imperialism'.[1]

Of course there had been, and would be, far more investment outside the Empire as Fieldhouse, for one, has stressed more than once; but 'from 1857 to 1865 the major movement of British capital was to India, to transform the land with public works. . . . And the effort that was made brought home with the dividends a spirit ripe for imperialism.'[2]

Cobden might lament that 'our Lancashire friends argue that unless we occupied India there would be no trade with that country . . . forgetting that this is the old Protectionist theory which they used formerly to ridicule', but they were able, none the less, to press the British to manipulate Indian tariffs to help the British cotton industry.[3] This of course only underlined in practice the argument that either colonization in some cases, or occupation and control in others, might be desirable as well as, or in some circumstances in preference to, trading with foreign and independent countries. In 1849 Russell had wondered why Cobden did not see that Canadian independence followed by 'the imposition of a duty from 30 to 40 per cent on British manufactured goods from the Mississippi to the St Lawrence would be a great blow to Manchester and Leeds'.[4] Six years later Gladstone declared that while 'the passing of unwise and bad laws in foreign countries

---

[1] Moore, op. cit., pp. 144–5 (below, pp. 194–5).

[2] Jenks, *Migration of Capital*, p. 207; cf. D. K. Fieldhouse, *The Theory of Capitalist Imperialism* (London, 1967), p. xvii, and '"Imperialism", an Historiographical Revision', *Economic History Review*, 2nd ser., XIV (1961), pp. 187–209.

[3] Cobden, 18 October 1857, quoted Morley, op. cit., II, p. 195; P. Harnetty, 'The Imperialism of Free Trade: Lancashire and the Indian Cotton Duties, 1859–1862', *Economic History Review*, 2nd. ser., XVIII (1965), pp. 333 and 348–9 (and cf. his article in *English History Review*, LXXVII (1962), pp. 684 ff.).

[4] Russell to Grey, 19 August 1849, quoted Galbraith, op. cit., p. 39 (below, p. 29).

B

may greatly restrict and hamper the extension of your trade
. . . with respect of a colony you have no such danger'.[1]

This doubt about foreign laws was an important factor in
the minds of some who preferred colonization to free trade as
a remedy for British economic difficulties. Wakefield, like Mill,
looked forward to both. Britain needed 'the use of more land'
to overcome declining profits, whether these were due to
'competition' *or* to diminishing returns in agriculture. Since in
effect this extra land could be obtained by exchanging domestic
manufactures for imported food, even from foreign countries,
this thoroughly justified the repeal of the Corn Laws. But an
increasing colonial population could likewise increase food
production without diminishing returns. Because it was increasing it would provide an increasing market for manufactures, and while the emigrants would produce food and
raw materials, emigration would reduce the surplus population
at home.[2] Though certainly the freer was world trade, the less
necessity there was for colonization, it is difficult to see the
necessity of Kittrell's argument that the two programmes
were 'competitive',[3] except on the assumption, so productive
of unnecessary and unfruitful controversy, that there can be
only one basis for every argument, or only one cause for any
event. In this case, as in so many others, both arguments are
perfectly logical, and both seem securely based on various
aspects of contemporary economic theory.

VI

Thanks to an efficient combination of labour and the division
of labour between the colony and the mother country, as
colonization proceeded the prosperity of all would inevitably
rise; but Mill supported Wakefield in stressing the benefit to
the colonists to be gained from forbidding the too easy
acquisition of land; this was

---

[1] Gladstone, 12 November 1855, quoted Knorr, op. cit., pp. 334–5.

[2] Wakefield, *Art of Colonization*, pp. 89–92; Buller, 6 April 1843, quoted ibid.,
p. 472. Cf. Winch, *Classical Political Economy*, p. 88; Knorr, op. cit., pp. 300–9,
and 339; Robbins, op. cit., p. 227; J. S. Mill, *Principles*, p. 739.

[3] Kittrell, op. cit., pp. 200 ff. (below, pp. 66 ff.).

a beneficial check upon the tendency of a population of colonists to adopt the tastes and inclinations of savage life, and to disperse so widely as to lose all the advantages of commerce, or markets, of separation of employments, and of combination of labour. . . . It keeps up a perpetual succession of labourers for hire . . . and . . . has produced a suddenness and rapidity of prosperity.[1]

To Karl Marx, keeping the colonist off the land in the new world in this way was as deplorable as the expropriation of the peasant and the creation of a dependant proletariat in the old.

> The expropriation of the masses of the people from the land forms the basis of the capitalist method of production. The essence of free colonization . . . [is] that the bulk of the land is still public property, and every settler can, therefore, turn part of it into his private property and individual means of production. . . . The wage worker of today will become tomorrow an independent peasant or handicrafts man, working on his own account.[2]

To Wakefield, anxious to transfer the stratified English society to the colonies, this dispersion was 'barbarizing' and had to be prevented; to Marx, if the 'numberless' independent producers prevented 'the centralization of capital' and so did away with the 'foundation of associated labour' which the capitalist required, this was a 'good thing'. Land ownership he thought a natural claim of the individual; there was no need for man to expropriate himself, or for 'systematic colonization to replace the spontaneous colonization which is its opposite', in order to prevent the dispersion or to foster 'accumulation'. Dr Pappé, in his discussion of the relationship between the theories of Marx and Wakefield printed below, points out that Marx was here the perhaps surprising bedfellow of Adam Smith and Thomas Jefferson among others,

[1] J. S. Mill, *Principles*, pp. 972–3.
[2] Marx, *Capital*, Chapter 23–5 (Everyman's edn., II, pp. 694 ff., 794–812, and 852–6).

who 'looked with favour' on an economy of free farmers; but whether or not a hierarchic society is desirable, Wakefield was undoubtedly right if one's object is to maximize production for the market.[1]

To create such a society demanded control from the mother country, and as time went on it became clear that over many colonies such control would be difficult, if not impossible, to exercise. But some powers of supervision remained everywhere, and considerable powers in many of the colonies. Political and economic relations with the colonies were closer than with most foreign countries. Although *The Economist* might firmly answer 'no' to the question of whether overseas territories would be 'less open to the reception of our superabundant population . . . if each had their own government and was a separate state',[2] despite outspoken radicals, nearly all M.P.s, Ministers and publicists, wanted to maintain colonial establishments. This was partly for the economic advantages we have been discussing, but partly because, as Gladstone insisted in 1855, in addition to a significant material benefit from the possession of colonies, 'their moral and social advantage is a very great one', and the work of founding 'free, growing and vigorous communities' was 'providentially assigned to Britain' and was 'a noble feature in the mission of this nation'.[3] Very broadly, in place of the old conception of empire, based largely on the alleged advantages of controlling imperial trade, which most political economists had attacked, a new one was arising, based on humanitarianism, migration

[1] H. O. Pappé, op. cit., p. 90 (below, p. 205). Cf. Adam Smith, *Wealth of Nations* (World's Classics edn., 1923), I, p. 421 ff., and II, p. 161 ff.; Mill, *Principles*, p. 121. Elsewhere Mill stresses the social value of small proprietors, e.g. Book II, Chapters VI and VII.

[2] *Economist*, 22 July 1848, quoted Schuyler, op. cit., p. 234.

[3] Address to the Mechanics Institute, Chester, 12 November 1855, in P. Knaplund, *Gladstone and Britain's Imperial Policy* (London, 1927), pp. 201 ff. Part of this address is quoted in Bennett, op. cit., p. 154. Cf. Gladstone's attitude in 1840 when he argued that Britain had a duty to maintain her colonies because they were 'receptacles for our surplus population', for whom 'we have an obligation to provide . . . what semblance we can of British institutions and a home as nearly as might be like that which the emigrants have left, and to which they continue to retain a fond attachment'. (29 May 1840, *Parliamentary Debates*, 3rd ser., XLIV, col. 730.)

and investment. This was not successfully criticized, and imperialism remained a basic feature of British policy.

VII

It seems doubtful if there was any period of anti-imperialism in nineteenth-century England. There were always anti-imperialist writers, but at no period did they represent the mood of very powerful political groups. The great expansion of the British Empire in India in the half century before the Mutiny in 1857 provoked the reflection that it would have been 'unjust to call on the people of England to make vast permanent sacrifices to impose a yoke on any foreign country from which no direct political advantage can be derived'.[1] Since the 1820s few economists had been hostile to imperial development, and most had actively supported it. Although one must not overlook the Sand River Convention in South Africa, the extension of local self-government and the policy of withdrawing imperial garrisons from the colonies, Professor MacDonagh, when looking for anti-imperialism, admitted that the pro-imperialist forces waxed more successful in the 1850s than perhaps in any other decade.[2] Since Professor Schuyler told us long ago that there were 'evidences that even before the formation of Gladstone's ministry [in 1868] a revival of imperialism was at hand', and that by 1869 to 1870, 'the British people, it was evident, were not ready to follow the doctrinaire disciples of the Manchester school',[3] successful 'anti-imperialism' must have been short-lived!

British rule in India, the 'imperialism of free trade', and the connection of the mother country with self-governing colonies offer different facets of British imperial policy, and to attempt to lump all together may cause confusion and misunderstanding. But they have common features. At most times there were differences of opinion about them. At all times there were both economic and non-economic arguments for all policies

[1] *Edinburgh Review*, CVII (1858), p. 37.
[2] MacDonagh, op. cit., p. 500 (below, p. 181).
[3] MacDonagh, op. cit., p. 272.

concerned with them. And throughout the century, opposition either to colonization or to imperialism, though vocal, was never voiced by more than a minority, in which only a minority of economists was represented.

1 Myths of the 'Little England' Era

JOHN S. GALBRAITH

[This article was first published in the *American Historical Review*, Vol. LXVII (1961).]

An appropriate motto for the student of British imperial history might be *caveat emptor*, for nowhere is there more widespread use of labels that delude rather than describe. Of the considerable mass of published work from Sir John Seeley's day to this on the anatomy of imperialism much has rested on the work of a previous 'authority' whose study was also derivative. Age has sanctified generalizations which, upon close analysis, have proved to be exaggerated, undocumented, or untrue. This perpetuation of half-truths and falsehoods is evident in interpretations of the middle quarters of the nineteenth century, conventionally called the 'Little England' era.

The years between Waterloo and the 1870s are frequently portrayed as a time when mercantilism died a lingering death, to be succeeded by a free-trade era which was dominated by a merchant-industrialist aristocracy dedicated to efficiency and *laissez-faire*. These new interests regarded with repugnance the anachronism of an empire sustained before 1849 by a system of preferential customs duties, and, before and after the repeal of the Navigation Acts, protected by troops paid by British taxpayers. The logical consequence of British industrial supremacy was the withdrawal of all financial support for the colonies, since the Empire no longer provided significant economic advantages. If the corollary of colonial self-support was secession, so much the better. Sir George Cornewall Lewis in 1841 wrote in his *Essay on the Government of Dependencies*, 'If a dominant country understood the true nature of the advantages arising from the relation of supremacy and dependence to the related communities, it would voluntarily recognize the legal independence of such of its own dependencies as were fit for independence; it would, by its political arrangements, study to prepare for independence those which were still unable to stand alone.'[1] Those who held such views were 'Little Englanders' or 'Separationists', and 'for thirty years after 1840 this opinion, though with variations, was widely held in England, not merely by academic theorists, but by leading statesmen like Gladstone and Granville, and by most of the officials responsible for the execution of colonial policy'.[2] Sooty Manchester had conquered Britain, and governments did its bidding. Free trade, *laissez-faire*, and low taxes all dictated an end to the maintenance of empire.

Yet in an era of anti-annexation the Empire continued to grow in India and elsewhere, and the colonies of settlement chose to remain within the imperial framework. The paradox is conventionally resolved by the explanation that most 'Little Englanders' excluded India from the scope of their argument and that other aberrations were caused by the actions of private individuals who defied government policy, as for example in New Zealand, or by the aggressiveness of governors who in their zeal for colonial security or in pursuit of glory violated the spirit or the letter of their instructions.

This conception of British policy in the mid-nineteenth century, like all distortions, contains an element of truth. Certainly some writers insisted that the Empire was an expensive anachronism, and some statesmen in moments of petulance – likely to be produced by an expensive and unproductive colonial war – might exclaim that the colonies were 'a millstone round our necks'. But no responsible statesman during the 'Little England' era embraced the view that separation of the colonies from Britain was a desirable prospect. Significantly,

[1] George Cornewall Lewis, *Essay on the Government of Dependencies*, ed. C. P. Lucas (Oxford, Eng., 1891), p. 324.

[2] H. J. Habakkuk, 'Free Trade and Commerical Expansion, 1853–1870,' in *Cambridge History of the British Empire* [hereafter cited as *C.H.B.E.*] (Cambridge, Eng., 1940), II, 751. See also C. A. Bodelsen, *Studies in Mid-Victorian Imperialism* (New York, 1925), which has often been cited as an authority by writers on British imperial policy.

the label of 'Little Englanders' was applied by politicians to opponents, not to themselves or friends. In the words of C. R. Fay, 'Every reflecting man from the Tories of the right to the Radicals of the left realized, in 1853 as in 1828, the ineluctable truth of [William] Huskisson's memorable words, "England cannot afford to be little. She must be what she is, or nothing."'[1]

Lord John Russell wrote to his Secretary of State for Colonies, Earl Grey, in 1849:

> As to Colonial Reform, as it is called, I am much in favour of it, but not of Cobden's reform—which wd. be a dissolution of the connection. Even in his own narrow view I wonder he does not see that the imposition of a duty of from 30 to 40 per ct on British manufactured goods from the Mississippi to the St. Lawrence wd. be a great blow to Manchester & Leeds. We must endeavour to make clear to our own minds what are the benefits w[ch] remain to us from the Col[l] connection, free trade being taken for granted. . . .[2]

It was the 'true interest' of Great Britain to maintain colonies,[3] Grey contended, and the president of the Board of Trade, Henry Labouchere,[4] agreed, as did other members of the Cabinet. But the objects of their attacks were at pains to disclaim the intentions attributed to them. Richard Cobden, who was usually singled out as being the high priest of 'Little England', rejected such doctrines, though his words, particularly when taken out of context, could support the contention that he wished Britain to rid itself of colonies. In 1850 he stated that 'the independence of the British Colonies is the best condition under which they can work out their own

[1] Huskisson's 'Speech on the Civil Government of Canada, 2 May 1828', quoted by C. R. Fay, 'The Movement Towards Free Trade', in *C.H.B.E.*, II, 414.

[2] Russell to Grey, 19 August 1849, in Grey of Howick Papers, University of Durham [hereafter cited as Grey Papers]. Copy in Russell Papers, P.R.O. 30/22/8, Public Record Office [hereafter cited as P.R.O.].

[3] Grey to Russell, 23 August 1849, ibid.

[4] 'I value the Colonies & wish to keep them as long as it is good for them & ourselves that we should remain united, & believe that may be done by frank language & direct policy to ensure this.' [1849], ibid.

destinies.' But he hastened to add, 'their severance from the country of their origin would be an evil', and he suggested imperial federation as a possible means of reconciling freedom and unity.[1] On another occasion, during a debate on the sugar bill in the House of Commons, he declared:

> . . . he was not opposed to the retention of colonies any more than hon. Gentlemen opposite. He was as anxious as any one that the English race should spread itself over the earth; and he believed that colonization, under a proper system of management, might be made as conducive to the interests of the mother country as to the emigrants themselves. But he also believed that the system upon which our colonial affairs were now conducted was one of unmixed evil, injustice, and loss to the people of this country.[2]

Cobden, like the 'Manchester School' of which he was frequently a spokesman,[3] did not express a consistent philosophy with regard to imperial policy. He was relatively unconcerned with the problems of Britain's relationships with colonies except regarding their economic implications. His great causes of free trade and peace involved certain corollaries in his views on empire, but on the British Empire as such he was uninformed. His emphasis on colonies varied from time to time depending on specific circumstances. On public occasions he often insisted that he was an enlightened imperialist. At Manchester in 1849 he said: 'People tell me I want to abandon our colonies; but I say, do you intend to hold your colonies by the sword, by armies, and ships of war? That is not a permanent hold upon them. I want to retain them by their affections. . . .'[4]

[1] James E. Thorold Rogers, *Cobden and Modern Political Opinion* (London, 1873), p. 258.

[2] Speech on 22 June 1843, *Parliamentary Debates*, 3rd ser., LXX, col. 205.

[3] The characteristics of the 'Manchester School' are also frequently misrepresented. See William D. Grampp, *The Manchester School of Economics* (Stanford, Calif., 1960).

[4] Cobden to Edward Ellice, 29 May 1856, private, Ellice Papers, National Library of Scotland; microfilm copy in Library, University of California, Los Angeles, reel 37.

But in private correspondence, Cobden sometimes sounded suspiciously like a Separationist, as in the following comment to Edward (Bear) Ellice in 1856:

> The idea of defending, as integral parts of our Empire, countries 10,000 miles off, like Australia, which neither pay a shilling to our revenue (to satisfy the Colonial views of Lord North) nor afford us any exclusive trade (to fulfil the demands of Lord Chatham) is about as quixotic a specimen of national folly as was ever exhibited. But I check myself —I am in a serious mood, & am talking common sense, which is utterly inapplicable to the politics of 1856.[1]

This statement is revealing not only of Cobden's views on the Empire but his assessment of British opinion. While he bemoaned the drain which colonies imposed on British resources, he admitted that his rational arguments were of little consequence in a British society seemingly dominated by irrationality.

William E. Gladstone was frequently labelled a 'Little Englander' during his long political career, and was so designated until recently.[2] Grey wrote to Russell, 'I entirely differ from Cobden and Gladstone (& I am glad to think that you agree with me) who seem by their speeches to think that our Colonial Empire is of no use to us.'[3] But Gladstone, allegedly the epitome of the Exchequer mentality, had a far more comprehensive view of Britain's relation to its colonies than most statesmen of his day. By the 1850s he had arrived at the conviction, which he never abandoned, that regulation of colonial problems from Westminster was disadvantageous to Britain and degrading to the colonies. Such control involved heavy burdens for the British taxpayer without benefiting the general welfare of the colonists. In a memorandum written about 1850 he contrasted unfavourably the colonial administration

---

[1] *Speeches on Questions of Public Policy, by Richard Cobden*, ed. John Bright and James E. Thorold Rogers (London, 1878), p. 248.

[2] One of the first to dissent from this description of Gladstone was Paul Knaplund, in his *Gladstone and Britain's Imperial Policy* (New York, 1947).

[3] Grey to Russell, 18 November 1850, Grey Papers.

with that which had been in effect before the American Revolution. 'The mind may be struck', he observed, 'with a rather painful impression that the school of discipline which we have provided for our later colonists has been less noble and less free than that in which Henry and Washington were reared.'[1]

Gladstone acknowledged Britain's obligation to protect its colonies by the fleet and to defend them against foreign aggression, but insisted that the use of imperial troops to maintain order between settlers and aborigines in such colonies as New Zealand and the Cape of Good Hope was an incitement to wars rather than a deterrent, for it encouraged the settlers 'to regard war as rather a luxury than a scourge, since though a scourge to those who are placed in its actual seat, it becomes a positive source of wealth to the colony at large'. He conceived the proper relationship between Britain and the colonies to be one of mutual interests, common ideals, and familial sentiments, not of paternalistic control and perpetual interference. He stated in his memorandum:

> We know by tradition that Colonies are beneficial, by experience that they are costly. We feel proud when we trace upon the map how large a portion of the surface of the earth owns the benignant sway of the British crown and we are pleased with the idea that the country which we love should so rapidly reproduce its own image, as it is said, in different quarters of the globe: but we are embarrassed when we see the actual relation of feeling is not always that which should subsist between a mother and her children and that a degree of dissatisfaction attaches to the administration of colonial affairs at home, irrespective of the particular qualities of the minister of the day, which is wholly without parallel in reference to any other department of the Government.[2]

When the sources of charges of 'separatism' against midcentury politicians are traced, they usually are found in

[1] Memo on colonies, undated, dated by Gladstone in 1888 as being 'period 1848–50 I think' (probably written in 1851), Gladstone Papers, British Museum, Additional Manuscripts, 44, 738.
[2] Ibid.

observations on colonial expenditures or references to the disadvantages of Britain's continued possession of Canada. And
since Canadian problems engaged the attention of British
ministries and the British Parliament in the period 1830–1860
more than those of any other colony, perhaps of the rest of
the Empire with the exception of India, it is easy to understand how such viewpoints could have been generalized to
imply a comprehensive outlook on empire. Lord Brougham
declared after the Canadian Rebellions of 1837 that an amicable
separation would be a 'positive gain' for Great Britain, and
some members of both parties in the House of Commons
expressed similar views.[1] For the next generation, writers and
politicians from time to time voiced the wistful thought that
Britain would be better off without the liability of British
North America. Such observations were particularly in evidence when Anglo-American relations were strained, for the
exposure of Canada to American attack obviously was a source
of embarrassment to the mother country so long as there was
an obligation for its defence. But no minister ever expressed
these sentiments, even in his most private communications
with his trusted friends. On the contrary, every government –
Whig or Tory, Liberal, or Conservative – sought to maintain
the connection and was dedicated to the proposition that
British North America must not fall into the hands of the
United States. Lord John Russell as Prime Minister in 1849
expressed the hope that by a federation the provinces of British
North America would be able to enter the international community as adults able to support themselves, but 'in strict
alliance' with Great Britain. The pressing danger was annexation to the United States, 'to which I never could give
my assent'.[2]

   Russell pointed out that the absorption of Canada into the
Republic would involve aggrandizement of American power
and the extension of the American trade barrier against British
manufactured goods.[3] His specific views on the solution of the

[1] Bodelsen, *Mid-Victorian Imperialism*, p. 15.
[2] Russell to Grey, 6 August 1849, Grey Papers.
[3] Russell to Grey, 19 August 1849, ibid.

'Canadian problem' were not necessarily shared by his colleagues[1] or by his successors, but there was no dissent among either that Canada belonged within the British rather than the American community.

It is hazardous to seek enlightenment on a statesman's viewpoints from public speeches or even from private letters; by selection from their speeches and writings it is possible to reach contradictory conclusions. But there is no evidence to support the assumption that doctrinaire 'Little Englandism' was ever influential in either Parliament or cabinet.

The myth of the 'Little England' era largely arises from a preoccupation with empire in a strictly political sense and a failure to recognize the importance of what has been called the 'informal empire' of trade and investment.[2] The early Victorians were indifferent or hostile to the extension of formal empire because political control involved costly administration and even more costly responsibility for defence. It was much to be preferred that the conditions requisite for trade and investment should be maintained without such expense. But there was no indifference to the commercial interests of British society. While a debate on 'colonial policy' would empty the House of Commons or reduce its members to utter boredom, debates on finance and commercial policy were certain to be conducted in an atmosphere of keen interest.

World conditions between 1815 and the 1870s favoured a more relaxed policy than was possible in the later years of the century. Before 1870 Great Britain enjoyed a freedom of access to the markets of the world unparalleled before or since. Other states, which in the last quarter of the century would become formidable competitors, were eager buyers of British

[1] Russell suggested to Grey for his consideration that the colonies might send members to the House of Commons in proportion to their contributions to the general expense of troops, barracks, and fortifications. Grey replied that this idea was 'startling at first' and required 'much consideration'. Grey to Russell, 23 August 1849, P.R.O. 30/22/8, P.R.O.

[2] The term 'informal empire' was given currency by C. R. Fay. See his 'The Movement Towards Free Trade', 388–414. For a perceptive discussion of the phenomenon, see John Gallagher and Ronald Robinson, 'The Imperialism of Free Trade', *Economic History Review*, 2nd ser., VI (August 1953), 1–15.

consumer goods and capital equipment. Powers which were to become leading participants in the scramble for colonies were either yet unborn (Germany and Italy) or were too preoccupied with internal problems to devote great energies to overseas expansion. France in 1830 had begun a campaign for the subjugation of Algeria, but the expenditure in men and resources was so great that 'Algeria' became to British politicians a symbol of all the follies of empire; France also displayed sporadic activity in the South Pacific. But with minor exceptions these were halcyon days for British commerce. The conditions that were to necessitate assertion of sovereignty over new dependencies did not yet exist; a large part of the world was within the British sphere of commercial empire; and as long as merchants enjoyed easy access to markets there was no necessity for expensive wars of subjugation and the paraphernalia of imperial administration. When profitable markets were disrupted by the breakdown of order or by the hostility of a government, this apparent indifference abruptly ended. The 'Opium War' of 1839 to 1842 was a demonstration that Britain in the free-trade area was prepared to use force, though as a last resort, to support trade.

If the term 'Little Englanders' is of doubtful value as a description of a significant British attitude at mid-century, so also is the label 'Colonial Reformer'. At first glance the Colonial Reformers appear a far more coherent group than their alleged opponents, and certainly their spokesmen were emphatic in denunciation of the evils of paternalism and lucid in argument for colonial self-government. The writings and speeches of Lord Durham, Edward Gibbon Wakefield, Charles Buller, and Sir William Molesworth are eloquent expositions of the case for colonial freedom. But it was characteristic of these 're-formers' to heighten the virtues of their arguments by overstating the defects of those who disagreed with them. Buller's sneering reference to Sir James Stephen as a dull, unimaginative clerk whose domination of colonial policy threatened to disrupt the Empire was characteristic of the treatment they meted out to those who dissented from their views in any respect. Wakefield and Buller used Wilmot-Horton as a foil, unfairly characterizing Horton's views as the 'shovelling out of paupers' to heighten the attractions of Wakefieldian systematic colonization.[1] Like other zealots they created their own image of their opponents in order to destroy them. They contributed in substantial degree to the myth of the 'Little Englander' as the antithesis of their own enlightened outlook. But the ideas they espoused belonged to the same family as the viewpoints of those they most vehemently denounced. The 'Colonial Reformers' argued that concession of colonial self-government would bind the colonies to Britain by ties of interest and affection and that a corollary of self-government was self-support; in other words, the colonies should maintain themselves rather than continue to be a drain on the imperial treasury. With some differences in emphasis such a viewpoint would have been endorsed by most members of the British Parliament. The antithesis of 'Colonial Reform' and 'Little England' bears no relation to reality. Molesworth is conventionally described as a 'reformer', and he had good claims to be so regarded, yet he found it necessary at times to defend himself against the accusation that he was a 'Little Englander'. In 1838 he told the House of Commons:

> . . . the saying, 'Emancipate your colonies', means with those who employ it most emphatically a great deal more than the mere words convey. It is used, by some at least, to express an opinion that a country like this would be better without colonies, and even that it would have been better for us if we had never had colonies. From this sentiment, notwithstanding my respect for some who entertain it, I venture to disagree altogether.[2]

In the 1830s he actively supported the South Australian and New Zealand schemes of systematic colonization, and a street in Wellington, New Zealand, commemorates his association with the foundations of that colony. Yet for all his disclaimers,

[1] The contributions of Wilmot-Horton to the idea of systematic colonization should be reassessed. His views were much closer to Wakefield than the Wakefieldians were willing to admit.

[2] *Parliamentary Debates*, 3rd ser., XLI, cols. 476–7.

the ideas expressed in Molesworth's writings and speeches frequently were indistinguishable from those attributed to the Separationists. His preoccupation, particularly after his return to Parliament in 1845 after a four-year retirement, was increasingly with the expense of colonies and the irrationality of buying customers for British products when the world at large was eager to trade. Britain did not require colonial dominion either to sell or to buy; in fact colonies exacted a tribute from Britain for which there was no economic return. In a speech in 1848 he argued that the only material benefit derived from the maintenance of colonies was the power to prevent the erection of hostile tariffs. But the total declared value of British exports was only about six million pounds, and the direct expenditure was approximately two million. No merchant would pay 6*s.* 8*d.* on the pound to insure that his goods would compete freely with those of his competitors, yet this was what the British Government was required to do to maintain its Empire. A dependent Canada was a source only of embarrassment and expense; an independent United States was more profitable to Britain than all its colonies combined. The implication of these arguments seemed to be that secession was desirable, but Molesworth refused to follow his logic to its ultimate conclusion. Rather he contended that if the colonies were granted self-government and required to support themselves, with Britain confining its protection to the oceanic trade routes, the result would in fact be a strengthening of the bonds of empire.[1] Molesworth did not seek the end of empire, but he sought the end of expensive paternalism. He spoke eloquently of the birthright of Englishmen to be free men; he invoked the shades of Benjamin Franklin, Patrick Henry, and the Adamses to prove that control meant the breakup rather than the preservation of empire, but his voice rang with special authority and conviction when he inveighed against expense. And the reaction of his fellow members of Parliament indicated that it was this aspect of his appeal which had struck a responsive chord. In 1850 a Colonial Reform Society was founded to campaign for local self-government 'for every dependency

[1] *Parliamentary Debates,* 3rd ser., C, cols. 830 ff.

which is a true colony of England', but the prospectus of the Society provided that 'it will be a main object of the Society's endeavours to relieve the Mother country from the whole expense of the local government of Colonies, except only that of the defence of the Colony from aggression by foreign powers at war with the Empire'.[1] This objective to its supporters was 'Liberal Imperialism'; to its opponents, 'Little England'. *The Times* enthusiastically endorsed the doctrines of the Society as opening the way to a new and more enlightened imperial relationship. Earl Grey, who as Colonial Secretary was the favourite target for the reformers' attacks, denounced their views as 'absurd' and 'absolutely inconsistent with the retention of the colonies at all'. It was obvious to Grey that *The Times* was either wrong-headed or deluded. He wrote to Clarendon, 'I can hardly believe that the conductors of the paper want to get rid of our Colonial Empire, yet undoubtedly they are doing their best to lead to this result and will succeed if they get the public to listen to them.'[2]

The spectrum of opinion on colonial policy was much narrower than the language of partisan politics would seem to indicate. The distance between the views of Russell and Grey and those of Molesworth and Gladstone was in fact small. The London *Evening Mail* perceptively observed after one spirited exchange between the Russell government and Molesworth that if actions rather than words were to be trusted, Molesworth had no more ardent supporters than the very ministers who denounced him for his 'Little England' views,[3] for all agreed on the principle of colonial self-government and reduction of British expenditures for colonial purposes.

The terms 'Little Englander', 'Colonial Reformer', and 'Liberal Imperialist' thus frustrate rather than facilitate comprehension of British colonial policy. They suggest a clash of opposites, which on examination proves to be non-existent. The labels 'humanitarian' and 'philanthropist' on the other hand do have some value as a description of a particular

[1] Klaus Knorr, *British Colonial Theories, 1570–1850* (Toronto, 1944), p. 354.
[2] Grey to Clarendon, 21 January 1851, Grey Papers.
[3] London *Evening Mail*, 11 April 1851.

philosophy. But these have been used as if they represented a community of viewpoint far broader than the facts justify. After 1834 there were no humanitarian influence in British colonial policy. There were humanitarian influences. Men who considered themselves 'humanitarians' advocated widely differing lines of policy.

Certainly the upsurge of evangelicalism in the late eighteenth and in the nineteenth centuries involved tremendous implications for British policy towards 'backward races', not only within the British Empire but throughout the world. Those who were caught up by the fervour of the evangelical movement in many instances experienced the mental and physical anguish of a tortured conscience followed by the ecstasy of spiritual rebirth. The effects of conversion were often startling. It could transform a former slave trader into a clergyman whose message to the world was poured out in the hymn 'How Sweet the Name of Jesus Sounds'.[1] The duty of the reborn was not only to cleanse the soul by prayer and good works but to witness to the benighted, and the great missionary societies that were formed at the end of the eighteenth century were expressions of this zeal for the conversion of the heathen. Cynics were quick to point out that the saints suffered from spiritual longsightedness, since their perception of social evils at the far ends of the earth was far clearer than their recognition of misery at home. Thomas Carlyle in *Past and Present* turned his fury on the maudlin sentimentalists of Exeter Hall who wept at the injustices to the savages, but were unaffected by scenes in their own society which to him were abhorrent:

> O Anti-Slavery Convention, loud-sounding long-eared Exeter Hall—But in thee too is a kind of instinct towards justice, and I will complain of nothing. Only black Quashee over the seas being once sufficiently attended to, wilt thou not perhaps open thy dull sodden eyes to the 'sixty-thousand valets in London itself who are yearly dismissed to the streets, to be what they can when the season ends'; or to

[1] John Newton quit the slave trade in 1755 at the age of thirty, experienced conversion, and became an Anglican clergyman and rector of Olney. With the poet William Cowper he wrote the *Olney Hymns*, published in 1779.

the hunger-striken, pallid, *yellow*-coloured 'Free Labourers' in Lancashire, Yorkshire, Buckinghamshire, and all other shires! These Yellow-coloured, for the present, absorb all my sympathies. . . .[1]

It is not within the province of this discussion to evaluate fully the justice of Carlyle's attack. But it is relevant to point out that 'humanitarianism' in the first half of the nineteenth century did not imply a reordering of the social and economic hierarchy; it did not attack the validity of the immutable laws of economics. The 'saints' were not unconcerned with evils at their doorstep, as Carlyle alleged, and humanitarianism did contribute to reforms which ameliorated the condition of the poor and, indeed, indirectly to the transformation of the society. But he was correct when he cried that they were stirred by the dramatic and the exotic far more than by subtle forms of injustice. Graphic descriptions of the horrors of the slave trade could evoke profound indignation, and attacks on legal slavery could produce a movement of power sufficient to cause Parliament to pass legislation to end such abhorrent practices. But the leaders of these campaigns tended to accept stereotypes of 'black Quashee' and of those who oppressed him which bore no relationship to flesh and blood human beings.

The preoccupation of Exeter Hall was not with understanding; it was engaged in a crusade against evil, and understanding would have blurred the issues. This characteristic gave it the power to destroy the institution of legal slavery in the British Empire, but it did not give it the wisdom to cope intelligently with the more complex forms of racial problems that remained after 1834. The missionary magazines of this era are filled with descriptions of the essentially noble qualities of the children of nature whom the missionaries sought to win for Christ. One article, typical of many, appeared in 1836 under the title 'The Humane and Generous Caffre', describing the heroism of a tribesman who had rescued a white child whose father had been killed by the Kaffirs during the war

---

[1] Thomas Carlyle, *Past and Present* (London, 1843), p. 278.

and had carried him to safety in Graham's Town. Despite this act of nobility, he was imprisoned as a spy.[1] The antithesis thus represented of the virtuous savage and the ignoble settler was a standard stereotype which provoked the anger not only of the white colonists generally but of those in the colonial society who were most concerned with the welfare of the tribesmen. Andries Stockenstrom, who was cursed by the frontiersmen of Cape Colony and commended by the missionaries as a 'humanitarian', in 1830 condemned the 'Exeter Hall' mentality in these terms:

> . . . experience has too well taught that independent of the ignorant, prejudiced and deluded part of the community in England (whose opinion we might contemn) even extensive circles amongst the truly worthy and respectable, whose approbation & support are in every respect desirable will at once set down as a narrow minded and oppressive enemy of the Aborigines and other coloured classes—and as hostile to their amelioration,—any man who shall presume in the least to differ with those . . . to whose views they have made their own reasoning powers entirely subservient.[2]

Even among the missionaries themselves there were those who condemned the 'humanitarians' of England for their unrealistic appraisal of the nature of tribal society and their lack of understanding of the complexities of the settler-tribesman conflict. In southern Africa such views were frequently expressed by representatives of the Wesleyan Missionary Society. One of their most prominent missionaries, the Reverend Mr W. B. Boyce, wrote that 'the undiscriminating and unreasonable prejudice of a class of philanthropists in Britain, has thrown back the Kaffer to his former degraded condition as the vassal of a tyrannical feudal lord'.[3] The Wesleyan and the London Societies were at times in a state of open hostility to each other, and the advice they offered

[1] *Missionary Magazine*, VI (November 1836), pp. 85–6.
[2] Remarks of the Commissioner General (Stockenstrom), 7 December 1830, CO 48/144, P.R.O.
[3] W. B. Boyce, *Notes on South-African Affairs* (London, 1839), p. 64.

governors for the resolution of the 'native problem' was frequently contradictory. The Select Committee on the Aborigines, which was dominated by its chairman Thomas Fowell
Buxton, quoted approvingly from the sermon of one evangelical minister that 'it is our office to carry civilization and
humanity, peace and good government, and above all, the
knowledge of the true God, to the uttermost ends of the earth'.[1]
Those objectives were not necessarily harmonious, and the
committee's report was of little use as a guide to policy.
Indeed, it was virtually ignored.

Humanitarians could agree that protection for the aborigines
should be afforded by the executive as representative of the
home government and could not safely be entrusted to a local
legislature; they were united in opposition to unjust seizure of
lands by European settlers and to a labour system which would
subject unsophisticated peoples to indefinite terms of servitude.
They believed that the salvation of these peoples in this world
and the next could be attained only through religious in-
struction and education. Their influence in defence of the
aborigines was of great significance. They contributed to the
emphasis which in the twentieth century was to develop into
the principle of trusteeship;[2] they appealed to the conscience
of British society against what many of their contemporaries
considered the natural law by which the strong exterminated
or enslaved the weak; and the violence with which they have
subsequently been condemned by white racists is a measure of
their effectiveness. But the cohesion of purpose and political
power of the humanitarians has been greatly exaggerated. The
principles of 'Exeter Hall' were so broad that their effect on
specific decisions in imperial policy after the Emancipation
Act was amorphous. The language of humanitarianism was
conventional in the Victorian Age and was used by those who
were hostile to the saints of Exeter Hall. Every respectable
Englishman believed himself motivated by Christian principles. Colonel George Gawler, writing to the commander of

[1] *Report from the Select Committee on Aborigines* (British Settlements), ordered by
House of Commons to be printed, 26 June 1837 (425), 76.
[2] George R. Mellor, *British Imperial Trusteeship, 1783–1850* (London, 1951).

his son's regiment, expressed gratification at the outbreak of
a Kaffir war, which would give the young man an opportunity
to do his duty, and concluded, 'I have always laboured to
impress upon him that, whether in or out of the Army, "the
Christian is the highest style of man"; and I am grateful to
God that my son, though far away, remembers my admoni-
tion.'[1] Sir Benjamin D'Urban, whose annexation of the territory of the Amaxhosa to the Kei River was attacked by the
London Missionary Society, asserted with conviction that his
opponents were pseudo philanthropists and that his measures
promoted the interests of 'humanity, policy, and real future
security' for both settlers and tribesmen.[2] His mercuric sub-
ordinate Harry Smith exploded that 'those Canting Ultra
Philanthropists will be the curse of the very people to serve
whom they are gulling the People of England, and making
a British Minister crouch to their d—d Jesuitical procedure'.[3]

An individual in different situations might be labelled a
'humanitarian' and an advocate of economy. Sir James Stephen
has been described by his biographer as a 'Christian humanitarian',[4] and that description fits him as well as any statesman
of his day. But in his counsel on policy in Cape Colony,
Stephen advocated retrenchment with all the vigour of the
most ardent disciple of Cobden and Bright. Earl Grey at times
expressed views indistinguishable from those advocated by
the missionary societies, as when he sought to promote the
organization of tribes north and west of the Vaal River for
defence against the Boer, and on other occasions his policy
seemed to be dictated by the Chancellor of the Exchequer.
These differences in emphasis do not imply a contradiction in
their philosophies. It would be a misconception to consider
'humanitarians' and 'Exchequer minds' as at opposite ends of a
spectrum of opinion. Few nineteenth-century humanitarians
would have been prepared to demand large levies on the

[1] Gawler to William Eyre, 13 June 1831, Eyre Papers, P.R.O. 30/46/3, P.R.O
[2] D'Urban to John Bell, 25 September 1835, D'Urban Papers, P-C2, Cape
Archives.
[3] Smith to D'Urban, 3 April 1836, very private, GH 34/8, Cape Archives.
[4] Paul Knaplund, *James Stephen and the British Colonial System* (Madison, Wis.,
1953), p. 17.

British treasury for the execution of their schemes for promoting the welfare of 'backward peoples'; they shared with the generality of the British middle classes a deep aversion to tax burdens for any purpose, colonial or domestic. They might contribute, and many contributed generously, in time and money to the work of a private society, but in their capacities as merchants, manufacturers, professional men, or landowners they expected vigorous economy in their government's budget. To the leaders of the humanitarians, as to Gladstone, economy was a religion.

Ministers showed public deference to the great missionary societies, and their dispatches were often couched in humanitarian language. But they could find humanitarian support for widely varying lines of policy. In South Africa some humanitarians opposed expansion; others supported the extension of British authority for the protection of tribes beyond the cape frontier. At times advocates of reduced imperial expenditures favoured expansion and at other times retreat.

A great diversity of interests wore humanitarian garb. The Hudson's Bay Company professed to be promoting the well-being of the Indians; the New Zealand Company stated that one of its principal aims was advancement of the welfare and civilization of the Maoris. English residents of Port Natal before the annexation of 1843 called for the dispatch of imperial troops partly on humanitarian grounds – the protection of tribesmen against the heartless Boers – though there was reason for suspicion that their own self-interest was a predominant consideration.[1]

Buxton's Select Committee of 1835 to 1837 opposed treaties with uncivilized peoples as a source of disputes rather than of mutual security; other humanitarians, including Dr John

---

[1] This humanitarian justification for self-interest continued after the arrival of the troops. The commandant of Port Natal wrote that 'the English residents, in order to get servants cheap, are willing to take them into their service without inquiry, and then to plead the cause of philanthropy in excuse'. Smith to Sir George Napier, 7 November 1842, in John Bird, *Annals of Natal* (2 vols., Pietermaritzburg, 1888), II, 125. C. F. J. Muller, *Die Britse Owerheid en die Groot Trek* (Cape Town, 1949), 216, states that of all the confirmed philanthropists, Sir James Stephen was far and away the most important.

Philip, superintendent in South Africa of the London Missionary Society, espoused such treaties. British governors professed to be following a humanitarian line when they adopted the treaty system in southern Africa. Whatever policy the government chose to pursue could be defended on the basis of humanitarianism. But the universal use of humanitarian language does not mean the universal ascendancy of humanitarian influences, and the humanitarians' own assessment is a most unreliable basis for determining their actual strength.

The 'humanitarians' and their detractors shared a conviction that British society had a higher destiny than the extension of its physical influence. Victorians long before Kipling's reference to 'the lesser breeds without the law' had a sense of moral and intellectual superiority, which often expressed itself as arrogance. But coupled with this conviction was an acceptance of obligation which even in an age of free trade and retrenchment was never entirely absent. British law, the most enlightened distillation of the best in the human intellect, was an article for export, and the conferral of British order, security, and justice was a priceless boon. Of this sense of destiny, the humanitarian movement was one, but only one, manifestation, and in recasting the interpretation of nineteenth-century imperial policy this broader 'missionary' impulse must be given greater recognition.

As is painfully evident to any serious student of imperial history, British policy in the nineteenth century was characterized by apparent inconsistencies which seem to defy coherent analysis. The labels of 'Little Englander', 'Colonial Reformer', and 'Humanitarian' are subject to indictment in large part because they produce a false impression of symmetry. Any new approach will require a creative imagination, but unlike earlier interpretations must be based upon careful examination of the facts.

2 The Development of the Theory of Colonization in English Classical Political Economy[1]

EDWARD R. KITTRELL

[This article was first published in the *Southern Economic Journal*, Vol. XXXI (1965).]

I INTRODUCTION

Unlike so much of the other topical discussions in classical economics, the debate on the colonization question in the classical literature met general apathy from the public and from the political leaders of the day. However, in contrast to this early apathy, modern students of the facet of classical economic thought that concerned colonization have attached considerable importance to the classical position in understanding the evolution of classical theory. Yet there is considerable ambivalence in this research. Generally speaking, the modern view is that the classical economists were incapable of recognizing the value of colonies to the mother country. The reason simply being that the classical theory placed great emphasis on the rate of interest as an effective regulator for keeping the rate of investment equal to the rate of savings. Full employment of the nation's resources was thereby maintained. Thus there was apparently no economic need for colonization. However, the very inadequate and impressionistic nature of this

[1] This article is taken from my unpublished doctoral dissertation 'The Development of the Theory of Colonization in English Classical Political Economy' (University of Chicago, 1962). I wish to acknowledge my indebtedness to the late Professor Abram L. Harris, and especially, George J. Stigler who initially suggested the investigation, and rendered valuable criticism throughout the course of the research, as well as in the preparation of earlier drafts of this article. The editors of this *Journal* have also been helpful.

modern thought on the classical position is well reflected in the fact that the alleged course of the economic thought that emerged in the discussion of colonization is regarded quite differently by different students. From one point of view, the theoretical structure of classical economics possibly became inconsistent, as the debate over colonization raised 'doubts concerning the efficiency of *laissez-faire* at the aggregative level', though unfortunately this never led 'to a reexamination or recasting of the central propositions of classical aggregative analysis'.[1] Yet another view maintains that the changes in attitudes of the economists to more favourable views on colonies were broadly paralleled by a transformation in their economic analysis which casts doubts on the validity of the classical macro-analysis.[2]

This article will show that there was no need for any such substantive change in the classical aggregative economic analysis in order to cope with the colonization question as it was presented in the classical era; that the theory did not undergo any such transformation; and that the salient question in the mind of the typical economist in this period respecting colonization was the political feasibility of the most important goal of classical economic policy, namely, free trade. The real doctrinal impediment to be faced by those advocating emigration and/or colonization was the population principle of wages. Once this obstacle had been overcome, the vexatious problem of financing the emigration and the possibility of the reform of restrictionist trade policies were the leading subjects for discussion among the economists studying the problem.

[1] B. A. Corry, 'Progress and Profits', *Economica*, May 1961, p. 210; D. N. Winch, 'Classical Economics and the Case for Colonization', *Economica*, November 1963, pp. 387–99.

[2] T. W. Hutchison, 'Robert Torrens and Classical Economics', *Economic History Review*, December 1958, pp. 317–18; idem, 'Bentham as Economist', *Economic Journal*, June 1956, p. 294 n. See also Brinley Thomas, *Migration and Economic Growth: A Study of Great Britain and the Atlantic Community* (Cambridge: Cambridge University Press, 1954), pp. 3–6; Bernard Semmel, 'The Philosophical Radicals and Colonization' in *Tasks of Economic History. Colonialism and Colonization in World History, Journal of Economic History*, December 1961, pp. 513–24.

To develop these views a cursory account is given first of certain aspects of the Smith–Ricardo legacy to the colonization discussion, and of the two most famous programmes that dealt with emigration and colonization, programmes so attractive to the leading economists of the time. Next, the important role played by the population principle of wages in the issue under question is discussed. This is followed by two concluding sections dealing with the classical position on colonization, and the importance of free trade in this discussion.

II THE LEGACY OF SMITH AND RICARDO

The period studied here – one roughly bounded by Adam Smith's *Wealth of Nations* and J. S. Mill's *Principles* – perhaps witnessed the greatest rate of economic growth in Britain's history. As is usual in such periods, the concomitant structural changes in the economy entailed a large amount of readjustment, distress, and social protest. Given the strong policy orientation of classical political economy, it was only natural that the followers of both Smith and Ricardo should have been concerned with these conditions. Both leaders were especially aware of the role of colonization in offsetting the decline in profits that was envisaged in their respective theoretical systems in the absence of legislative and institutional reforms; and to their followers they bequeathed a framework that could simultaneously be critical of colonization, yet recognize its great value under extenuating political conditions.

Smith's severe critique of colonies is well known: the gains from colonization were gains made in spite of past colonial policy. The exclusive trade of the mother country with the colonies resulted in a mal-allocation of resources, and impeded investment as well as inducing profligacy and prodigality among the favoured merchants. The colonies, under the present system of government, had only been a source of war and a great source of expense since the mother country must bear the expense of defending the colonies without any compensation from them to defray the expenses of civil government in the home country. The successful colonies were so by chance – events 'which no human wisdom could foresee'.[1]

But there were other aspects of Smith's colonial thought that allowed a more favourable view towards colonization. Aware of the costliness of colonies, and cognizant that only a 'visionary enthusiast' would advocate the rightful course of voluntary separation of the colonies, he therefore maintained that for any colony to be of value to the mother country it must contribute a net revenue to her. Though by no means a liberal imperialist, Smith suggested an Imperial Federation with representation based on tax contributions, such representation to grow with augmented revenues. The mother country's compensation to the colonies was an extension of freedom of trade to all members of the Federation.[2]

The most important element of Smith's thought on colonization was his view of its relationship to the overall rate of profit. As is well known, Smith envisaged a decline in the rate of profits that followed a competition of capitals which lowered prices and raised wages. Smith was not as perturbed as some of his successors over this phenomenon if the decline were brought about through the 'natural effect of . . . prosperity'. With proper institutional reforms he believed that the desire of one to better himself and the principle of the division of labour increasing productivity would be sufficient to insure continuing prosperity for an indefinite period. However, to his successors who still had to live with the legacy of mercantilist commercial restraints, he suggested the role of colonization in arresting the distress. 'The acquisition of new territory,' Smith wrote, 'or of new branches of trade, may sometimes raise the profits of stock, and with them the interest of money, even in a country which is advancing in the acquisition of riches.'

[1] Adam Smith, *An Inquiry into the Nature and Causes of the Wealth of Nations*, Edwin Cannan (ed.) (New York: The Modern Library, 1937), pp. 531, 533–8, 540–2, 547, 555, 558–9, 560, 572, 575, 576, 578, 590, 626, 899.
[2] Ibid., pp. 581–90. Cf. Klaus E. Knoor, *British Colonial Theories, 1570–1850* (Toronto: University of Toronto Press, 1944), pp. 185–95.

Smith even gives a historical example substantiating his view.

> For some time after the conclusion of the late war, not only private people of the best credit, but some of the greatest companies in London, commonly borrowed at five per cent, who before had not been used to pay more than four, and four and a half per cent. The great accession both of territory and trade, by our acquisitions in North America and the West Indies, will sufficiently account for this. . . .[1]

The Philosophical Radicals, led by Bentham, and later James Mill, agreed with Smith that on balance the colonies were burdensomely expensive, a cause of war, and sanctuaries for privilege. Indeed, they embellished his argument by relating colonization to their theory of government. The real reason for colonies, so Mill states in his classic 'Colony' article, is the fact of bad government: The 'ruling few' dominate the 'subject many', and through bad government maintain colonies for the sake of the few against the many.[2]

Ricardo approved of the Radical position, albeit with qualifications. Nevertheless, Ricardo's theoretical system could also offer support to those seeking colonization through emigration. In the Ricardian system the fall in profits is due to diminishing returns from the necessary cultivation of inferior qualities of land. But the arrival of the stationary state could be offset indefinitely. For 'if . . . in the progress of countries in wealth and population,' Ricardo writes, 'new portions

[1] Smith, op. cit., p. 93.

[2] James Mill, 'Colony', *Supplement to the Fourth, Fifth, and Sixth Editions of the Encyclopaedia Britannica* (Edinburgh: Archibald Constable, 1924), III, pp. 257–73. However, indicative of the complexity of the classical position on colonization, it is interesting to note that this Radical criticism pertained to colonization through emigration, and not to those colonies, especially like India, obtained through conquest. The latter type were considered as valuable in that they offered areas for experiments in Radical reform. Bentham had visions of trying his Panopticon in Calcutta. His legal reforms and James Mill's land rent taxation programme were also developed in India, with Mill having a direct hand in the proceedings. I am indebted to conversations with Prof. Abram L. Harris for this observation.

of fertile land could be added to such countries, with every increase of capital profits would never fall, nor rents rise'.[1]

To Ricardo, there were at least two methods of overcoming the obstacle to economic development posed by a shortage of fertile land. The first method, universal free trade, formed the basis of Ricardian policy proposals. When a country reaches the limits of its increase in both capital and population, Ricardo declares, then foreign commerce would enable such a country for an 'indefinite time' to increase in wealth and population, 'for the only obstacle to this increase would be the scarcity, and consequent high value, of food and other raw produce'.[2]

However, should free trade in corn not be permitted, Ricardo's theory predicted a different course of events. His remark that 'if with every accumulation of capital we could tack a piece of fertile land to our Island, profits would never fall', could afford justification for colonization along Ricardian lines. Ricardo even attempted an analysis of the relationship of domestic accumulation and colonization, an effort that was to be corrected in Mill's famous chapter on the fall of the rate of profits. Ricardo wrote that the decline in profits is the

effect of a constantly accumulating capital, in a country which refused to import foreign and cheaper corn. But after

[1] *The Works and Correspondence of David Ricardo*, Piero Sraffa (ed.) with the collaboration of M. H. Dobb, 10 vols. (Cambridge: Cambridge University Press, 1951–5), IV, p. 18; I, pp. 110–28; VI, p. 162. Mill once considered asking Ricardo to write the 'Colony' article, VII, p. 195; also cf. ibid., pp. 231, 244, 249; however, see p. 241. On this classical view towards India, see also J. R. McCulloch, *A Dictionary, Practical, Theoretical, and Historical, of Commerce and Commercial Navigation*, 2 vols. (Philadelphia, Pa.: Thomas Wardle, 1840), I, pp. 630–3. Respecting the general issue see R. Torrens, *An Essay on the Production of Wealth: with an Appendix, in which the Principles of Political Economy are Applied to the Actual Circumstances of this Country* (London: Longman, Hurst, Rees, Orme, and Brown, 1821), pp. 229–31; John Stuart Mill, *Representative Government*, in *On Liberty, Representative Government, the Subjection of Women*, with an introduction by Millicent Garrett Fawcett (London: Oxford University Press, 1954), Chapter xviii.

[2] Ricardo, *Works*, op. cit., IV, p. 179.

profits have much fallen, accumulation will be checked, and capital will be exported to be employed in those countries where food is cheap and profits high. All European colonies have been established with the capital of the mother countries, and have thereby checked accumulation.[1]

Thus when political economists of a later period turned to the colonization question, their respective masters in the classical school had provided a framework and a precedent within which the problem could be quite easily handled. This is clearly seen in the economists' evaluations of the competing plans of emigration and colonization.

III SYSTEMATIC EMIGRATION AND
SYSTEMATIC COLONIZATION

Sir R. J. Wilmot-Horton was the founder of the programme for emigration in the twenties that became known as Systematic Emigration. This programme is of interest to students of economic thought because of its influence upon classical economists and the contrast it affords with the Wakefield system of colonization.

Wilmot-Horton's argument for emigration used a straightforward wages-fund approach: wages are depressed because the supply of labour is greater than the demand for labour. Therefore, to insure a ratio of labour to capital favourable to a higher rate of wages, surplus labour should emigrate. Although the proponents of this programme would allow for selective emigration (i.e. emigration of all social and economic classes), they concentrated on a 'shoveling out of paupers' as the Wakefieldians contended. There was an attempt, however

---

[1] Ricardo, *Works*, op. cit., IV, p. 16 n. Also see [James Mill], 'East Indian Monopoly', *Edinburgh Review*, November 1811, pp. 232–3, 240. Quite early, critics, as well as followers, explicitly recognized this aspect of Ricardian economics. See Godfrey Higgins, 'Observations on Mr. McCulloch's Doctrines Respecting the Corn Laws, and the Rate of Wages, etc., etc.,' *The Pamphleteer*, LIII (1826), p. 244; and [signed] W., 'The Ricardo School. To the editor of *The Spectator*', *The Spectator*, 26 November 1836, p. 1132. Cf. John Elliot Cairnes,' Colonization and Colonial Government', in *Lectures Delivered Before the Dublin Young Men's Christian Association in Connexion with the United Church of England and Ireland: During the Year 1864* (Dublin: Hodges, Smith, and Co., 1865), pp. 300–3.

to bring some order into an otherwise desultory process of emigration. Under the plan of Systematic Emigration, the destitute, primarily agricultural labourers were to be provided passage to Canada. The emigrant was to be given a grant of one hundred acres of land subject to the land being cultivated. He was also to be supplied with provisions for one year along with farming implements, and established immediately as a landholder and prospective employer of labour. As the colonies were short of labour, the emigration was to be confined to the empire. The gains to the mother country were those of relief to her redundant population and the creation of a market for her produce. And although the Malthusian population principle forced him to admit that the population redundancy would set in again after the emigration had removed the surplus of labour, Wilmot-Horton argued that this would not take place before the expenses of the emigration were more than covered since these costs would be less than the expenses of maintaining the pauper in idleness at home.[1]

In fact, the aspect of Wilmot-Horton's programme that received the greatest scrutiny, and which was to be the reason for its rejection in favour of Wakefield's competing programme, had to do with the vexatious problem of financing the emigration. The tergiversation of Wilmot-Horton on this problem reflects the general concern of both political leaders and economists. At first he argued for the entire costs to be borne by the parish. Later, he asked that the emigrant bear part of the expense. The report of his emigration committee in 1827 recommended a loan to the emigrant which was to be

[1] Wilmot-Horton's plan is discussed in Richard Charles Mills, *The Colonization of Australia 1829–42: The Wakefield Experiment in Empire Building*, with an introduction by Graham Wallas (London: Sidgwick and Jackson, 1915), Chapter II; and R. N. Ghosh, 'Malthus on Emigration and Colonization: Letters to Wilmot-Horton', *Economica*, February 1963, pp. 46–50. Cf. Robert Wilmot-Horton, *The Causes and Remedies of Pauperism: Fourth Series. Explanation of Mr. Wilmot-Horton's Bill, in a Letter and Queries Addressed to N. W. Senior, Esq., Professor of Political Economy in the University of Oxford; With His Answers: Dedicated to the Rate-Payers of England and Wales* (London: Edmund Lloyd, 1830); idem, *The Causes and Remedies of Pauperism: Second Series, Containing Correspondence with M. Duchatel, Author of an Essay on Charity*, 2nd ed. (London: Edmund Lloyd, 1831); *Sessional Papers: Third Report from the Select Committee on Emigration from the United Kingdom*, v (1827), pp. 228, 265.

gradually repaid by him. Two years later Wilmot-Horton advocated a quit-rent of two pence per acre on colonial land at the end of five years to meet local expenses in the colonies. However, because of severe criticism, he reverted to his former plan whereby the financing was to be met by government loans to parishes which in turn would mortgage the poor rates for this purpose, again the argument being that these emigration expenses would actually be less than the cost of maintaining the otherwise destitute labourers at home. In 1832, all aspects of the plan were rejected officially on the grounds of its costliness. Also, the plan was thought to entail undue risks in lending upon the security of repayments by emigrants, as well as increasing the national debt through the provision for mortgaging the poor rates.[1]

To the proponents of Systematic Emigration, colonization was simply the only means they saw of coping with the economic distress prevalent in Britain, and should a better method present itself, Wilmot-Horton said it would be most welcome.

This mundane scheme of Systematic Emigration was a sharp contrast to Edward Gibbon Wakefield's ambitious programme which had a broader purpose. Here, an attitude of empire building in lieu of 'mere emigration' was advocated, a development requiring a more extensive discussion of colonial relations with the mother country and of internal colonial polity, as well as offering a means-alternative to Wilmot-Horton's plan for meeting the expense of the emigration and colonization. Wakefield's plan of Systematic Colonization was offered as much more than a substitute for Wilmot-Horton's emigration scheme (which, according to the Wakefieldians,

---

[1] See Mills, op. cit., pp. 32–4; and R. N. Ghosh, op. cit., pp. 47, 50. Prior to the Systematic Emigration programme, private philanthropy and the bearing of the expenses of emigration immediately by the emigrant were most often recommended. See [Anon.], 'Emigration Report', *Westminster Review*, October 1826, pp. 347–52; [Anon.], 'Emigration', *Eclectic Review*, August 1827, p. 250; [James Spedding], 'New Theory of Colonization', *Edinburgh Review*, July 1840, pp. 284–5; Nassau W. Senior, *Industrial Efficiency and Social Economy*, S. Leon Levy (ed.), 2 vols. (New York: Henry Holt and Co., 1928), I, p. 342; *Sessional Papers: Report of the Emigration Commissioners*, XXXII (1831–2), p. 211; and also Mills, op. cit., p. 47.

had biased the case against emigration because of its costliness and its emphasis on pauper emigration).[1]

Wakefield believed that past colonial policies which permitted the sale of colonial land at very low prices were the cause of an uneconomical dispersion of colonies on the land, a dispersion that precluded establishment of an efficient combinable supply of labour. This condition would be reflected in the retarded state of the division of labour in the colonies resulting in a low rate of wages and profits that discharged and repelled both capital and labour from the colony. The failure of the colony was deemed inevitable. Thus Wakefield sought a relatively high and restrictive price on the colonial land sufficient to prevent the colonists from becoming landowners 'too soon'. Under this programme, a combinable supply of labour to capitalists would be assured. In Wakefield's system, everything else was incidental to this doctrine of the sufficient price. But, as will be shown in a subsequent article, very germane to an understanding of his influence upon the classical economists was Wakefield's plan advocating the use of the proceeds from the sale of the colonial lands and from the taxes upon rents in the colonies, as an emigration fund to defray the costs of emigration. Moreover, in order to cope best with the different problems which population posed at both ends of the emigration process, he sought 'selective emigration', i.e. the emigration of young childless couples between the ages of eighteen and twenty-four, from all social strata. As he considered all social classes to be in a depressed state, his goal of making the colonies '*Extensions* of an old society' seemed much easier than would be the case with pauper emigrants. In addition to these economic and social aspects of his programme, there was a political side in that he desired colonial self-government. Following Smith, he felt that this was the

---

[1] [Edward Gibbon Wakefield], *England and America: A Comparison of the Social and Political State of Both Nations* (New York: Harper and Bros., 1834), pp. 280–1 n.; 310 n.; idem, *A View of the Art of Colonization, with Present Reference to the British Empire in Letters Between a Statesman and a Colonist* (London: John W. Parker, 1849), p. 39; Mills, op. cit., pp. 31, 48–52. However, see Douglas Pike, 'Wilmot-Horton and the National Colonization Society', *Historical Studies, Australia and New Zealand*, May 1956, pp. 205–10.

cheapest mode of government for both the colony and the mother country. Wakefield also believed that the colonies would be better governed if power were placed in the hands of the most interested parties, i.e. the colonists; this would expedite the policy of selective emigration, since a self-governing colony would attract the independent personalities requisite to govern them. Finally, since independence was inevitable, he thought the granting of self-government to the colonies impeded their outright separation from the mother country.[1]

The other important aspect of Wakefield's thought, and one that has attracted inordinate attention among students of economic thought pertaining to colonization, concerns Wakefield's views on the possibility of a super-abundance of capital. Neither he nor his followers explained why capital should accumulate after the interest rate had fallen to very low levels. Nevertheless, colonization was recommended as providing an extension of the market for the surplus produce of the mother country, and as affording a relief to her surplus population as well as her superfluous capital. In Wakefield's words, 'a progressive enlargement, partly domestic and partly colonial, of the field for employing capital and labour'.[2]

The programme seemed to have a self-regulating, or self-supporting, feature that had appeal even after Wakefield publicly denied any such characteristic to his programme. Given a sufficient price that took account of the savings habits and the wage rates of the labourer (lest the price be so low as to be not sufficiently restrictive), the augmented productivity on the land encouraged the extension of agriculture by existing landowners as capital accumulated. Concomitantly there was added investment in agriculture by labourers who now were able to purchase land after completing their terms of service (usually three to four years) as propertyless labourers. These new land

---

[1] Edward Gibbon Wakefield, *A Letter from Sydney and Other Writings*, introduction by R. C. Mills (London: J. M. Dent & Sons, Ltd., 1929), pp. 70–9, 82–6, 89–90, 100–6; idem, *England and America* . . ., pp. 259–309; idem, *Art of Colonization* . . ., pp. 338, 374; Mills, op. cit., pp. 99, 102, 112–13, 117–20, 129–31.

[2] Wakefield, *England and America* . . ., pp. 225, 238–55.

sales would produce revenue for new immigration, and the process would proceed anew, conditions by the success of establishing a new sufficient price.[1] This price also created the conditions in the colony requisite to attract foreign capital and labour.

IV THE POPULATION PRINCIPLE OF WAGES AND
   COLONIZATION

Before the programmes of Wilmot-Horton and Wakefield could have been seriously considered by the economists of the day, the population principle of wages had to be re-considered and more weight given to the preventive check than Malthus would sanction. Ironically, Malthus was the chief witness before Wilmot-Horton's emigration committee in 1827. The committee's report of that year expressed the belief that the case for emigration had been 'strengthened throughout by general reasoning and scientific principles', i.e. by the principle of population. As a matter of fact, the population principle as expounded by Malthus himself was the most important obstacle in the way of a positive emigration and/or colonization programme.

To be sure, Wilmot-Horton obtained Malthus' approval for several prevalent viewpoints in favour of emigration: it would increase the wealth of the empire, furnish a market for British goods, and prevent the secession or conquest of the colonies. Further, emigration was desirable if the expenses of emigration were less than the expense of supporting the unemployed at home; and should the two costs be equal, emigration would still be an object for government assistance provided the occasion did not recur. Malthus also thought that a legal provision denying poor relief to labourers refusing the opportunity to emigrate was a decided reform in the poor law.

Yet even in this testimony and in correspondence with Wilmot-Horton, Malthus remained true to convictions he had expressed in the very first edition of his *Essay on Population* by

[1] Mills, op. cit., pp. 107–9; Wakefield, *England and America . . .*, p. 288.

making it clear that he considered emigration could be only a temporary solution to the problem.[1] Of course, he made some well-known concessions to emigration. In the second edition, he maintains that the only reason emigration has been proposed as a remedy for population pressure is that proponents know that it will not work. But as 'a partial and temporary expedient', emigration should not be prevented by government, even if it is arguable that governments do not have the responsibility to actively support it.[2] In the fifth edition he added another important concession. Where there was a disequilibrium in the labour market caused by a cessation in demand that has been giving stimulus to population for ten or twelve years, then publicly supported emigration was desirable, a 'temporary relief'; for in this case, though equilibrium in the labour market could be restored, 'the interval must be marked by the most severe distress. . . .'[3] And as late as 1827, he could write to Wilmot-Horton that his objections to a National System of Emigration did 'not apply to a great temporary sacrifice in the encouragement of emigration made at particular times'. He had in mind 'to alleviate the misery attendant upon the accomplishment of some specific desirable object, such as an alteration in the mode of managing landed estates, or some change in the mode of applying the Poor Laws'.[4]

Nevertheless, two fundamental characteristics of Malthus' general thought on the population principle always remained to thwart any long-term plans for emigration. Early in the *First Essay* Malthus claimed family connections, friends, and attachment to one's native land presented obstacles to emigration. But he adds: 'to make the argument more general and less interrupted by the partial views of emigration, let us take

---

[1] *Sessional Papers: Third Report from the Select Committee on Emigration from the United Kingdom*, p. 233; and Qu. 3294–5, p. 542; Qu. 3299–3300, p. 542; Qu. 3251, p. 539; and Qu. 3277, p. 541; Qu. 3350, p. 546; Qu. 3380, p. 548.

[2] T. R. Malthus, *An Essay on Population*, introduction by Michael P. Fogarty, 2 vols. (London: J. M. Dent and Sons, Ltd., 1958), Vol. II, p. 36. Cf. 1, pp. 69, 270–1.

[3] Ibid., Vol. II, p. 37.

[4] Ghosh, op. cit., p. 50.

the whole earth, instead of a spot, and suppose that the restraints to population were universally removed'. Malthus never relaxed this 'world view' approach. Though he was aware that a new country could advantageously receive the skills, knowledge, disciplines, and the like from the old countries, he nevertheless reasoned within a model that made no distinction between the relations of total resources and total population of the world, and the resources and total population on a national level.[1] Therefore emigration was pre-empted from serious consideration in the economic policy of a particular region.

The other facet of Malthus' thought became a byword for those who were critical of emigration and colonization in general. Referred to as the 'vacuum theory' of emigration, it was succinctly stated by *The Times* in its review of the report of Wilmot-Horton's emigration committee. 'Is it to be supposed,' *The Times* asked, 'if a district were cleared of what may be called its redundant labourers, by sending them abroad, that the vacuum would remain, and never be filled up?' The facts prove the contrary: 'There is nothing which nature replenishes with such rapidity as those unnatural lacunae made in society. . . .'[2] Some Malthusians even questioned the ethics of a policy that would simply transfer the excessive population to another region in 'a process that hastens onward every country to the same consummation'.[3]

However, by the time Systematic Emigration became an issue, Malthus was being severely criticized. Ricardo practically ignored the population principle in his analysis of wages

[1] E. F. Penrose, 'Malthus and the Underdeveloped Areas', *Economic Journal*, June 1957, p. 224 f. Cf. Malthus, *Essay on Population*, Vol. I, p. 10; Vol. II, pp. 21–2.

[2] *The Times*, 13 October 1827; also see Ghosh, op. cit., pp. 50, 51, 52; Malthus, *Population: The First Essay*, with a Foreword by Kenneth E. Boulding (Ann Arbor, Mich.: The University of Michigan Press, 1959), p. 39.

[3] Thomas Chalmers, *On Political Economy in Connection with the Moral State and Moral Prospects of Society*, 2nd ed. (Columbus: Isaac Whitting, 1833), pp. 300, 305, 309, 500. On p. 184 he speaks of Britain's colonies as 'showy appendages'. For other supporters of the vacuum theory of emigration, see, e.g. [Mrs Marcet], *Conversations on Political Economy in Which the Elements of that Science Are Familiarly Explained* (London: Longman, Hurst, Rees, Orme, and Brown, 1819), p. 166; 'Emigration Report', loc. cit., p. 347.

in the *Principles*, and conceded that the market rate of wages could remain above the subsistence rate for an indefinite period because the growth of capital could proceed faster than the growth of population. Even the natural rate of wages itself was variable, assuming different values at different times in the same country, and differing materially among different countries.[1]

McCulloch, as early as 1825, had maintained that subsistence grows faster than population. And further anticipating Senior by several years, he claimed that to 'retrograde is not natural to man. The desire to improve our circumstances, and to acquire an increased command over the necessaries and luxuries of life, is deeply rooted in the human breast', and this 'has been found sufficiently strong to counteract one of the most powerful instincts of our nature. . . .'[2]

Some of Malthus' critics argued that there were checks to population not covered in Malthus' trilogy of misery, vice, and moral restraint.[3] Others drew on Adam Smith to argue that population was both a cause and effect of economic growth. Thus dense population enhanced productivity by creating conditions for a better division of labour.[4] With the

[1] Ricardo, *Works*, Vol. I, pp. 94–7, 100; Vol. VIII, p. 368; Vol. IX, pp. 49–50.

[2] See J. R. McCulloch, *The Principles of Political Economy: With a Sketch of the Rise of the Progress of the Science* (Edinburgh: William and Charles Tait, 1825), pp. 346–7; idem. 'Taxation and the Poor Laws', *Edinburgh Review*, January 1820, p. 163. In his *Principles . . .*, pp. 206–7, McCulloch even considered the prudential check as actually being the most important check to population.

[3] *Literary Remains, Consisting of Lectures and Tracts on Political Economy*, of the Late Rev. *Richard Jones*, ed. with a Preface by the Rev. William Whewell (London: John Murray, 1859), pp. 95–6, 100, 110–13. Similarly T. R. Edmunds, *An Enquiry into the Principles of Population, Exhibiting a System of Regulations for the Poor: Designed Immediately to Lessen, and Finally to Remove, the Evils Which Hitherto Pressed upon the Labouring Classes of Society* (London: James Duncan, 1832), pp. 79–86; cf. pp. 86–7.

[4] Thomas Attwood, *A Letter to the Right Honourable Nicholas Vansittart, on the Creation of Money and on Its Action upon National Prosperity* (Birmingham: R. Wrightson, 1817), pp. 17, 47, 48, 76, 80; Joseph Lowe, *The Present State of England in Regard to Agriculture, Trade, and Finance; with a Comparison of the Prospects of England and France* (London: Longman, Hurst, Rees, Orme, and Brown, 1822), p. 210; J. S. Eisdell, *Treatise on the Industry of Nations; or, the Principles of National Economy and Taxation*, 2 vols. (London: G. B. Whittaker and Co., 1839), Vol. I, pp. 558, 592, 603.

influence of the population principle on the wane, economists were more encouraged about the lasting benefits from emigration. While it was still maintained that emigration could never be a substitute for prudence, emigration was now to become 'a remedy preparatory to the adoption and necessary to the safety of every other'[1] plan permanently to allay the population-employment problem since it 'would give time for reflection'.[2] This interim period of improvement, valuable even if the 'vacuum' were to refill, was to create those attitudes of prudence and foresight that would prevent the 'vacuum' from refilling and thus ensure a permanent improvement in the moral and economic conditions of the masses.[3]

Of course this critical trend in the attitude towards Malthus was not shared by all economists. A number were to continue to argue that only a large-scale emigration could have any permanent results, since any improvement in the small would only encourage population,[4] and that colonization must be 'cautiously and sparingly used, as it may stimulate population,

---

[1] Nassau William Senior, *Three Lectures on the Rate of Wages, Delivered Before the University of Oxford in Easter Term 1830. With a Preface on the Causes and Remedies of the Present Disturbances*, 2nd ed. (London: John Murray, 1831), p. v; cf. idem, *A Letter to Howick, on a Legal Provision for the Irish Poor; Commutation of Tithes, and a Provision for the Irish Roman Catholic Clergy*, 2nd ed. (London: John Murray, 1831), p. 10; [Anon.], 'Colonization', *Edinburgh Review*, January 1850, p. 8.

[2] John Wade, *History of the Middle and Working Classes with a Popular Exposition of the Economical and Political Principles Which Have Influenced the Past and Present Condition of the Industrious Orders*, 2nd ed. (London: Effingham Wilson, 1834), pp. 340-1.

[3] Senior, *Three Lectures on the Rate of Wages . . .*, pp. xvii-xviii; [J. R. McCulloch], 'Dr. Chalmers on Political Economy', *Edinburgh Review*, October 1832, p. 55; Wade, loc. cit., pp. 340-1. [E. G. Wakefield], 'Letters on the Colonies: To the Lord Howick', *The Spectator*, 4 June 1831, pp. 458-9; Archibald Allison, *The Principles of Population, and Their Connection with Human Happiness*, 2 vols. (Edinburgh: William Blackwood and Sons, 1840), Vol. II, pp. 404-5.

[4] William Thomas Thornton, *Over-population and Its Remedy: Or, An Inquiry into the Extent and Causes of the Distress Prevailing Among the Labouring Classes of the British Islands, and Into the Means of Remedying It* (London: Longman, Brown, Green, and Longmans, 1846), p. 287; John Hill Burton, *Political and Social Economy: Its Practical Application* (Edinburgh): William and Robert Chambers, 1849), pp. 340-3.

and the advantages accruing to the mother country so far proportionately diminished'.[1]

When J. S. Mill lent his authority to the population principle in his *Principles*, the vacuum theory, by now vigorously criticized, received new impetus.[2] Thus Torrens voiced the sentiments of many when he so correctly warned of the nihilistic implication of Malthus for colonization or other remedial policies when, as late as 1844, he rewrote his warning of early years. 'Were this [population principle] true, all endeavours to improve the condition of the people by emigration or otherwise would be completely idle and abortive.'[3] How interesting this is for the argument of this paper. Torrens had long been a critic of the population principle. As shown below, he was now lending support to the stagnationist views on the effects

[1] Travers Twiss, *View of the Progress of Political Economy in Europe Since the Sixteenth Century*. A Course of Lectures Delivered Before the University of Oxford in Michaelmas Term, 1846, and Lent Term, 1847 (London: Longman, Brown, Green, and Longmans, 1847), p. 220; idem. *Two Lectures on Machinery, Delivered Before the University of Oxford in Lent Term 1844* (Oxford: John Henry Parker, 1844), p. 60.

[2] John Stuart Mill, *Principles of Political Economy with Some of Their Applications to Social Philosophy*, ed. with intro. by Sir William Ashley (London: Longmans, Green, and Co., 1929), pp. 161, 349, 352, 367, 372, 383, 719, 721–4. Mill later became more sanguine, however. But for the Malthusian theme, see e.g. Henry Fawcett, *Manual of Political Economy*, 3rd ed. (London: Macmillan and Co., 1860), pp. 134–5, 218; John Lancelot Shadwell, *A System of Political Economy* (London: Trubner and Co., 1877), p. 71.

[3] R. Torrens, *The Budget: A Series of Letters on Financial, Commercial, and Colonial Policy* (London: Smith, Elder, and Co., 1841–4), p. 127. Cf. *Substance of a Speech Delivered by Colonel Torrens in the House of Commons, 15 February, 1827, on the Motion of the Right Hon. Robert Wilmot-Horton, For the Re-appointment of a Select Committee on Emigration From the United Kingdom* (London: Longmans, Rees, Orme, Brown, and Green, 1828), pp. 39–44. Senior had said the same thing, *Two Lectures on Population, Delivered Before the University of Oxford in Easter Term 1828. To Which is Added, A Correspondence Between the Author and the Rev. T. R. Malthus* (London: Saunders and Otley, 1829), pp. 80–1. Later, *Industrial Efficiency . . .*, I, 340, 349, he refers to emigration and colonization as the 'remedial check' to population. Wade, op. cit., 4th ed., 1842, pp. 195–6, had to counter the Malthusian theory in arguing for emigration. Similarly, Wilmot-Horton, *Causes and Remedies of Pauperism: Second Series . . .*, pp. 34–40; *Allison*, op. cit., pp. 403–4. Even some Wakefieldians recognized that Malthus was the major threat. Thus, William Hutt, *Emigration and Colonization, A Speech Delivered at a General Meeting of the National Colonization Society, June 1830* (London: Effingham Wilson, 1832), p. 4.

of accumulation – even developing an economic rationale for colonization on these grounds. Yet through it all he remained cognizant of the real enemy, the Malthusians. In turn, the Malthusians, systematic developers of the stagnationist argument, understandably never utilized their alternative to the orthodox model of the self-adjusting economy in their discussion of colonization. And if this were not enough, the leader of the Birmingham School, a school which came closest to modern under-consumptionist theory and national employment policy, actually opposed colonization because it was believed that the emigrants would be primarily just those 'unproductive' labourers deemed so necessary to insure the consumption of the produce of the 'productive' sector of the economy, thus maintaining full employment.[1]

V CLASSICAL MACRO-ANALYSIS AND COLONIZATION

The view that macro-analysis was used by the classicists to oppose colonization goes back at least to Wakefield, and he specifically singles out Mill, Bentham, and McCulloch for criticism. His strictures were indeed properly directed against Mill and Bentham, and he could have included Francis Place, who was even more dogmatic and misinformed than Wakefield. Place was unequivocal in his theory and history:

So far from the Political Economists calling 'boldly and loudly' for emigration, there is not a single writer of eminence on the subject of Political Economy who has not condemned every one of the projects which have been, started to promote emigration. Every one of them has . . . doubted that emigration could be beneficial to the working

---

[1] Attwood, *A Letter to . . . Vansittart . . .*, pp. 70–5, 86, 112; idem, *Observations on Currency, Population, and Pauperism in Two Letters to Arthur Young, Esq.* (Birmingham: R.Wrightson, 1818), p. 70n.; cf. p. 74. Of greater interest is the fact that Attwood believed that free trade could be a substitute for colonization (pp. 2–3, 55–6) though he did not desire such a development. Thomas Joplin, *Views on Currency* (London: James Ridgway, 1828), p. 100, desired the colonial relationship on the familiar grounds that the colonial trade was more secure than that trade which depended on foreign supplies.

people on any practicable scheme whatever. Emigration, or any thing which removes the surplus population, would no doubt benefit those who remained; and if they did not, increase again too fast they would continue well off; but there are two very serious objections to Emigration which have never been removed: (1) that emigration cannot be carried on to a sufficient extent; (2) that if it could, the capital expended on emigration would prevent the employment of people here. This is really the way in which Political Economists have expressed themselves on the subject of emigration.[1]

But a few trees do not make a forest, and this was a gross misrepresentation of the views of economists. The theory of the wages-fund was a tool, not a doctrine, and various economists used the tool to fashion policy proposals on emigration. Thus, as noted above, emigration was often recommended on the ground that the expenses of maintaining the labourers at home were greater than the expenses of emigration. Senior, who held this view, added that if the expenses of the emigration were greater than the expense of pauper support, the emigration was still justifiable if it were insurance against political instability and attack on property resulting from des-

[1] Francis Place, *Illustrations and Proofs of the Principle of Population*, critical and textual notes by Norman E. Himes (London: George Allen and Unwin, Ltd., 1930), p. 323, 329 n; also, Wakefield, *England and America . . .*, p. 250; Torrens, *Colonization of South Australia*, 2nd ed. (London: Longman, Rees, Orme, Brown, Green, and Longmans, 1836), pp. 229–30. Cf. *The Works of Jeremy Bentham*, John Bowring (ed.), 11 vols. (Edinburgh: William Tait, 1843), Vol. IV, pp. 410–16; and Alexander Bain, *James Mill: A Biography* (London: Longmans, Green, and Co., 1882), pp. 358–9. Mill was not in opposition to colonization if productivity in the colonies was higher than in the mother country; and if they were not far distant, otherwise the transportation expense would be exorbitant. However, Wakefield was not averse to using this capital loss-unemployment theme when it suited his purpose. See his *A Statement on the Principles and Objects of a Proposed National Society for the Cure and Prevention of Pauperism, by Means of Systematic Colonization* (London: James Ridgway, 1830), pp. 5–6; and Charles Tennant [E. G. Wakefield], *Letters Forming Part of a correspondence with Nassau William Senior, Esq., Concerning Systematic Colonization, and the Bill Now Before Parliament for Promoting Emigration; also, a Letter to the Canadian Land Company, and A Series of Questions, in Elucidation of the Principles of Colonization* (London: J. Ridgway, 1831), p. 35.

titution.[1] He then proceeded, with James Stephen, to prepare a draft of a plan for emigration similar to that of Wilmot-Horton.[2] The proponents of emigration also claimed that these expenses would be more than recouped by the markets created for the mother country's produce in the newly settled land.[3] Mill and Place aside, when the Ricardians opposed emigration it was never on the grounds indicated by Wakefield and others after him. Ricardo at first opposed the emigration of the Irish population since he felt that as long as the people remained uneducated and indolent, emigration of the Irish would simply cause an equal reduction in food production. McCulloch felt (in 1822) that any vacuum created in the Irish population through emigration would be refilled unless the emigration policy was supplemented by a tax on cottages and the consolidation of farms. Later, Ricardo agreed to grant money for one Peter Robinson's emigration expedition to Canada 'by way of experiment' with the provision that 'he would not consent to any *large* grants for this purpose hereafter'.[4] Moreover, both McCulloch and Ricardo expressed approval of Wilmot-Horton's plans for emigration.[5] Even in the middle twenties

---

[1] Senior, *Three Lectures on the Rate of Wages . . .*, pp. xvi–xvii; similarly, George Poulett Scrope, *Principles of Political Economy, Deduced from the National Laws of Social Welfare, and Applied to the Present State of Britain* (London: Longman, Rees, Orme, Brown, Green, and Longmans, 1833), pp. 334–8. On the role of emigration in assuring political stability, see [Anon.], 'Colonization,' pp. 2–5, *et passim* ; also Wakefield, *England and America . . .*, p. 253.

[2] [N. W. Senior and James Stephen], *Remarks on Emigration with a Draft of a Bill* (London: R. Clay, 1831).

[3] Senior, *Industrial Efficiency . . .*, p. 347; cf. Edmonds, op. cit., p. 278; George Poulett Scrope, *Extracts of Letters from Poor Persons Who Migrated Last Year to Canada and the United States ; Printed for the Information of the Labouring Poor, and Their Friends in This Country*, 2nd ed. (London: James Ridgway, 1832), p. v.

[4] Ricardo, *Works*, loc. cit.; R. D. Collison Black *Economic Thought and the Irish Question 1817–1870* (Cambridge: Cambridge University Press, 1960), p. 134; p. 207 and note. [J. R. McCulloch], 'Ireland', *Edinburgh Review*, June 1822, p. 108. The italics in the quotation are added.

[5] Lionel Robbins, 'A Letter from Ricardo', *Economica*, May 1956, pp. 172–4; [J. R. McCulloch], 'Emigration', *Edinburgh Review*, December 1826, pp. 49–74. Yet some years later Wilmot-Horton depicted both Ricardo and McCulloch, and their wages-fund argument, as hostile to emigration, claiming that he himself had long opposed this position. See his *Ireland and Canada ; Supported by Local Evidence. Dedicated, to Her Majesty the Queen* (London: John Murray, 1839), pp. 32–8.

the Radical view had been scuttled by McCulloch. Before a parliamentary committee in 1825, McCulloch stated that it would be 'sound policy to lay out a *very large sum* in carrying away the surplus population of Ireland to other parts of the world', provided that measures were taken to prevent sub-division of the farms (e.g. assurance that the cottages of the emigrating tenants would not be filled up for fifteen to twenty years). He considered it 'an object of great importance, that the government should not be stinted or scrupulous about furnishing the means'. Thus in the following year he could recommend expenses for emigration totalling £27,694,000, which approximated eight per cent of his own estimate of the national income.[1]

VI CLASSICAL ECONOMICS, COLONIZATION AND FREE TRADE

Enough has been said to show that the glut controversy was not a central issue in the extensive discussion of emigration and colonization by the economists of the period. The economic case for or against colonies in the whole classical era did not turn on the relevance of the argument that all savings are automatically invested. Indeed some classical economists, impressed by the importance of cyclical disturbances in the

---

[1] See, *Sessional Papers ; Minutes of Evidence Before the Select Committee on the State of Ireland*, VIII (1825), pp. 817–20, 830–1; and his 'Emigration', pp. 66, 70, where he sanctions emigration even if the costs of emigration were actually twice those estimated (at £13,847,000). This was approximately 8 per cent of his own estimate of the national income. See [idem], 'Taxation and the Poor Laws', p. 178. Senior, *Three Lectures on the Rate of Wages . . .*, loc. cit., was prepared to recommend at least £12,000,000 to meet the expenses of emigration. Perhaps the best single statement of the issue in question was that of Herman Merivale in his Oxford lectures. As he correctly warns, attention must not be exclusively devoted to capital in the wages-fund formulation: 'it must be remembered . . . [emigration] cannot be effected without some sacrifice of capital in *transporting* [the emigrants]. Of course . . . the economical success of that experiment depends on whether the abstraction of capital, and consequent diminution of employment for labour, over-balances or not, the relief which emigration gives to the market for labour.' *Lectures on Colonization and Colonies: Delivered Before the University of Oxford in 1839, 1840, and 1841*, 2 vols. (London: Longman, Orme. Brown, Green, and Longmans, 1841), Vol. I, p. 139. Also, Mill, 'Colony', p. 262.

economy, sought a remedy for this distress in colonization.[1] Even Wakefield and Torrens, leaders of the 'new' thought advocating colonization as an outlet for the country's superfluous capital, recognized the dominance of the free-trade argument in the discussion, and in the final analysis had to rely on institutional factors to substantiate their programme of colonization. When they were first confronted with the free-trade argument they did not deny the principle at all. Its practicality was questioned. 'Here again the question of dominion is mixed up with the question of existence,' Wakefield wrote in 1833. 'Independent states! which are the independent states that could produce very cheap corn for the English market?' After rejecting a list of suggested countries as possible British markets and raw materials sources, he concluded by classifying the United States, along with Canada, as a British colony, though independent! It was here that a market for British manufactured goods could be established as well as a suitable supply of corn,[2] since the spreading of English culture would ensure the dominance of the 'colonial' market.

Wakefield still had to face the issue some years later, and he fared no better. As late as 1849, when Wakefield was still asking for colonization, he noted that obstacles to foreign countries' 'food-exporting, goods-importing power' still persisted. In some countries agricultural improvement is so slow that food perhaps will not increase more quickly than their own population. Moreover, a great many such countries exclude British manufactured goods through hostile tariffs, or they are in such a state of political convulsion as to diminish their food exporting power. But, Wakefield continues, there remain countries like North America and the British colonies where fresh lands open up a practically unlimited source of food.

[1] Thus, some writers tied in partial gluts with the need for emigration and/or colonization. See Merivale, op. cit., Vol. I, pp. 175–9; G. R. Porter, *The Progress of the Nation; In Its Various Social and Economical Relations from the Beginning of the Nineteenth Century to the Present Time*, 3 vols. (London: Charles Knight and Co., 1836–43), Vol. II, pp. 95–6; Vol. I, p. 303; Vol. III, p. 369; Francis William Newman, *Lectures on Political Economy* (London: John Chapman, 1851), pp. 197–8, 204.

[2] Wakefield, *England and America . . .*, pp. 247–8.

It does seem possible, therefore, that Great Britain, without Corn Laws, might enlarge her whole field of production more quickly than her population could increase.

But this is an unsolved problem; and time is required for its solution. But in the meanwhile, at all events, there must be a pressure of all classes upon their means of subsistence, the field of production [for all factors] must be too small . . . and mischievous competition must last.[1]

Torrens, long impressed with the idea that the colonial trade was more secure from tariff and other restrictive policies than an erstwhile free trade, embellished Wakefield's views into an analysis that provided a rationale for a policy of reciprocity and a British Zollverein.[2] Torrens also believed that the excessive accumulation of capital could not be utilized through free foreign trade because the domestic country could not cause the foreign capital employed in producing raw materials to increase in the same proportion as the domestic capital employed producing the goods for the foreign market. Even if this obstacle were met, the domestic country 'could not prevent foreign countries from imitating the examples we have set them, and from imposing high protecting duties on the importation of manufactured goods', thereby forcing the

---

[1] Idem, *Art of Colonization* . . ., p. 90. Wakefield, as opposed to the Ricardians, desired the complete repeal of the Corn Laws in one fell swoop. See *England and America* . . ., pp. 131–49. However, given the international restrictionist policies, this would still not be enough. Thus, see the speech of Charles Buller, one of the Wakefield's ablest followers: 'I must not . . . be understood to propose colonization as a substitute for free trade. I do not vaunt its efficacy as superior; indeed I admit that its efficacy in extending employment must be slower. But, on the other hand, it will probably be surer; and will be liable to no such interruptions from the caprice of others, as trade with foreign nations must always be subject to.' *Parliamentary Debates*, 6 April 1843, p. 501. Also see R. Torrens, *A Letter to the Right Honourable Sir Robert Peel, Bart., M.P., etc., on the Condition of England, and on the Means of Removing the Causes of the Distress* (London: Smith, Elder, and Co., 1843), pp. 9–10; and his earlier *Substance of a Speech Delivered by Colonel Torrens* . . ., p. 15. Similarly, *The Spectator*, 1 November 1834, pp. 1038–9.

[2] Torrens, *The Economists Refuted; or, An Inquiry into the Nature and Extent of the Advantages Derived from Trade* (London: S. A. Oddy, 1808), pp. 34–6; idem. *An Essay on the Production of Wealth* . . ., pp. 222–48; Lionel Robbins, *Robert Torrens and the Evolution of Classical Economics* (London: Macmillan and Co. Ltd., 1958), Chapter vi-vii.

foreign country's increasing supplies of food and raw material to be utilized in its own market.

If the home capital employed in preparing cotton goods increases faster than the foreign capital employed in producing equivalents to be exchanged for cotton goods, the home capital employed in preparing woolen goods may increase faster than the foreign capital employed in producing equivalents for their purchases. The like may simultaneously occur in all the other branches of foreign trade. In all, manufacturing capital may increase faster than the foreign capital which raises the materials of manufacture; and thus, in all the departments of industry supplying goods to the foreign market there may be a contemporaneous overtrading, a consentaneous [*sic*] home competition, occasioning a general fall of prices, of profits, and of wages, want of employment, and destitution.[1]

The result of this disproportionate production was an adverse turn in both the factorial and the commodity terms of trade. Torrens felt that the adverse turn in the factorial terms of trade demonstrated the imbalance of domestic production with the foreign market and the subsequent general glut of capital, over-trading, etc., in the domestic economy.

Because of these restrictions on trade, Torrens believed that there were no real alternatives to colonization. The substantive change in his theory that concerns the colonization issue pertained to his converted belief in the possibility of excessive accumulation and the relief afforded this excess through colonization. But this development was secondary to the importance he attached to his long-held views on the insecurity of non-colonial trade. The addition of the views on the excessive accumulation of capital simply augmented his position on the desirability of colonies. He always 'found in economics an outlet for his concern with the imperial greatness of

[1] Torrens, *A Letter to Rt. Hon. Peel* . . ., pp. 16–17; idem, *Colonization of South Australia*, pp. 233–8; 274.

Britain',[1] irrespective of his views on the efficacy of the classical macro-analysis at the particular time.

Others were impressed with the argument for colonies based on this security-of-trade view, and yet adhered to international free trade as the ultimate substitute for colonization. There was no inconsistency in pleading for colonies to remove the 'surplus' of labour and capital, to develop those sorely needed raw materials for Britain's economic welfare, to provide a relief from political turmoil that was latent in pauperism, and yet claiming that with proper political and institutional reform there would be no need for colonization, and with some writers, even for emigration. Thus to the many-sided Charles Poulett Scrope, emigration and colonization were necessary to the home country because of 'the imposition of legislative shackles which cramp the exertion of its inhabitants, and interfere with the natural, that is, the *free* direction of their industry, and the natural and equitable distribution of its produce'.[2] Accepting the classical macro-analysis as a valid long-term principle, he argued that it was the politics and not any chronic defects in the economic mechanism that necessitated colonization. This view, expressed in the following statement, had the deepest sympathy of many of the economists of the day who were advocating colonization. Scrope wrote:

> To a certain limited extent, the argument as to the expediency of encouraging the production within our own territorial limits of the commodities required for the satisfaction of our wants, is sound and perfectly admissible. Until nations are perfectly convinced of their community of interest – until all mutual jealousy and animosity is extinguished which it places in the way of foreign commerce be prevented, it will be safer for a nation to produce within its own limits the commodities it requires.[3]

[1] Frank Whitson Fetter, 'Robert Torrens: Colonel of Marines and Political Economist', *Economica*, May 1962, pp. 152–65. Cf. the references in footnote 2, p. 68.

[2] Scrope, *Principles of Political Economy* . . ., p. 379.

[3] Ibid., pp. 372–3; also p. 392. In pleading for colonies, Scrope gives the same argument that Torrens gave pertaining to the disproportionate growth of the complementary productive capacities in the foreign, relative to the domestic,

It is no surprise, then, that some forty years later the aged Scrope even argued against publicly supported emigration from England since past emigrants were sending remittances back to Ireland for emigration. The natural stimulation given to emigration by the Australian and California gold discoveries, as well as the control of colonial waste lands by local authorities, were also important factors in his changed policy views, although the substantive content of his theory remained the same throughout.[1]

The pivotal role of voluntary emigration in the later classical discussion of colonization is graphically reflected in some views of J. S. Mill which have been overlooked by most commentaries. These display yet another facet of the variegated texture of classical thought on the issue in question.

One could paint a picture of Mill as the outstanding convert to Wakefield's scheme as a device to resolve the population problem. All are familiar with his statement that colonization 'in the present state of the world is the best affair of business, in which the capital of an old and wealthy country can engage'. And his just retort to Wakefield's claim for breaking new

country and the resulting adverse turn in the terms of trade (p. 382). He had argued this thesis earlier, and had pleaded for colonization on this basis. See his 'The Political Economists', *Quarterly Review*, January 1831, pp. 24–5. For other economists who adhered to some variant of a self-adjusting aggregate market mechanism, but who advocated colonization because universal free trade seemed politically unattainable, see John Rooke, *An Inquiry into the Principles of National Wealth Illustrated by the Political Economy of the British Empire* (Edinburgh: A. Balfour and Co., 1825), pp. 1–14, 78–9, 103, 141–2, 150, 372–3; Edmonds, op. cit., p. 56; G. R. Porter, op. cit., Vol. III, p. 318; Vol. II, pp. 95–6; Vol. III, p. 369; Eisdell, op. cit., Vol. I, pp. 316–17; Allison, op. cit., Vol. II, pp. 367–400, also advocated a policy of reciprocity; Newman, op. cit., pp. 189, 197–8. Merivale, op. cit., Vol. I, pp. 162–81, followed the Scrope-Torrens argument on the security of the colonial trade and Torrens on the possibility of general gluts, but he qualifies the latter's argument as a temporary phenomenon, and did not seem to begrudge the crumbling of the Empire later in his life. See his 'The Colonial Question in 1870', *Fraser's Review*, February 1870, pp. 155–64. For an interesting account of where the theory changed but the views on colonization remained the same, see *The Spectator*, 19 July 1834, pp. 681–4; and especially, *The Spectator*, 19 November 1836, p. 1111; *The Spectator*, 26 November 1836, p. 1132. Throughout the transformation, *The Spectator* was a vigorous supporter of Wakefieldian policy.

[1] G. P. Scrope, *Political Economy for Plain People Applied to the Past and Present State of Britain*, 2nd ed. (London: Longman, Green, and Co., 1873), pp. 279–80.

ground with his emphasis on the 'field of employment', meaning agricultural land, as a factor in the determination of the
rate of profits, was that this was not contrary to the 'principles
of the best school of preceding political economists [but]
instead being . . . corollaries from those principles'.[1] Also, he
placed greater emphasis in his *Principles* on colonization than
on free trade to provide the necessary cheap imports to maintain Britain's economic advance. But Mill, too, had to rely on
scepticism concerning the ability or willingness of the foreign
sources of food to meet Britain's import demands, and concluded that if Britain's population and capital continue to
increase at their present rate, 'the only mode in which food
can continue to be supplied cheaply to the one, is by sending
the other abroad to produce it'.[2] Perhaps Mill's long association
with the Wakefield programme, and his acceptance of all parts
of the system in contrast to the limited support given by other
Wakefieldians, is a factor accounting for the careless reading
of even Mill's own *Principles* respecting the fibre of the classical
theory as it was confronted with Wakefield's programme. Even
as late as 1866 he wrote that he was in favour of public loans
for colonization if they are deemed necessary, and in 1869 he
wrote to an Australian colonist that in 'regard to [colonial]
lands, I am still, like yourself, in favour of the Wakefield
system'. Finally, in early 1870, he thought that the separation
of the colonies would be a great shock to the English public.
For his own part, he felt that the severance of the colonial tie
would be disadvantageous to the world in general, and to
England in particular.[3]

[1] Mill, *Principles of Political Economy* . . ., pp. 728; and pp. 739, 746, 971.
Ricardo, following Malthus, used instead the term 'arena'. See *Works*, Vol. II,
p. 293; Vol. VI, p. 103. Cf. Robbins, *Robert Torrens* . . ., p. 248: 'The Ricardians
feared the declining rate of profit because they thought it would stop accumulation; Torrens and Wakefield feared it because they thought that nevertheless
accumulation would be attempted but would find no realization in investment.'
But in the absence of a universal free trade, this analytical difference was not
paralleled by a substantive difference on the need for emigration and colonization.

[2] Mill, *Principles of Political Economy* . . ., pp. 737–8, 739.

[3] See *Letters of John Stuart Mill*, ed. with an introduction by H. S. R. Elliot,
2 vols. (London: Longmans, Green and Co., 1910), Vol. II, pp. 59, 201, 237–8,
267–8 respectively.

Yet one gets a mistaken view of Mill's position on colonization, as well as a false impression of the classical tradition on
this issue, if such evidence is cited out of the total context
of Mill's colonization views. From the time of his *Principles*
until his death some twenty-five years later, a substantive
change occurred in his views on the need for a publicly supported plan of colonization that was independent of any substantive change in his economic theory. He remained a
Wakefieldian only in the sense that *if* publicly supported
colonization were to be put into effect, he believed the best
technique would be that of the Wakefield system. Already, in
earlier editions of his *Principles*, he had become more tepid on
the need for colonization. Even in the initial edition he felt
that colonization was more limited in alleviating the Irish
poverty than in the case of Scotland and England because of the
unsuitability of the Irish temperament for colonization, and
because of his view that the Irish civilization, being the least
advanced, was the least suitable one to form the basis for a
new world civilization.[1] In 1852 he noted that the spontaneous
Irish emigration, 'at once voluntary and self-supporting', was
being fed by the funds granted to emigrants from the earnings
of those connections and relatives who had gone before. Also
voluntary emigration had been aroused by the new gold discoveries, though he added in 1865 that as both streams of the
source of emigration had recently slackened, Wakefield's
system might again have to be pushed by the government.[2]

But Mill also maintained that the lowering of transportation
costs, and the spreading of the knowledge of employment
opportunities of remote parts of the world to all classes of
people, may occasion spontaneous emigration which 'without

[1] Mill, *Principles of Political Economy* . . ., p. 382 n. Cf. [Anon.], 'Colonization',
p. 14 and references therein.

[2] Mill, *Principles of Political Economy* . . ., pp. 974–5 and note. See also J. R.
McCulloch, *A Treatise on the Circumstances Which Determine the Rate of Wages and
the Condition of the Labouring Classes Including An Inquiry into the Influence of Com-
binations*, 2nd ed. (London: G. Routlege and Co., 1854), pp. 24–5; Rev. Thomas
Jordan, 'Effects of Emigration; Can It Be Made a Means of Relieving Distress?'
Journal of the Dublin Statistical Society, October 1856, p. 384; James Dunn, 'On
Emigration; and Its Effects on Commerce', *Transactions of the Manchester Statistical
Society, Session 1853–54*, pp. 59–63.

any national measure of systematic colonization, may prove sufficient to effect a material rise of wages in Great Britain, as it has already done in Ireland, and to maintain that rise unimpaired for one or more generations'. This spontaneous emigration, 'together with the flush of prosperity occasioned by free trade', had given to overcrowded Great Britain a temporary breathing spell, 'capable of being employed in accomplishing those moral and intellectual improvements in all classes of the people, the very poorest included, which would render improbable any relapse into the over-peopled state'.[1]

Moreover, Mill's desire to maintain the colonial tie reflects his classical free-trade convictions. This is explicitly brought out in his *Representative Government*, published in 1861. Here he is critical of sending colonial representatives to the British legislature and of imperial confederation on the grounds that neither knows the other's interest, nor has confidence in the conduct of the other. He adds that Britain does not need colonies for protection, and that Britain would be in a much stronger and more dignified position were she to become separated from the colonies instead of being a single member in a confederation. He then gave an aside that his father could easily have written:

> Over and above the commerce which she might equally enjoy after separation, England derives little advantage, except in prestige, from her dependencies; and the little she does derive is quite outweighed by the expense they cost her, and the dissemination they necessitate of her military forces, which in case of war, or any real apprehension of it, requires to be double or treble what would be needed for the defenses of this country alone.[2]

Two years before his *Representative Government*, he had vigorously protested against the view that English prosperity was based on economic imperialism and a consequent policy devoid of international morality. Such an attitude, he claimed, was

[1] Mill, *Principles of Political Economy* . . ., p. 384.

[2] Ibid., *Representative Government*, pp. 404–6.

without basis in the laws of national wealth and in all the facts of Britain's commercial condition.[1] So in 1861 he maintains that if colonies desire to sever the tie with the mother country they should be so permitted; but, if agreeable to both parties, there are reasons for maintaining the colonial tie. In his *Principles*, he pleaded for commerce because it substituted trade in place of war as the principle means of communication between nations. This culmination of classical thought is reached in his *Representative Government*. Here he is of the opinion that the colonial tie, in the present world condition,

> is a step as far as it goes, towards universal peace, and general cooperation among nations. It renders war impossible among a large number of otherwise independent communities; and moreover hinders any of them from being absorbed into a foreign state, and becoming a source of additional aggressive strength to some rival power, either more despotic or closer at hand, which might not always be so unambitious or so pacific as Great Britain. It at least keeps the markets of the different countries open to one another, and prevents that mutual exclusion by hostile tariffs, which none of the great communities of mankind, except England, have yet completely outgrown.[2]

Another factor is added by Mill which had not been so explicitly stated hitherto by the writers considered in this paper, but which was to become more important in coming decades:

> And in the case of the British possessions it has the advantage, specially valuable at the present time, of adding to the moral influence, and weight in the councils of the world, of the Power which, of all in existence, best understands liberty – and whatever may have been its errors in the past, has attained to more of conscience and moral

[1] [J. S. Mill], 'A Few Words on Non-intervention', *Fraser's Magazine* (December, 1859), reprinted in *Dissertations and Discussions: Political, Philosophical, and Historical*, 4 vols. (New York: Henry Holt and Co., 1874), Vol. III, p. 245.

[2] Idem, *Representative Government* . . ., p. 406; cf. his *Principles of Political Economy* . . ., p. 581.

principles in its dealing with foreigners, than any other great nation seems either to conceive as possible, or recognize as desirable.[1]

All in all, then, given the classical analytical apparatus, the classicists could and did advocate colonization within this framework; but given free trade, the classical economists did not see any economic need for colonization. Only with this consideration in mind is there any sense in discussing the role of classical theory respecting colonization. And with free trade, the classical idea of colonization becomes similar to the Greek idea of colonization: the spreading of race and culture, wherein common interest assured peace and trade between the mother country and the 'colony' with no design on either part for imperial union. Thus a frequent view was that 'the English language and the commerce of the world are now almost coextensive'.[2] Why have the cumbersome and costly political tie when the market in the newly founded countries will be assured Britain because the transplanted cultural body will have the tastes for the mother country's industry? By spreading civilization, one also created a supply of raw produce and the demand for finished produce.

[1] Mill, *Representative Government*, loc. cit. In a letter to J. E. Cairnes, dated 15 June 1862 Mill wrote: 'I think it very undesirable that anything should be done which would hasten the separation of our colonies. I believe the preservation of as much connexion as now exists to be a great good to them; and though the direct benefit to England is extremely small, beyond what would exist after a friendly separation, any separation would greatly diminish the prestige of England, which prestige I believe to be, in the present state of the world, a very great advantage to mankind.' *Mill-Taylor Collection* (London: London School of Economics), Vol. IV. Cf. Cairnes, op. cit., pp. 322–6. These views would presumably come as a surprise to some students. Thus, see Frank Whitson Fetter, 'Robbins on Torrens', *Economica*, November 1958, p. 348. Cf. A. V. Dicey, *Lectures on the Relation Between Law and Public Opinion in England During the Nineteenth Century* (London: MacMillan and Co., Ltd., 1905), pp. 455–6; and Sir Robert Giffen, *Economic Inquiries and Studies*, 2 vols. (London: George Bell and Sons, 1904), Vol. II, pp. 401–4. Prof. Abram L. Harris kindly provided the reference for the Mill letter.

[2] Dunn, op. cit., p. 74; also Jordan, op. cit., p. 379; [Anon.], 'Colonization', op. cit., p. 18; McCulloch, *A Treatise . . .*, loc. cit.; Merivale, op. cit., Vol. I, p. 386; Vol. II, p. 294; Burton, op. cit., pp. 335–6.

3 The Philosophic Radicals and Colonialism

B. SEMMEL

[This article was first published in the *Journal of Economic History*, Vol. XXI (1961).]

In 1948, in an address before this association, the late J. B. Brebner spoke of *laissez-faire* as a 'myth', describing it as a battle cry of the middle classes in their struggle with the landed aristocracy, and noting particularly that the Philosophic Radicals – the Benthamites – were proponents not of *laissez-faire*, as they have been represented to be, but of a new bureaucratic collectivism.[1] It is becoming clear that the reputed mid-Victorian policy of 'anti-colonialism' is likewise a myth, as two Cambridge dons argued in an article in 1953, for England continued to extend her empire – both 'formal' and 'informal' – during the middle years of the nineteenth century.[2] Was the policy which led to the extension of the empire in direct contradiction to the ideas of the men who had revealed the absurdities of the 'Old Colonial System' in the bright beam of the new science of political economy and had brought about the repeal of the Corn Laws in 1846 and of the Navigation Acts in 1849? Or is the 'anti-colonialism' of Radical doctrine also a myth? I hope to show that Benthamite Radicals, far from being ideological opponents of colonialism, as they are usually depicted,[3] were advocates of positive programmes of empire,

[1] See J. B. Brebner, 'Laissez-Faire and State Intervention in Nineteenth-Century Britain', *The Tasks of Economic History*, Supplement VIII of *The Journal of Economic History*, 1948, pp. 59–73.

[2] J. Gallagher and R. Robinson, 'The Imperialism of Free Trade', *Economic History Review*, vi, No. 1 (1953), 1–15.

[3] There are many works which uphold this position. See, for example, R. L. Schuyler, *The Fall of the Old Colonial System* (New York: Oxford Univ. Press, 1945).

and, grounding their argument upon the new economic science, constructed and maintained a set of doctrines of which the keystone was the necessity of empire to an industrial England.

I

It is, of course, well known that the Benthamite 'Colonial Reformers', men like Roebuck, Durham, Sir William Molesworth, Charles Buller, and Edward Gibbon Wakefield, and their staunch ally, John Stuart Mill, did not share the view of colonies usually associated with mid-Victorian liberalism, that they were 'millstones about the neck of the mother country'; indeed, they were advocates of schemes for the colonization of Australia and New Zealand. More significant, however, and not so well understood, was that, foreshadowing later theories of economic imperialism, they had become convinced that the processes of the new capitalism had made it essential that Great Britain have ready access to undeveloped lands – both inside and outside the formal empire – to which she could send her superfluous population, which would consume the excess capacity of her factories, and to which she could export the surplus capital which was driving down the domestic rate of profit – and all this as early as the 1830s. They maintained, furthermore, that without a positive programme to extend the 'field of production', England faced disastrous social revolution.

The chief formulator of this Benthamite 'ideology' of colonialism was Edward Gibbon Wakefield. Wakefield was born in London in 1796, the son of a Pall Mall land agent – employed frequently by Ricardo and other Radicals – who had written a highly regarded survey of Ireland, and was an intimate of both James Mill and Francis Place. In 1826, Edward, always a rebel, had, by a stratagem, enticed an heiress into a Gretna Green marriage, and as a result was sentenced to three years in Newgate prison. During his imprisonment he began his study of colonial affairs, and seized upon the famous principle of 'systematic colonization', which he set forth in *A*

Letter from Sydney, in 1829. It was a principle worthy of a land agent's son. Previous efforts at colonization had failed, Wakefield observed, because the man with capital to invest in colonial lands had been unable to hire labourers. The migrant had found it all too simple to obtain land free or at such a low price that he could set himself up as a proprietor almost immediately. The result was disastrous, since the most productive farming required the proper combination of capital and labour, and capital would not migrate unless assured of adequate labour. The answer for Wakefield was the setting of a 'sufficient price' upon colonial lands so that the working-class migrant could not obtain land until he had served for some years as a labourer. The alternative to such a system, Wakefield stressed, was slavery which was to be found in virtually all successful colonies producing exportable crops. Through such 'systematic colonization', furthermore, it would be possible to have all the advantages of civilization, a product of the concentration of population (as opposed to the barbarous diffusion of, say, the American backwoods).[1] Of course, a 'sufficient price' and the concentration of population would also mean that the organizers of the colony would gain considerably through the rise in real estate values and the sale of land. There was a good deal of unfriendly talk about Wakefield as a land speculator, and a part of the Wakefield correspondence, unfortunately, lends some credence to these charges.[2]

Yet 'systematic colonization' is not what primarily concerns us – though it is the only one of Wakefield's economic ideas of empire which is generally known, and Marx was to devote a chapter of *Das Kapital* to a 'triumphant' proof that the 'bourgeois' Wakefield, by setting forth this theory, had 'inadvertently' revealed the truth about the dependence of capitalism upon the exploitation of labour.[3] Systematic colonization was only a corollary of what might be called a 'general theory' of empire, a theory rooted in Wakefield's

[1] For descriptions of the land schemes, see Wakefield's *A Letter From Sydney* (London, 1829), and *The Art of Colonization* (London, 1849).

[2] Wakefield papers. British Museum, 25, 261, Folio 20.

[3] Karl Marx, *Capital* (Chicago: Charles H. Kerr, 1906), Vol. I, Chapter XXXIII.

disbelief in Say's Law, so dear to the orthodox. Say's Law held that since goods produced represented a demand as well as supply, goods exchanging for goods, a general over-production or glut was impossible; similarly, a glut of capital was regarded as a brief and transitory phenomenon by the followers of Say and Ricardo. Wakefield, with greater insight into monetary phenomena, saw England chronically beset by the possession of more capital than could be profitably employed. The resulting competition among capitalists, he observed, tended to drive down the rate of profit, and was the cause of crisis, business failure, and widespread misery. During the Napoleonic wars this 'supera-bundance of capital' had been wasted and, consequently, the rate of profit had not been depressed; with peace, however, the more rapid accumulation of capital had caused difficulties. Wakefield, in the manner of the heterodox Malthusian school, urged 'expenditures' on the part of capitalists, instead of 'investitures in trade'. More particularly, he urged – as the method of absorbing the surplus of capital, and the excess of production to which it gave rise – the expansion of the 'field of production'.

The vital question, Wakefield explained, was 'the proportion which population and capital bear to the land, or what may be termed, the field of employment for capital and labour'. Production 'is limited not merely by capital', as the Ricardians insisted, 'but also by the field of employment for capital itself' – that is, the land, which was 'the chief element of production'. Where, as in the United States, capital bore a large proportion to labour, and a small proportion to the field of production, wages and profits were both high. Where capital bore a small proportion to labour and a great proportion to the land, the the result was, as in England and other advanced commercial societies, both low wages and low profits. There was a remedy. An advanced commercial system which had outgrown its 'field of employment', required new lands for its population and new fields in which to invest its rapidly accumulating capital, and, consequently, must build an empire. Despite an increase of national wealth, 'the state of capitalists and labourers may grow worse, provided that the field of production be not extended at the same rate with the increase of people and capital'. This had been the source of Britain's distress in the years between 1815 and 1830. Unlike the Malthusians, Wakefield offered a programme which would permit, and even encourage, 'the most rapid increase of people and capital' through the formation of colonies.[1] In addition, Wakefield advocated the repeal of the Corn Laws to assure England of an 'informal' trade empire, as well as a formal colonial one. Repeal would make possible a permanent division of employment between England and America, for example, 'equally useful to both': 'Americans would raise cheaper corn than has ever been raised; and, no longer wanting a tariff, might drive with the manufacturers of England the greatest trade ever known in the world.' Furthermore, he suggested, American agriculture would be a most useful field for investment of super-abundant English capital.

The social and political context of Wakefield's economics was to be found in his book *England and America* (1833) – one of the great 'anticipatory' works of the nineteenth century. Foreshadowing certain portions of the analysis of Marx, Wakefield observed that Great Britain possessed a more numerous working class than any other country, a working class 'whose only property is their labour', and which was compelled to sell this in a market 'overstocked with labour', consequently realizing 'the minimum of wages', a sum 'which will barely supply the labourer with necessaries'. This class, composing 'the bulk', 'the vast majority of the people', lived in a state of misery – they were 'white slaves' – and 'if the English had been a martial people', they 'would either have destroyed the classes whom they considered their oppressors or have perished in a servile war'. Yet, for the time being, such gross inequality was necessary. The rich were performing a function of considerable utility, for if 'the capital of the society was equally divided among all,' he observed, 'it would be impossible to undertake any of those works which require the employment of many hands and a fixed capital'. England

[1] See the notes to Wakefield's edition of Smith's *Wealth of Nations* ((London, 1835), Vol. I, pp. 223–41, 251–3, 390, 395.

owed its great riches to this type of economic organization. In addition to the capitalist and the worker, there was what Wakefield called 'the middle or uneasy class', consisting of 'three-fourths, or rather perhaps nine-tenths of all who engaged in trades and professions', as well as the many smaller capitalists. All the professions, all the trades were overcrowded, and this middle class was especially hard pressed by the low rate of profit, which brought them to 'ruin, or, at least the constant dread of ruin', and the haunting fear of submersion into the working classes. The kinship to later Marxism is abundantly evident in all this.

Under these circumstances, in Wakefield's view, social revolution was an ever-present danger; yet the organization of England's economic system was extremely delicate – so much depended 'upon confidence and credit' – that he believed that all would be lost in case of class violence. Consequently democracy would soon have to be granted, rather than risk the consequences of class conflict. If granted immediately, however, democracy would be perilsome, for the working-class majority would opt for 'a revolution of property' disastrous to production. The solution was, first of all, to 'render the English working class comfortable, satisfied, and as wise, at least, as the working class in America'. Parliament would have to act 'to raise wages'. How could this be done? By extending the field for the employment of English capital and labourers, that is, by establishing a trade empire and colonies. 'The whole world is before you,' Wakefield declared. 'Open new channels for the most productive employment of English capital. Let the English buy bread from every people that has bread to sell cheap. Make England, for all that is produced by steam, the workshop of the world. If, after this, there be capital and people to spare, imitate the ancient Greeks; take a lesson from the Americans, who as their capital and population increase, find room for both by means of colonization.' It was only in this way that England could resolve the contradictions of its economy and 'escape from that corrupting and irritating state of political economy, which seems fit to precede the dissolution of empires!' Dwelling upon questions of distribution, he declared, made for 'bad blood between the two classes', when by examining production 'we may prove that masters and servants have one and the same interest'. Through a system of colonies, both formal and informal, both capitalist and worker could prosper.[1]

II

As early as the 1830s, then, Wakefield advocated a programme of empire very similar to that which Hobson and the Marxists were to accuse capitalism of following three-quarters of a century later, and, as has been noted, the Benthamite economist had largely anticipated their subsequent analysis of the economic necessity for such a programme. Nor was Wakefield a forlorn and forgotten ideologist. His general theory became a part of the programme of the leading philosophic Radicals. The first to be converted by Wakefield was Jeremy Bentham himself. The view long associated with Bentham, and the Ricardians generally, was that it was the quantity of capital rather than the extent of the market which determined the size of the trade in which a nation could engage; this view held colonies to be a drain upon the capital of the mother country.[2] Wakefield, quite early, set out to convince Bentham that this view was erroneous – sending his early anonymous writings to the old man while still in Newgate prison[3] – and he succeeded, at last, in overcoming Bentham's economic objections. Writing in 1833, Wakefield was delighted to report

[1] *England and America* (New York, 1834), 23–30, 42, 47, 61–3, 68, 82–4, 93–130, 190–8, 224–31. (London edition published in 1833.)

[2] See J. Bentham, 'Emancipate Your Colonies! Addressed to the National Convention of France, Anno 1793,' (first published in 1829) in J. Bowring, ed., *The Works of Jeremy Bentham* (Edinburgh, 1843), Vol. IV, pp. 407–18. Yet Bentham's view upon the subject of colonies was a bit ambiguous, and he offered a most fertile subject for 'conversion'. See 'The True Alarm', (1801) in W. Stark (ed.), *Bentham's Economic Writings* (London: Allen & Unwin, 1954), Vol. III, pp. 65–216; and 'Institute of Political Economy', (1801–4) in ibid., Vol. III, pp. 309–80, especially pp. 352–5. Also T. W. Hutchison, 'Bentham as an Economist', *Economic Journal*, LXVI (June 1956), 288–306.

[3] The British Museum's copy of an anonymous pamphlet by Wakefield, *Sketch of a Proposal for Colonizing Australasia, &c.* (n.p., n.d.), bears the inscription in Bentham's handwriting: 'Jeremy Bentham/13 July 1829/Received From the unknown author/without accompanying Note.'

that, in the summer of 1831, Bentham had finally become persuaded that colonization was 'a work of the greatest utility', and that Bentham had agreed to frame a charter for a society whose purpose it would be to settle parts of Australia upon the lines set by the programme of 'systematic colonization'.[1] The Bentham manuscripts at University College, London, include such a charter, drafted in Bentham's uniquely cumbersome style and followed by a general unfolding of the scheme dedicated to 'transferring individuals in an unlimited multitude from a state of indigence to a state of affluence'. Characteristic of Bentham was the setting down of the most detailed rules of settlement; he went so far as to specify exercises for prospective settlers during the long voyage to Australia![2]

After Bentham died in 1832, there was a split among the philosophic Radicals between Bowring and Perronet Thompson on the one hand, and James and John Stuart Mill, George Grote, Molesworth, and Buller on the other, and one of the grounds of division was 'systematic colonization'.[3] During the period (1829–36), when Bowring and Thompson controlled the *Westminster Review*, that journal was vociferous in denouncing Wakefield's ideas:[4] the remaining Benthamites, decidedly more influential, founded the *London Review* in 1833 and supported Wakefield. Grote became the first secretary of the Colonization Society, which had determined to establish a settlement in Australia upon the Wakefield principle.[5] Both Molesworth and Buller – the famous 'colonial reformers', the formulators and advocates, along with Wakefield himself, of the Durham report – served as spokesmen for Wakefield's

[1] Wakefield, *England and America*, note, p. 252.

[2] Bentham papers. University College, London, Folder No. 8, dated 1831, pp. 149, 152, 161–91.

[3] See E. Halévy, *A History of the English People in the Nineteeth Century* (New York: Peter Smith, 1950), Vol. III, pp. 231–2.

[4] See 'New South Australian Colony', *Westminster Review* (October 1834), XXI; 'South Australian Colony', *Westminster Review* (July 1835), XXIII.

[5] See [E. G. Wakefield] *The New British Province of South Australia* (London, 1838), pp. 156–61; see also letter of Grote to John Lefevre, 21 March 1834, in *Second Report from the Select Committee on South Australia*, June 1841, 1841 (394), IV. 9, Appendix, p. 35.

views in the House of Commons. Wakefield was himself unable – because of his sojourn at Newgate prison – to assume an open political role, but was always behind the scenes, with his rather considerable powers of persuasion. An opponent of the colonial reformers at one time referred to Molesworth as 'one of Mr Wakefield's speaking-trumpets',[1] and in truth he, as well as Buller and other Benthamites, could justly be regarded as disciples of Wakefield on matters of economics and empire who defended Australian colonization, or Corn-Law repeal, or other related policies in accordance with the 'ideology' set forth in *England and America*.

The adoption of the Wakefield ideology – again note its startling resemblances to the later Marxist one – by leading philosophic Radicals is evident in a host of parliamentary addresses. There is, for example, a speech upon colonization which Buller delivered in 1843, in which he attributed England's economic distress not to 'temporary' or 'partial', but to chronic conditions of 'over-production', and 'idle money', and saw 'in the constant accumulation of capital, and the constant increase of population within the same restricted field of employment' a 'permanent cause of suffering'. As a result, he continued, 'every kind of business is more and more passing into the hands of great capitalists, because they can afford, on their large amounts, to be content with a rate of profit, at which smaller capital would not produce a livelihood'. The cry of fair wages had to be answered, Buller told the members of the House of Commons, 'if you wish to retain your own great advantages of position and property'. What was required was 'a wider field of employment', and this could be obtained by 'colonization', a true 'remedy against the distress of the country'.[2] Wakefield's influence was to be seen in the Radical campaign against the Corn Laws, the repeal of which was believed necessary if England was to make good a position as 'workshop of the world'. (In 1836, a group of London Benthamites – Molesworth, Charles Villiers, Grote, Roebuck, and

[1] *Sidney's Emigrant Journal*, I, No. 26 (29 March 1849), 202.
[2] *Parliamentary Debates* (*P.D.*), House of Commons, 3rd Series. 6 April 1843, LXVIII, 486, 488, 491, 495, 499.

D

Joseph Hume – organized the Anti-Corn Law Association, which, despite the formation of Cobden's much grander Anti-Corn Law League in 1837, led the parliamentary fight for repeal.) The Wakefieldian cadences of the Molesworth speeches for repeal were in contrast to the free-trade optimism of Cobden. 'There is a tendency in labour and capital to augment more rapidly than the means of employing them,' Molesworth observed to the House of Commons in 1837, 'and consequently to produce hurtful competition' which brought distress. 'Labour and capital are super-abundant compared to land', and 'consequently both wages and profits are low'. 'A free importation of corn would be equivalent to the addition of so much land to this country', and were it possible, England 'might perpetually import food from other countries in return for our manufactures'. Molesworth asserted that it was 'only by means of a repeal of the Corn Laws', and 'of proper schemes of colonization' that 'the field for the productive employment of labour and capital can be continually enlarged', and only in this way could England 'render the inevitable progress of democracy in this country as safe and peaceable as it is in America'.[1] In 1838, again speaking on behalf of Corn-Law repeal, Molesworth depicted the ruin of 'smaller capitalists' as a result of competition and the 'general fall of profits'. These ruined capitalists would be 'absorbed in the labouring class; and if this severe competition were to continue, the community would ultimately consist only of two classes – labourers and the possessors of immense capitals'. The solution for Molesworth – as for Wakefield and Buller – was 'to augment . . . the field of employment', through colonization and repeal of the Corn Laws.[2]

Buller and Molesworth, while crediting Wakefield with the authorship of 'systematic colonization', accepted the other aspects of his general theory of empire as a part of their political baggage, without seeming to be especially aware of the novelty or the inner unity and consistency of this body of doctrine. The same was true of other Radicals who parroted

[1] *P.D.*, Commons, 16 March 1837, xxxvii, 597–601.
[2] *P.D.*, Commons, 15 March 1838, xli, 928–32.

these ideas – H. G. Ward, for example, the M.P. for Sheffield, and the editor of the *Weekly Chronicle*, or R. S. Rintoul, the editor of the *Spectator*.[1] One point emerges clearly: much of what has been regarded as characteristically Marxist doctrine was already common Radical belief when Marx came to England in 1849. The Benthamites – unlike other 'anticipators' of Marx – were not 'socialists' resting their argument upon an extension of the labour theory of value. Yet in their view of the relationship between master and man under the new industrialism, in their description of a society faced with a growing polarization of wealth, in which competition was driving down the rate of profit and pushing smaller capitalists into the ranks of the working class, a society on the brink of revolution, Buller, Molesworth, Ward, Rintoul, and others, following the major lines of Wakefield's analysis, had pre-empted the socialist economist. With this picture of industrialism in mind, fearing immediate democracy as a danger to the new economic system, the philosophic Radicals, in the 1830s and 1840s, sponsored an imperial programme to relieve mounting social pressures.

While the Cobdenite was 'orthodox' – and it was the orthodoxy of the optimistic economic harmonies of Frederic Bastiat[2] – the philosophic Radicals, as I have noted, saw the industrial and commercial system as operating most inharmoniously and requiring a constant expansion of the fields of production and employment if it were to survive. It was this severely amended classicism which formed the basis for the economic theories of empire of Wakefield and his disciples as well as for those of John Stuart Mill, the foremost Benthamite economist. In Parliament, in 1849, in the course of acknowledging his own debt to Wakefield, Molesworth had observed

[1] For Ward, see *P.D.*, Commons, 25 June 1839, XLVIII, 842–68; also *P.D.*, Commons, 13 June 1843, LXIX, 1496–1504. For the *Spectator*, see 'Emigration and Its Fraudulent Detractor', *Spectator*, XIV, No. 702 (11 December 1841), 1188–9.

[2] See letter of Cobden to Bright, 1 October 1851, quoted in John Morley, *The Life of Richard Cobden* (London: Fisher Unwin, 1905), p. 561.

that 'by his writings' Wakefield had 'produced a profound impression on the minds of some of the ablest men of our day, as for instance, John Mill, Grote, and others'.[1] Mill freely admitted Wakefield's influence, but he was not – like Molesworth, Buller, and their associates – a convert to Wakefield's sociology and political philosophy. In his *Principles of Political Economy*, in 1848, in which he paid a generous tribute to Wakefield, Mill declared that 'Colonization, in the present state of the world, is the best affair of business, in which the capital of an old and wealthy country can engage.' In advanced countries, Mill observed, largely following Wakefield's economic analysis, not capital, but 'fertile land' was deficient, and the legislator ought not to promote 'greater aggregate saving, but a greater return to savings . . . by access to the produce of more fertile land in other parts of the globe'. In specific terms, he observed that if 'one-tenth' of England's workers and capital were 'transferred to the colonies', wages and profits would benefit from 'the diminished pressure of capital and population upon the fertility of the land'. Acknowledging, in non-orthodox manner, that a surfeit of capital in England was pushing profits to the 'minimum', he asserted that one of 'the counter-forces which check the downward tendency of profits' was 'the perpetual overflow of capital into colonies of foreign countries'. 'I believe this to have been for many years one of the principal causes by which the decline of profits in England has been arrested.' Indeed, capital export, for Mill, was a precondition to the healthy functioning of advanced economies: 'As long as there are old countries where capital increases very rapidly, and new countries where profit is still high, profits in the old countries will not sink to the rate which would put a stop to accumulation.' 'The exportation of capital' was 'an agent of great efficacy in extending the field of employment' for the capital which remained at home, and would help to put off the advent of what the classical economists called the 'stationary state'.[2]

---

[1] *P.D.*, Commons, 26 June 1849, CVI, 940.

[2] J. S. Mill, *Principles of Political Economy* (London: Longmans, Green, 1909), pp. 727–8, 738–9, 741–2, 746, 748, 749. The first edition appeared in 1848.

III

The ideas of the Cobdenites conform more readily to the usual view – one common to such diverse students of the period as Professors Schuyler and Langer, and Lenin – of a mid-Victorian anti-colonialism. Yet, as Gallagher and Robinson have told us, despite the misleading adoption of Cobdenite cant by the major English leaders – even by Disraeli – in the fifties and sixties, and seventies, their views did not generally prevail. Those of the philosophic Radicals were much more in harmony with what actually happened, and the Benthamites even succeeded, on occasion, in urging a somewhat lethargic England on to more positive imperial activity.

The old colonial system – the system of mercantilist restrictions – was buried, but the Benthamites did not support the negative idea of empire of Richard Cobden and the men of Manchester, but a number of positive ones – systematic colonization was one of these – in this as in other areas of legislation. The Benthamites wished, by means of a universal free trade, to preserve England's position as the 'workshop of the world' – to maintain a trade empire which the German protectionist Frederick List and his American counterpart Henry Carey charged was designed to make the entire globe subservient to England.[1] Britain, content with its technological superiority and immense productive capacities, wanted free access to the markets of the world and new fields for the investment of its surplus capital. It was no longer necessary to impose a rigid colonialism upon undeveloped areas, as it had been during the period of the mercantile wars of the seventeenth and eighteenth centuries. Yet the philosophic Radicals believed England needed a formal empire as well for investment and market conditions of special safety; but they thought in terms of a different sort of imperial system than formerly. I have noted the settlement of Australia and New Zealand, largely under the auspices of the philosophic Radicals. Though the 'colonial reformers' urged that such colonies of settlement

---

[1] See F. List, *The National System of Political Economy* (New York, 1904); H. C. Carey, *Principles of Social Science* (Philadelphia, 1858); *The Way to Outdo England Without Fighting Her* (Philadelphia, 1865).

be given responsible government, they saw them tied so securely by sentiment and economic necessity to an imperial metropolis, which alone could provide manufactured goods for their agricultural exports, that it was no longer necessary to restrict colonial trade by legislation. There were, however, some, like the Benthamite Roebuck, who wished to prohibit the colonies from erecting tariffs against Britain,[1] and others, like the economist Robert Torrens, another Wakefield disciple though not a Benthamite, who proclaimed, sixty years before Joseph Chamberlain, the necessity of an Imperial Zollverein.[2]

These goals of the philosophic Radicals are different from those of the 'imperialism' of the years between 1880 and 1914, a product of the growing competition of industrial nations for colonies. Such a programme of aggressive expansion was not required when England possessed an industrial monopoly, and was the leader of world finance and commerce. But the Benthamites were not free of the animus which contemporary opinion associates with an active colonialism. In 1833, for instance, Wakefield suggested that England, by appropriate threats, obtain special privileges from China, including islands off its coast, to be used as emporia,[3] thus anticipating the policy of the Opium War, in 1839–40, which secured the island of Hong Kong. The war, though opposed by Tories like Peel, was actively supported in Parliament by Buller, Ward, Hume and other Radicals.[4] (Hume even spoke in favour of the war in the Punjab, in 1849, to protect Indian trade.)[5] The parliamentary campaign of Molesworth and Buller and other 'colonial reformers' in the forties against the interference of the Colonial Office and its permanent Under-Secretary, James Stephen ('Mr Mother-Country') in the affairs of overseas colonies was not simply an early step towards the Statute of

---

[1] J. A. Roebuck, *The Colonies of England* (London, 1849), p. 153.

[2] See R. Torrens, *The Budget* (London, 1844); see also L. Robbins, *Robert Torrens and the Evolution of Classical Economics* (London: Macmillan, 1958), Chapter VII.

[3] Wakefield, *England and America*, pp. 150–89.

[4] *P.D.*, Commons, 8 April 1840, LIII, 781–90 (Buller); 824–30 (Ward); 27 July 1840, LV, 1051–2 (Hume).

[5] *P.D.*, Commons, 5 March 1849, CIII, 168; 24 April 1849, CIV, 752–3.

Westminster, as it is usually regarded by historians, but a protest against the efforts of the Colonial Office and missionary
bodies to halt the policy of land grabbing and the local wars
of extermination which New Zealand colonists were waging
against the Maori.[1] The Welensky government and the Alger-
ian *colons*, today, would also like to be free of the interference
of the metropolis.

I have not, however, been primarily concerned in this short
paper with the influence of the philosophic Radicals upon the
actual formulation and execution of policy, but with their
development of a theory of free-trade colonialism – a doctrine
which helps to clarify imperial policy during the decades of
Britain's trade monopoly and prosperity, which was readily
converted, under the pressure of foreign competition, to the
liberal imperialism of Rosebery, Haldane, and Mackinder,
about the time of the Boer War,[2] and which, finally, brilliantly
anticipated twentieth-century theories of imperialism. How
may the understanding of the 'ideology' of Wakefield and his
disciples affect the lines of future research? So far as the history of economic ideas is concerned, the acceptance, among the
philosophic Radicals – who were the parents, godparents, and
indulgent relatives of classical economics – of opinions regarded as heresy when later proclaimed by Hobson and Keynes,
deserves more attention. It would be helpful to investigate the
provenance of Marxist economic doctrines from the standpoint of these Benthamite colonial views. More important,
these Benthamite doctrines provide useful insights into the
early relationship of industrialism and 'imperialism', and raise
further substantial questions concerning the leading theories
of colonialism and imperialism. For example, do they not provide additional ground for questioning Schumpeter's brilliant
if contrived, theory that the *fin-de-siècle* imperialism was an
atavism, thoroughly out of line with the temper of capitalism
in its classic period? Does it not arouse serious doubts about

[1] *P.D.*, Commons, 17 June 1845, LXXXI, 665–726; 21 July 1845, LXXXII,
807 ff; 23 July 1845, 970–1011; 30 July 1845, 1239.

[2] B. Semmel, *Imperialism and Social Reform* (Cambridge: Harvard Univ. Press,
1960), Chapters III, VII, VIII.

the Marxist idea – developed by Luxemburg, Hilferding, and others – that 'imperialism' was a product of *spätkapitalismus*, of a capitalism in its 'highest-stage', in which 'finance' not 'industry' was predominant? The Benthamite economists presented an acute analysis of the process of empire building and its motivations and, unlike more recent theories, a comparatively disinterested one. The keenness and comparative freedom from polemics of their description of the economic relationship between an industrial England and a predominantly agricultural world may even be a help in our understanding of the present-day relationship between advanced and underdeveloped nations.

4 Classical Economics and the Case for Colonization

D. N. WINCH

[This article was first published in *Economica*, Vol. XXX (1963).]

In the 1830s a case for reviving the 'lost art of colonization' was put forward by the Colonial Reform movement; the histories of South Australia and New Zealand bear ample testimony to its practical successes. This article considers the nature and significance of the economic arguments employed in the advocacy of colonization by Edward Gibbon Wakefield, the leader of the movement. They are of interest in the history of economic thought for several reasons. First, the case for colonization was largely developed as an attack on Ricardian orthodoxy; it belongs, therefore, to an active underworld which has attracted comment in recent years. Secondly, in their search for an approach to capital accumulation, investment opportunities, and expanding markets which would be more relevant to British economic problems than Ricardian prescriptions, the colonizers looked back to Adam Smith. Thirdly, Wakefield gained widespread support from contemporary economic writers; and in particular from John Stuart Mill, the last major Classical spokesman.

I

It would have been possible to construct a case for colonization on Ricardian lines; it could, for instance, have been built on Ricardo's remark that 'if with every accumulation of capital we could tack a piece of fertile land to our Island, profits would never fall'.[1] But the Ricardians did not look on colonies in

[1] *Works and Correspondence of David Ricardo*, ed. P. Sraffa, Vol. VI, p. 162.

this way, as places where the return to British capital and labour in agriculture was higher than at home. A strong presumption against the creation of new colonial responsibilities existed among Classical writers prior to Wakefield's campaign. They placed their faith in the repeal of the Corn Laws as the best means of arresting the decline of profits. Nevertheless the question remains not only why Wakefield chose not to make use of Ricardian arguments but also why he considered it necessary to attack the orthodox Classical macroeconomic position as represented by the writings of Ricardo, McCulloch, and James Mill.

Several opinions have been offered on this point already. J. S. Mill, as will be stressed later, refused to consider that Wakefield's views contradicted 'the principles of the best school of preceding political economists'.[1] Dr G. S. L. Tucker, influenced perhaps by Mill's comment, has said that Wakefield's anti-Ricardianism was a 'peculiar feature' of his writings, and concluded that he 'simply did not understand the theories that he criticized so confidently'.[2] Another view of the matter has been taken by Lord Robbins, who argues that Mill failed to see the non-Ricardian element which is inherent in Wakefield's position.[3]

Wakefield was not impressed by the Ricardian analysis of the British economic situation; he was more drawn to the underconsumptionist views of Malthus's disciple, Thomas Chalmers.[4] He subscribed, in his own words, to 'a sort of heresy in political economy which has thrown light on many points which had been left in total darkness by those who imagine that the science was perfected by Ricardo'.[5] He believed that

[1] *Principles of Political Economy*, Ashley edn., p. 728.

[2] *Progress and Profits in British Economic Thought, 1650–1850*, 1960, p. 184.

[3] *Robert Torrens and the Evolution of Classical Economics*, 1958, pp. 247–8. To this should be added Dr Corry's criticism of Tucker for insufficient sympathy with Wakefield's difficulties. See 'Progress and Profits', *Economica*, Vol. XXVII (1961), p. 207.

[4] He described Chalmers' *On Political Economy* as a work which 'so abounds in novel and important speculations, that no one, who has derived his knowledge from other books on political economy, can truly suppose that he has mastered that science. . . .' See his edition of the *Wealth of Nations*, 1833 (4 vols.), Vol. I, p. 243.   [5] Ibid., p. xiii.

the main problem facing the British economy in the 1830s was shortage of profitable investment opportunities. In spite of technological advance (and because of artificial barriers like the Corn Laws), the limits of the 'field of employment' for capital had not expanded sufficiently to absorb, at existing rates of profit and wages, the increase in capital accumulation and population which had taken place since 1815.

> The field, the capital, and the people, may increase, yet if the enlargement of the field be not more rapid than the increase of capital, no alteration of profits will occur; nor any alteration of wages, unless the field be enlarged and capital be increased, at the same time, more rapidly than people shall increase. Though in such a state of society, both capitalists and labourers will increase in number, though new means of communication will be opened, though fresh towns will arise, though the increase of population and of national wealth may be striking; nevertheless the rate of profits may still be low, the rate of wages but just sufficient to permit an increase of labourers, the majority of the capitalists in a state of uneasiness, and the whole body of labourers miserable and degraded.[1]

Britain was suffering from a general glut of capital; all trades were 'overstocked' and no mere distribution of capital could bring relief. Losses were widespread and profits so low that capitalists were forced either to leave their funds lying idle or to squander them in speculative foreign ventures. Yet capital accumulation continued and the only relief came from 'occasional destruction of capital on the greatest scale'.[2] The evidence presented in support of this view was not very substantial or systematically organized, a common fault in several of the crucial discussions of this period. It consisted chiefly of instances of 'wasteful' loans to South American republics,

[1] *England and America*, 1833 (2 vols.), Vol. I, p. 129; see also pp. 12–14, 85–9 and Note IV.
[2] See *Art of Colonization*, 1849, pp. 75–6, and *England and America*, pp. 88–9, 17–18.

mining ventures and scattered evidence of the low rate of return on capital in a number of trades.[1]

Wakefield was not always successful, or interested, in stating precisely in theoretical terms where he differed from the Ricardians. Some of his criticisms of their position were crude and unfair, which lends support to Tucker's charge. He accused them of having concentrated on the division of the total product between capital and labour while ignoring the 'field' in which they are employed and the growth of total product. He ridiculed dogmatic statements by James Mill that 'wages depend on the proportion between labour and capital', and the view that profits fall as wages rise. They would not, he believed, have been able to explain the simultaneous existence of low profits and low wages in Britain and high profits and high wages in America.[2]

Although the Ricardians would not have favoured the term 'field of employment' they would certainly have agreed with Wakefield's application of it to the Corn Laws.[3] Moreover, it is obvious that Wakefield did not or would not understand the special sense in which Ricardians spoke of high wages and low profits.[4] When questioned by J. A. Roebuck as to whether he realized that they were speaking only of 'proportionate quantities' and not absolute levels, Wakefield replied that 'some of them have endeavoured to give that explanation since the doctrine was attacked', but before this had implied 'that the only possible way in which the conditions of the bulk of the people in an old country can be improved, is by increasing the quantity of capital'.[5] Here again Wakefield was unfair

[1] See *England and America*, particularly Note III where Wakefield deals extensively with the 'distress' among the middle classes and all those living on small capitals.

[2] See *England and America*, Note IV, and his edition of the *Wealth of Nations*, Vol. I, Notes to Book I, Chapters VII and IX.

[3] Wakefield seems to have recognized this in his discussion of the theory of rent in his edition of the *Wealth of Nations*, Vol. II, Note to Book I, Chapter XI; but he conveniently overlooked it in his attack on their other views.

[4] Wakefield's partner Torrens understood this notion and gave an excellent explanation of Ricardo's position in his *Colonization of South Australia*, 1835, pp. 27–8.

[5] *Select Committee on the Disposal of Land in the British Colonies*, B.P.P., 1836, XI, Q. 977.

to their position. Ricardo plainly foresaw the possibility that further accumulation under some circumstances might not be beneficial.[1]

But it is easy to see how it was possible for Wakefield to consider the Ricardians 'as a new sect who have set up a new god, which is called Capital, and which they worship devoutly'.[2] They created the impression that, so far as Britain was concerned, further accumulation was desirable, and any loss, waste or export of capital was to be deplored.[3] Adherence to Say's Law ensured that the process of accumulation would be self-regulatory; in Ricardo's words, 'at the same time that capital is increased, the work to be effected by capital, is increased in the same proportion'.[4] Even in the stationary state stagnation was impossible, as a mechanism existed to switch savings into consumption once profits reached the minimum.[5]

It was this position which Wakefield believed to stand in the way of recognition of the need for colonization which involved the export of capital. The real point of difference between him and the Ricardians concerned the theoretical possibility and actual existence of secular stagnation in Britain. He was denying the assumption of Say's Law by arguing that the demand or 'field of employment' for capital was not co-extensive with its supply, and that capital accumulation could take place in the absence of profitable investment opportunities, making possible the simultaneous existence of redundant capital and labour.[6]

To understand Wakefield's reasons for attacking Ricardianism it is necessary to bear in mind the objection which had

[1] *Works*, Vol. I, p. 99.

[2] *England and America*, Vol. I, p. 114.

[3] See Tucker, op. cit., pp. 125–6, 142–3, and 162. Concerning the export of capital see Ricardo, *Works*, Vol. I, pp. 136–7, 247–8, 396–7; Vol. III, p. 274; Vol. IV, pp. 16 n, 237; Vol. V, p. 38.

[4] *Works*, Vol. I, pp. 289–90.

[5] See *Works*, Vol. IX, p. 25 for a clear statement of the distinction between the stationary state and stagnation. For comment on this doctrine, see M. Blaug, *Ricardian Economics*, 1958, pp. 90–3.

[6] For a similar interpretation of Torrens' views, see L. Robbins, op. cit., pp. 175–81. For Ricardo's denial of the possibility of redundant capital *and* labour, see *Works*, Vol. VIII, pp. 185; also Vol. II, pp. 426–7.

been made by members of the Classical School to schemes for assisting emigration to British colonies put forward by Wilmot-Horton in the 1820s. It was most clearly expressed by James Mill.[1]

It has been often enough, and clearly enough, explained that it is only capital which gives employment for labour; we may, therefore, take it as a postulate. A certain quantity of capital, then, is necessary to give employment to the population, which any removal for the sake of colonization may leave behind. But if, to afford the expense of that removal, so much is taken from the capital of the country, that the remainder is not sufficient for the employment of the remaining population, there is in that case, a redundancy of population, and all the evils which it brings.

It was in response to this objection that Wakefield gave the best statement of the issue separating him from his opponents. He maintained that James Mill's argument was based on the assumption 'first, that no labour is employed save by capital, secondly, that all capital employs labour'. He denied the second assumption:[2]

It does not follow that, because labour is employed by capital, capital always finds a field in which to employ labour. This is a *non-sequitur* always taken for granted by Bentham, Ricardo, Mill, McCulloch and others. Adam Smith on the contrary, saw that there were limits besides the limit of capital, to the employment of labour, the limits, namely of the field of production, and the market in which to dispose of surplus produce.

Horton was handicapped in his reply to the charge of capital loss because in his case for emigration he had made use

[1] Article 'Colony' for the *Supplement to the Encyclopaedia Britannica*, p. 13. His argument assumes wage rigidity downwards.

[2] *England and America*, Vol. II, p. 103 n. He considered that Bentham's *Manual of Political Economy* was responsible for bringing to the fore the principle of 'the limitation of production and trade by the limitation of capital'. The idea can be found in the *Wealth of Nations*, Cannan edition, Modern Library, pp. 421–5; but Bentham's *Manual* was built around the principle.

of the wage-fund doctrine upon which it is based.[1] Wakefield was interested in removing the basis of the charge altogether because even though he contended that his system would make emigration self-financing, he wished to portray colonization as the best means of enlarging the field of employment for capital as well as labour. The conclusion which he drew from his analysis was 'that capital, for which there is no employment at home, might be spent on emigration without diminishing employment for labour to the slightest extent. I use the word *spent* instead of *invested*, in order to save the trouble of explaining at length, that if capital so employed were utterly lost, that loss of capital need not diminish employment for labour.'[2] In fact he regarded colonization, if conducted according to his principles, to be the means of reducing the pressure of accumulated capital on profits in Britain by providing new investment opportunities.

II

In making his criticisms of Ricardianism Wakefield claimed to find support in Adam Smith for his view of the relationship of capital accumulation, profit decline, and stagnation.[3] This may appear to be a strange claim in view of the fact that Smith is generally regarded as having laid the foundation for the orthodox Classical macroeconomic position in his doctrine of 'saving is spending'.[4] Smith had expressed no concern about further capital accumulation or even the decline of profits; he certainly had not considered the possibility of stagnation and was never under pressure, as Ricardo was from Malthus, to do so. But his interpretation of the decline of profits in terms of 'competition of capitals', as a simple demand and supply phenomenon, allowed for the possibility of 'excess' capital

[1] See his *Causes and Remedies of Pauperism*, Introductory Series, 1830, pp. 65–70.

[2] *England and America*, Vol. II, pp. 98–100.

[3] In his edition of the *Wealth of Nations* Wakefield set out 'to vindicate some of (Smith's) doctrines which modern writers have impugned', Vol. I, p. xiv. For his defence of Smith's theory of profits, see ibid, Vol. I, pp. xvi, 244–6; and *England and America*, Vol. I, pp. 115–16, and Vol. II, p. 103 n.

[4] See e.g. Tucker, op. cit. p. 123 and B. A. Corry, *Money, Savings and Investment in English Economics, 1800–1950*, 1962, pp. 19–25.

accumulation in relation to investment opportunities. Ricardo recognized this loophole and went to some lengths to close it.[1]

Wakefield was not alone in his appeal to Smith's authority; other critics of Ricardo, like Malthus, did the same.[2] And by the 1840s there were others who were sympathetic to Wakefield's revival of Smith's theory of profits. Herman Merivale provides us with judicious comment on the issues at stake as it appeared to an informed contemporary observer.[3] He acknowledged the formal correctness of Ricardo's model but considered that 'under the actual circumstances of society' Smith's idea of 'competition of capitals' had much to commend it. He accepted the idea that capital accumulation does not necessarily increase the field of employment, for he claimed that when profits fell to a certain minimum 'any further savings out of its return must be spent unproductively or left idle'. His conclusion was:[4]

> . . . although the inferior quality of newly-cultivated soil be the immediate cause of the diminution of the rate of profits, it is nothing but the competition among the capitalists which drives capital to seek the inferior soil, and induces its owner to be content with a lower profit. When population has increased so far as to demand the cultivation of fresh soil, from whence is the capital derived which is to be employed upon it? From the accumulations made by the capitalists at the old rate of profit. What, then, induces the

[1] Ricardo, *Works*, Vol. I, Chapter XXI, *passim*.

[2] See Tucker op. cit. p. 130. See Malthus, *Principles of Political Economy*, 1820, pp. 308–11, 326, 331. In the *Additions to 4th and Former Editions of an Essay on the Principle of Population*, 1817, there is a more overt parallel with Wakefield when he says: 'This country, from the extent of its lands, and its rich colonial possessions, has a large *arena* for the employment of an increasing capital' (p. 117).

[3] Merivale's account is free from the distortion which sometimes occurs when past controversies are viewed through modern eyes. Wakefield has already suffered from this; witness J. B. Condliffe's statement that Wakefield's views on the field of employment come 'very close indeed to the concept of national income which has been emphasized by J. M. Keynes and his followers since 1936'. *The Commerce of Nations*, 1950, p. 256.

[4] See *Lectures on Colonies and Colonization*, Oxford University Press reprint, 1928, pp. 170–4, and his review of McCulloch's edition of the *Wealth of Nations*, *Edinburgh Review*, No. CXLII, January 1840, p. 443.

capitalist to be content with a lower rate of profit from his new investment? The fact that he cannot otherwise employ his savings at all. He is content with a lower rate of profit rather than consume them unproductively.

Wakefield returned to Smith for remedies as well as analysis. To someone anxious to stress the value to Britain of new colonial markets and investment opportunities, Smith's more dynamic approach to the gains from foreign trade was attractive. The differences between Ricardo and Smith on this question have been noted by Allyn Young, J. H. Williams and, more recently, Hla Myint.[1] The point is worth stressing in this context since it has an important bearing on the case for colonization. Myint has pointed out that Smith speaks of two types of gain from trade: first, the gain through increased productivity, and secondly, the gain via the 'vent for surplus'. Widened markets increase productivity by permitting and stimulating greater division of labour and the use of improved techniques. The notion of 'vent for surplus', or the idea that trade 'carries out that surplus part of the produce of . . . land and labour for which there is not demand at home', clearly assumes that prior to the opening of trade resources are not fully employed. It follows that trade has a direct impact on the level of economic activity and that exports can be increased without reducing domestic production. Smith did not justify this assumption; it is dealt with as part of his conjectural history of growth and is treated as a generalization open to empirical observation. He implies that it is due to poor communications, 'indivisibilities', and insufficient 'penetration' of the market in the early stages of development.[2]

Smith's formulation found little favour among the Ricardians. It conceded too much to the business man's view of

[1] Allyn Young, 'Increasing Returns and Economic Progress', *Economic Journal*, Vol. XXXVIII (1928), pp. 527–42; J. H. Williams, 'The Theory of International Trade Reconsidered', reprinted in *Readings in the Theory of International Trade*, 1950, pp. 253–71, and Hla Myint, 'The "Classical Theory" of International Trade and the Underdeveloped Countries', *Economic Journal*, Vol. LXVIII (1958), pp. 317–37.

[2] See *Wealth of Nations*, Cannan edition, Modern Library, pp. 18, 353–4, 384–6, 415–16, 574–5.

markets as an expansive force and gave comfort to those who argued the need for measures to stimulate the demand for output. It contradicted two of the basic assumptions of the theory of comparative costs; internal factor mobility and full employment of all resources before the opening of trade. This theory was an improvement in the analysis of the reasons for international specialization; but for the Ricardians it had the additional significance of being fully in accord with the assumption of Say's Law. It explained the gains from trade without leaving the door open for their under-consumptionist critics. This is borne out by the fact that even before the enunciation of the idea of comparative cost we find those holding to some version of Say's Law consistently denying the importance of new markets to the level of economic activity.

This can be seen in Bentham, who in his early work on political economy developed a form of Say's Law as applied to agriculture. He held that since agricultural products 'constantly and necessarily produce a market for themselves' it was impossible for a country to have too much agriculture. In other words, unlimited investment opportunities existed so that capital withdrawn from, say, the colonial trade, would find equally profitable employment at home.[1] His position is summarized in the following quotation:[2]

> Trade is the child of capital. In proportion to the quantity of capital a country has at its disposal, will, in every country be the quantity of its trade. While you have no more capital employed in trade than you have, all the power on earth cannot give you more trade. . . . It may take one shape or another shape, it may give you more foreign goods to consume, or more home goods . . . but the quantity and value of the goods . . . will always be the same. . . . It is the *quantity of capital*, not *extent of market* that determines the quantity of trade. Open a new market, you do not, unless by accident, increase the sum of trade. Shut up an old market, you do not, unless by accident, or for the moment, diminish the

[1] See *Bentham's Economic Writings*, ed. W. Stark, 1952–4, Vol. I, pp. 215–18.

[2] *Emancipate Your Colonies!* in *Collected Works*, ed. J. Bowring, 1843, Vol. IV, p. 411.

sum of trade. In what case, then, is the sum of trade increased by a new market?

A similar idea was expressed by James Mill in his reply to Spence which contains one of the classic statements of Say's Law. In this we find a striking comment on the unimportance of foreign trade to the level of economic activity.[1]

> ... no exact estimate can be made of what any nation gains by commerce. It may, however, be safely concluded that its importance is in general greatly overrated. Every arm could be employed and every article of the annual produce could be sold, if the country were surrounded by Friar Bacon's Wall of Brass, a thousand feet high. The labour of the nation would not be so productive; the annual produce would not be so large; the people would not be so cheaply, that is, liberally supplied with commodities; neither individuals, nor the government, could spend so much without turning back the progress of the country. But every labourer would find work, and every shilling of capital would find employment.

Ricardo's statement of the issue is more subtle. With his theory of comparative costs he was able to give a more detailed account of the gains from international specialization. It was also necessary for him to consider the relationship of new markets to the central problem of declining profit. He denied that the general level of profits could permanently be affected by new markets for goods or outlets for capital. In fact it seems to have been an argument by Malthus linking markets and profits that elicited from Ricardo the first clear statement of his own theory of profits.[2] His conclusion was:[3]

> Foreign trade, then, though highly beneficial to a country, as it increases the amount and variety of the objects on which

---

[1] *Commerce Defended*, 2nd ed., 1808, pp. 106–7.

[2] See his letter to Trower stating the issue between himself and Malthus *Works*, Vol. VI, pp. 103–5. Time and again they came back to this problem; see e.g. Vol. VI, pp. 110–11, 113–15, 119, 128–9, 140, 162–3, 167, 170, 223. See also G. S. L. Tucker, 'The Origin of Ricardo's Theory of Profits', *Economica*, Vol. XXI (1954), pp. 320–33.

[3] *Works*, Vol. I, p. 133. See also p. 291 n, for his views on Smith's theory of foreign trade.

revenue may be expended, and affords, by the abundance and cheapness of commodities, incentives to saving, and to the accumulation of capital, has no tendency to raise the profits of stock, unless the commodities imported be of that description on which the wages of labour are expended.

Given the assumption of full employment, the opening of new markets merely leads to the rearrangement of existing factors of production among different employments. Where a new market was opened up say by the removal of trade barriers, the re-allocation of resources was beneficial to consumers since more commodities would be obtained from the same outlay of domestic factors of production. The closing of markets would likewise affect adversely the allocation of world resources, but would not, except perhaps temporarily, affect the level of employment; resources released by the closure would be re-absorbed at existing rates of reward.[1]

The assumption of full employment by later Classical writers made it possible for them to make a division in their subject matter which is very modern in spirit. A major part of their inquiry dealt with the problem of growth treated macro-economically in terms of capital accumulation and profits. Separate from this, and most clearly developed in the theory of international trade, there is the line of inquiry which is most akin to modern welfare economics in that it is concerned with microeconomic allocative efficiency or the problem of obtaining the best use of given full-employed resources. The two questions are not completely separated because Ricardo acknowledged that the 'efficiency' gains from foreign trade would give incentives to saving. He also made it clear that he saw no conflict between 'efficiency' gains and those to be derived from arresting the fall of profits, thus protecting accumulation and the future growth of the system as a whole: the problem of growth *versus* choice did not exist for him. 'It is quite as important to the happiness of mankind, that our enjoyments should be increased by the better distribution of

---

[1] Perhaps the clearest statements of the Ricardian position in relation to that of Smith are by J. R. McCulloch in *Edinburgh Review*, No. LXXXIV, August 1825, pp. 287–8, and J. S. Mill, *Principles*, pp. 579–80.

labour, by each country producing those commodities for which by its situation, its climate, and its other natural or artificial advantages, it is adapted, and by their exchanging them for the commodities of other countries, as that they should be augmented by a rise in the rate of profits.'[1]

In terms of logical coherence and analytical sophistication the Ricardian theory marked a definite advance on the work of Smith. But these improvements were bought at a price which many have considered too high in terms of loss of explanatory content. Ricardo was notoriously cavalier in his treatment of 'disturbing factors' and adjustment processes; in Professor R. S. Sayers's words, he was addicted to the assumption of 'instantaneous adjustment to a long-run equilibrium'. Smith's less rigorous, quasi-historical approach to growth had much to commend it; a common-sense link was forged between capital accumulation, investment opportunities, and expanding markets. J. S. Mill might consider Smith's treatment of foreign trade to be a 'surviving relic of Mercantile theory'; but as Allyn Young has said, 'the business man's mercantilistic emphasis upon markets may have a sounder basis than the economist who thinks in terms of economic statics is prone to admit'.[2]

It was precisely this mercantilist emphasis which attracted Wakefield to Smith's approach.[3] He felt that the Ricardians had given insufficient importance to the new markets that would be created for British capital and manufactured goods by colonization. Unlike them, he did not feel that repeal of the Corn Laws alone would be sufficient to provide cheaper food for Britain's growing population.[4] Colonization provided the

[1] *Works*, Vol. I, p. 132.

[2] Loc cit., p. 537.

[3] 'If (the Mercantilist writers) did not know scientifically, that all improvements in the productive power of industry, that industry itself, is limited by the extent of the market, still they felt that every new colony . . . increased by so much the means of exchanging the produce of English labour, and by so much increased the wealth of England.' *England and America*, Vol. II, p. 81.

[4] *England and America*, Vol. I, Note VI; Vol. II, pp. 87–95. He recommended immediate repeal on the interesting grounds that a sudden reduction in the price of bread, money wages remaining constant, would lead via the income-effect to a rise in the demand for other domestic foodstuffs like meat, thereby cushioning the impact of repeal on British farmers.

means whereby European skills and capital could be combined to extend cheaper sources of food and raw materials and make them more secure. He was not in favour of the old colonial system nor did he support Torrens' idea of a colonial Zollverein; his point was simply that although it was not necessary to govern colonies to trade with them, it was necessary for colonies to exist.

It is important to recognize that despite certain parallels Wakefield was not simply another under-consumptionist critic of Ricardo. He occupies a middle position. Speaking of the two camps he says: 'Neither clan admit the possibility of enlarging the field of employment for capital and labour so as to permit without injury to any one, and with benefit to all for ages to come, the most rapid increase of people and capital.'[1] He did not support any of the standard under-consumptionist remedies because he held that in colonization the means existed to provide a positive long-term solution to British problems. In this respect he was like Smith, for he believed that widened markets would guarantee unlimited investment opportunities. Unlike Smith, however, he did not regard the 'negative' solution of removing trade barriers to be an adequate method of releasing the forces of growth: the creation of colonies required some positive state action.

III

Although several prominent economists, notably Torrens, Senior, Merivale, and Whateley, gave their support to Wakefield's schemes for systematic colonization, J. S. Mill is of particular interest.[2] He always treated Wakefield's ideas with great respect and gave them prominence in his *Principles* long after systematic colonization had passed from the scene as a public issue.[3] Since Mill was so sympathetically inclined to Wakefield's ideas, the question is raised as to what influence

[1] See his edition of the *Wealth of Nations*, Vol. I, p. 253.

[2] For a thorough examination of Wakefield's supporters, see D. Pike, *Paradise of Dissent: South Australia 1829–1857*, 1957. The part played by Robert Torrens is dealt with in L. Robbins, op. cit., Chapter VI.

[3] See e.g. Book I, Chapter VIII, and pp. 381–4, 727–39, 963–6, 969–75.

the anti-Ricardian arguments associated with the advocacy of colonization had on his theoretical and policy position.

Mill attempted to bring the case for colonization within the orthodox fold by accepting Wakefield's ideas on the relationship of accumulation to profit decline simply as corollaries of Ricardian principles. He acknowledged, however, that they were 'corollaries which, perhaps, would not always have been admitted by [the best school of preceding political economists] themselves'.[1] He acceded to the policy implications of Wakefield's case while retaining a thin veneer of theoretical consistency with his earlier expositions of the fall of profits in Ricardian terms and his defence of Say's Law. In this way the basic Classical macroeconomic analysis was maintained intact, even though, as Professor T. W. Hutchison has indicated, in going so far towards Wakefield's position he 'completely undermines the relevance of his theoretical analysis of the impossibility of general over-production'.[2] The possibility of stagnation is denied but the spectre of the stationary state is admitted to be real. Instead of being a theoretical construct of at most a remote contingency, we find that owing to the rapid rate of accumulation possible in a secure and mature economy 'the rate of profit is habitually within, as it were, a hand's breadth of the minimum, and the country therefore on the very verge of the stationary state'.[3] This situation is avoided only by the destruction of accumulated capital during the depression phase of the business cycle; by improvements in technology or the opening up of new markets which cheapen goods purchased by wage-earners; and by the export of capital in search of higher profits.

One of the most far-reaching effects of Mill's acceptance of Wakefield's position concerning capital accumulation was that it led him to re-consider the question of the effects of government expenditure and to repudiate the 'Treasury View'.[4]

---

[1] See e.g. Book I, Chapter VIII, p. 728.
[2] *Review of Economic Doctrines, 1870–1929*, 1953, p. 353.
[3] *Principles*, 731.
[2] Ibid., p. 740.

The theory of the effect of accumulation on profits, laid down in the preceding chapter, materially alters many of the practical conclusions which might otherwise be supposed to follow from the general principles of Political Economy, and which were, indeed, long admitted as true by the highest authorities on the subject. It must greatly abate, or rather altogether destroy, in countries where profits are low, the immense importance which used to be attached by political economists to the effects which an event or a measure of government might have in adding to or subtracting from the capital of the country.

Ricardo's fears concerning the export of capital, and the argument that state support of emigration entailed loss to those who remained at home, were swept away. The export of British capital to America and colonies of European settlement becomes the natural complement to repeal of the Corn Laws.[1]

As Dr Corry has pointed out, another significant feature of the colonization discussion is that it shows that Mill recognized the possibility of flaws in the *laissez-faire* process of growth in capitalist economies.[2] If colonization was an economic necessity for Britain, then it would require government support. Mill took a surprisingly strong stand on the question of assisted emigration; despite the fact that the majority of the emigrants of this period went privately, he seems to have had difficulty in believing that unaided emigration, except in the Irish case, could have any real effect on the population problem. As late as 1865 he argued that 'it is not certain that the aid of government in a systematic form . . . will not again become necessary to keep the communication open between hands needing work in England, and the work which needs hands elsewhere'.[3]

---

[1] *Principles*, pp. 739–42. This should be taken in conjunction with his earlier statement that trade with colonies should be regarded as akin to trade within a country; colonies were regions where Britain found it convenient to produce raw materials and to which British capital flowed freely (pp. 685–6).

[2] Corry, *Money, Savings and Investment . . .*, pp. 37–8.

[3] *Principles*, pp. 971, 975. He retained this passage in the 1865 edition even though he had stated (p. 385) that the need had declined owing to cheaper transport, etc.

Mill appears to have acquired from Wakefield's writings a new appreciation of the importance of expanding markets to economic growth, in both mature and underdeveloped economies. This can be seen in the chapter which he devoted to Wakefield's analysis of the 'political economy of new countries' and in his recognition of a special category of gain to be derived by underdeveloped economies from foreign trade.[1] But he was always careful to state that in allowing new markets to play a larger rôle he was not abandoning the idea that 'a market for commodities does not constitute demand for labour'.[2] This balancing act provides an answer to the question why Wakefield's attack on orthodoxy did not have a more lasting effect on Classical macroeconomic theory. Mill's acceptance of the prescriptions while overlooking the theory behind them muffled the impact; when colonization faded as a public issue nothing was left except the reference in Mill's *Principles*; if the subject was mentioned by later writers it was as an obscure example of an exception to the *laissez-faire* rule.[3]

But it is no exaggeration to say that Wakefield's work induced Mill to re-consider a range of expansive forces that were part of Smith's inquiry into growth, but were excluded or pushed into the background by the Ricardians. In this way Wakefield played a part in making Classical political economy more relevant to the conditions of mid-nineteenth-century Britain by bringing attention to factors such as the export of capital and the opening up of new markets and sources of supply, which were important to the growth of the British economy up to 1914.

[1] *Principles*, Book I, Chapter VIII, and pp. 118–22, 681.

[2] Ibid., pp. 120, 579–80.

[3] See e.g. H. Sidgwick, *Principles of Political Economy*, 1883, pp. 466 ff.; H. Fawcett, *Manual of Political Economy*, 5th ed., 1876, pp. 59–63.

5 The Colonization Controversy: R. J. Wilmot-Horton and the Classical Economists

R. N. GHOSH

[This article was first published in *Economica*, Vol. XXXI (1964).]

In a recent article Dr D. N. Winch has presented an interesting discussion of the ideas of the classical economists concerning colonies and colonization.[1] His discussion revolves around Wakefield, who, in spite of his un-Ricardian views on saving and investment, was successful in persuading many contemporary economists, especially Torrens and John Stuart Mill, to support his economic arguments for colonization. The rôle of Wakefield in the history of British colonization is generally known.[2] The role of Wakefield's rival, Horton, on the other hand, is not properly appreciated.[3] In the 1820s Horton was certainly the leading advocate of colonization, who made the acquaintance of most of the contemporary classical economists, including Malthus, James Mill, Torrens, Senior, and Mc-Culloch, and induced several of them to examine and approve the need for a scheme of systematic emigration as a means to relieve over-population at home.

Our knowledge of Horton has been limited, and has also been somewhat distorted because of the charges made against him by Wakefield and his followers in the columns of the

[1] D. N. Winch, 'Classical Economics and the Case for Colonization', *Economica*, Vol. XXX (1963), pp. 387–99.

[2] R. C. Mills, *The Colonization of Australia, 1829–1842*, 1915.

[3] The only known full biography of Horton is an unpublished thesis (1936) of Bristol University, by E. G. Jones. I am considerably indebted to this work.

Spectator. In the present article, which is based largely on the Horton Papers,[1] an attempt is made to re-assess Horton's contributions to economic thought on emigration and colonization. The aim is three-fold: first, to examine the economic arguments Horton used to support his scheme of state-aided emigration; second, to trace the nature of the Horton-Wakefield controversy over colonization; and third, to consider the role of the classical economists in this controversy.

I

The widespread economic distress in Britain which followed the Napoleonic wars was generally attributed to an excessive increase of population. Possibly because this increase of population occurred at the same time as British colonial expansion, it was thought by some that the emigration of surplus population to the colonies might be a possible remedy for the econ-omic distress in the mother country. Among the economists, Malthus in his *Essay on Population* (1817 edition), Torrens in *A Paper on the Means of Reducing Poors* [*sic*] *Rates* (1817), and thereafter David Buchanan in an article on Emigration in the *Supplement* to the *Encyclopaedia Britannica* (1824) were prepared to support emigration in certain circumstances. Yet, in general, suggestions in favour of colonization and pauper-emigration were received with suspicion, although, compared with the situation in the closing years of the eighteenth century, the climate of opinion was certainly becoming less hostile. It was during these years that R. J. Wilmot-Horton appeared on the scene, and by his own efforts and indomitable energy was able to arouse intense public interest in problems of emigration and colonization.

Horton succeeded Henry Goulburn in December 1821 as Under Secretary of State for War and the Colonies. Shortly after joining the Colonial Office he drew up a plan of colonization,

[1] The Horton Papers are now in the Central County Library, Derby. A list of some items in the Horton Papers was given in the Appendix to my article, 'Malthus on Emigration and Colonization: Letters to Wilmot-Horton', *Economica*, Vol. XXX (1963), pp. 45–62.

an enlarged version of which was published with two Appendices in the *Report of the Parliamentary Select Committee on the Employment of the Poor in Ireland*, 1823. The basic object of the plan was that the poor-rates should be mortgaged by parishes to secure loans from the government for financing the emigration and settlement of paupers as peasant-proprietors in the unoccupied land of Canada. By its nature the scheme was generally to be restricted to the agricultural population, but it could also be applied to deal with any permanent redundancy of the industrial population. Any person taking advantage of the scheme would have to give up for himself and his children all claims upon parochial support, present and future. The financial implications of the plan underwent changes from time to time. Horton finally adopted the principle that the burden of repaying the government loans should fall on the parishes.

The substance of Horton's economic arguments in support of emigration is summarized in the remaining paragraphs of this section.

In a country where 'property is appropriated' there would always be people who have been deprived of the means of production and have nothing except their labour to offer in exchange for the means of subsistence. Now the price paid for labour, like that of any other commodity, is determined by the forces of demand and supply. When labour is brought to the market in excess of its demand, its value inevitably depreciates. In other words, an excess supply of labour tends to depress wages. There is, however, one 'material' difference between labour and other commodities. When in excess supply, the price of all the units of a commodity 'falls to one equally low price'. But when labour is in excess supply, it is possible that the labourers in employment receive a rate of wages much higher than 'the allowance received by those surplus labourers who are reduced to the condition of parish paupers'.[1] Horton thought that it was not difficult to explain this situation. Labourers generally become accustomed to a standard of living such that if wages were to fall below it, they would work

[1] R. J. Wilmot-Horton, *Lectures on Statistics and Political Economy*, 1831 Lecture I, p. 8.

'unwillingly' and 'inefficiently' although they would 'continue to work'. The employer would lose 'in the diminished results of labour, what he might gain in the reduced amount of wages',[1] and therefore the employer might not risk to reduce wages below the level to which labourers as a class had become accustomed at any given time. The existence of a large body of unemployed workers, willing to work at a rate lower than the current rate of wages, would, however, in the long run progressively reduce this 'standard of living' of the working class, and continue to reduce wages until they were just sufficient to provide for physical existence. Therefore, the conditions of employed labourers could never be stable so long as there was 'a mass of unemployed labour *behind them*, beating down their wages by competition'.[2]

Hence redundancy of population is always dangerous. But the existence of a large body of unemployed workers acts not only as a potential threat to the stability of the condition of those who are employed but also as a positive burden on society. This burden, or the 'tax', as Horton preferred to call it, is there simply because the unemployed poor consume a portion of the national output without making any contribution to its generation. They live on the produce of the other classes. The amount of this 'tax' in England could be measured directly at that time by the amount of expenditure on poor relief. For Ireland and Scotland, where the system of poor relief did not exist, it was difficult to determine exactly the size of the 'tax'. But it would be a 'delusion to suppose' that these countries could escape the burden of maintaining the paupers: 'Such a doubt would be as irrational, as to doubt that evaporation takes place from the surface of the earth, and reforms those clouds which had previously descended in rain, although such a process is invisible to the naked eye.'[3]

Given the fact of redundancy of population in the sense of

[1] R. J. Wilmot-Horton, *Lectures on Statistics and Political Economy*, 1831, Lecture 1, p. 9.

[2] Ibid., Letter from Horton to Dr Birkbeck, p. 16.

[3] R. J. Wilmot-Horton, *An Inquiry into the Causes and Remedies of Pauperism*, first series, 1829, pp. 36–7.

an excess supply of labour, the cure would obviously be a speedy adjustment of supply to demand, or of demand to supply, or of both adjustments simultaneously.[1]

Now Horton thought that it would be impossible to stimulate demand by artificial means. The demand for labour is determined by the availability of the wages-fund, or more generally, by the rate of capital accumulation.[2] But there was no 'natural and unforced means' to increase the rate of capital accumulation: he seems to have believed that only voluntary savings create capital.[3] In fact, he thought that even the normal process of capital accumulation was disturbed throughout Britain, but especially in Ireland, by an acute flight of capital abroad, engendered by a sense of political insecurity. In 1822, there were some organized political disturbances in the southern districts of Ireland, and Horton was quick to attribute them to the existence of a large body of unemployed and dissatisfied persons. He believed that a plan to dispose of this surplus population, for instance by emigration, would restore political 'tranquillity'. He argued that, at least for Ireland, any plan for increasing the rate of capital accumulation or for increasing the flow of capital could be taken up successfully only 'after the absorption of part of the redundant population, by the means of a well-regulated emigration'.[4]

Horton then turned to the question of the reduction in the supply of labour. The classical economists generally viewed this question with little optimism. They generally thought that a speedy adjustment of the supply of labour to a diminished demand was impossible, and that in any case it would involve great sufferings for the labouring classes. This idea was well expressed by McCulloch in his article on Taxation in the *Supplement* to the *Encyclopaedia Britannica* (1824):

[1] See Horton's speech, *Hansard's Parliamentary Debates*, Vol. XXI, 4 June 1829, col. 1724.

[2] See Horton, *Letter to Sir Francis Burdett: In Reply to His Speech in Opposing a Parliamentary Grant of £30,000 for the Purpose of Emigration*, 1826, pp. 2–3 and also 19.

[3] *Lectures*, 1831, Resolution 4. Correspondence between Horton and a Select Class of the London Mechanics' Institution.

[4] See Horton's evidence before the *Select Committee on the State of Ireland*, 1825, pp. 15–17.

But it is equally impossible suddenly to diminish the number of the labourers. . . . Such a diminution cannot . . . be effected otherwise than by the operation of increased mortality, or by a decrease in the number of births. But unless the fall were very sudden and extensive, it would require a considerable number of years to render the effects of increased mortality very apparent; and it is so difficult to change the habits of a people, that, though the demand for labour were to decline, it would notwithstanding, continue for a while to flow into the market with nearly the same rapidity as before. Nor would the ratio of the increase of the population be sufficiently diminished, until the misery occasioned by the restricted demand on the one hand, and the undiminished supply on the other, had been generally felt.[1]

Horton, however, disagreed, and he held that a rapid adjustment of an excess supply of labour was possible. It could be done by a process of 'abstraction' of all surplus labourers from the glutted labour market, without influencing the mortality or the fertility rates of the population. This process of speedily restoring the equilibrium between the supply of labour and its demand could be effected by home colonization and/or by colonization abroad.

Horton was not opposed to the idea of home colonization, that is the reclamation and cultivation of waste land either by government or by private enterprise. He thought that the reclamation of bogs in Ireland 'as a national work, would be an advantageous one', and added: 'I have not the slightest doubt that it might be carried into effect without any material difficulty. It would undoubtedly employ a very considerable number of the population during the process'.[2] What he urged, however, was that the reclamation of waste land might not prove to be economically profitable, although the great social

---

[1] *Supplement to the Encyclopaedia Britannica*, 1824, p. 621. Horton wrongly attributed the authorship of this article to Ricardo. See Horton, *Lectures . . .*, 1831, Lecture I, p. 9; also Lecture II, p. 7, and Lecture IV, p. 12.

[2] R. J. Wilmot-Horton, *Causes and Remedies of Pauperism*, 1829, Part I, pp. 49–50.

benefit of the measure might far outweigh the purely monetary losses. That it was 'unprofitable, was proved by the circumstance, that no capitalists were found to engage in such an enterprise'.[1] Furthermore, as home colonization could not effectively prevent the colonists from re-entering into competition with the remaining labourers, it could not be depended upon as a safe method for the 'abstraction' of labour from the market.[2] It would have an additional danger – children born to the home colonists would very soon be a burden in the labour market.[3]

On these grounds, although he was not opposed to the reclamation of waste land at home, the weight of his support was for a policy of emigration and colonization abroad. Nevertheless, he stated almost categorically:

> Colonization abroad, as a remedy for the evils of a relatively redundant population, is, and has been, with me, only a subordinate object of enquiry. I consider it only as the best and cheapest mode of disposing of that superfluous labouring population from the general labour market, which I contend to be the main remedy for the distressed condition of the labouring classes of the United Kingdom, inasmuch as it is that superfluous labour which is not wanted by any party as a means of production, which deteriorates the condition of the whole labouring classes collectively.[4]

Horton went on to add that he was not prepared to consent to any compromise in regard to 'abstraction', but that if it could be shown that 'the superfluous population so abstracted can be disposed of more economically and more advantageously at home than abroad', then he would 'never be found to press for a moment the remedy of Colonial Emigration'.[5]

Thus the *rationale* of colonization could be laid down in Horton's own formula:

[1] Horton's speech, *Hansard's Parliamentary Debates*, Vol. 18, 17 April 1828, col. 1551.

[2] *Lectures . . .*, 1831, Lecture IV, p. 18.

[3] See *Causes and Remedies of Pauperism*, fourth series, 1830, p. 43.

[4] *Causes and Remedies of Pauperism*, first series, 1829, pp. 22–3.

[5] Ibid., first series, pp. 23–4.

In our own empire it was indisputably true, that the proportion between capital and manual labour had not been preserved; and the consequences was, that the labouring classes did not receive that remuneration for their exertions which was consistent with their prosperity, and hardly with their existence. The conclusion, therefore . . . was most sound and just; one part of our dominions required population, which the other could bestow with advantage, and the wants of one country could thus be supplied by the superfluities of the other.[1]

II

Wakefield's attitude to Horton at first was favourable. In his first pamphlet on colonization entitled *Sketch of a Proposal for Colonizing Australasia* (1829) he referred to Horton's scheme of pauper-emigration as a 'benevolent plan'. Through his friend Roger Gouger, later Secretary of the National Colonization Society, he sent a copy of this monograph to Horton, and wrote in the accompanying letter:

> The mode of Emigration recommended in the paper which I have the honour to enclose, was originally suggested to my mind by your works on that subject, amongst which I include the excellent Report to Parliament.[2] They establish that the people of this Empire are redundant, not merely in proportion to capital, according to the general theory of Mr. Malthus, but specially, in proportion to territory. They establish, therefore, that Emigration is the proper remedy for the excessive pauperism of this people.[3]

Subsequently, mainly through Wakefield's influence, Horton was approached to become one of the original members of the National Colonization Society formed in 1830.

However, differences between the Wakefield group and

[1] Horton's speech in Parliament, *Hansard's Parliamentary Debates*, Vol. 16, 15 February 1827, col. 480.

[2] This refers to the *Report of the Select Committee on Emigration from the United Kingdom*, 1826–7. Horton was the chairman of this committee.

[3] Horton Papers: Copy of letter from the author of the *Sketch of a Proposal for Colonizing Australasia*. The letter is undated.

E

Horton soon began to develop.[1] In April 1830, after a meeting of the Provisional Committee of the Society, it was resolved 'That the Statement of the principles and objects of the proposed Society . . . be published.' This Statement was published as a pamphlet of less than one hundred pages. After a brief reference to 'the zealous exertions of Mr. Wilmot-Horton' to popularize the emigration movement, it was alleged in it that he had failed to answer his critics on two main points, namely that the vacuum created by emigration tends to fill up quickly, and that the cost of emigration throws too great a burden on the mother country. These criticisms were regarded as 'absolute and fatal objections' to his proposals. As an alternative, therefore, a new scheme of colonization, clearly identifiable as the Wakefield System, was put forward. The two basic features of the new plan were stated as: (i) the creation of an emigration-fund by the sale of colonial land to which value would be given by 'forced concentration'; and (ii) the selection of young married couples as emigrants.[2] It was claimed that these new measures constituted a definite improvement as they were expected 'first, to encourage the greatest possible increase of people, without any excess for generations to come, and secondly, to render emigration absolutely costless to the State'.[3]

The pamphlet of the Society upset Horton greatly. For almost a decade he had carried out a single-handed campaign against public apathy towards emigration. Now he found that his authority in the field of colonization was challenged by Wakefield and his disciples, who, paradoxically, were also pledged to popularize it. At first he refused to believe that the new principles of the Society really stood in opposition to his own, but gradually he found it impossible to accommodate the views of Wakefield and his followers. The controversy became

[1] For a detailed account of Horton's association with the National Colonization Society, see E. G. Jones's unpublished thesis, op. cit. See also Douglas Pike, 'Wilmot-Horton and the National Colonization Society', *Historical Studies – Australia and New Zealand*, Vol. 7 (1956).

[2] See *A Statement of the Principles and Objects of a Proposed National Society for the Cure and Prevention of Pauperism by Systematic Colonization*, 1830, pp. 17–21, 43, and 46.

[3] Ibid., pp. 66–7.

so intense within the Society that it ultimately had to be dissolved, although the process of its dissolution may have been accelerated by financial difficulties.[1]

What was the real trouble between Horton and Wakefield? On minor points, of course, their differences were apparent. First, Horton proposed only such an amount of emigration as would save the cost of maintaining able-bodied paupers in idleness at home; Wakefield, on the other hand, considered emigration of little use unless it had the effect of permanently raising the wages of labourers in the mother country to an acceptable level. Second, Horton proposed that the cost of emigration should be met by the parishes, while his opponent advocated a scheme in which the cost would be met by the colonists themselves. Third, Horton proposed that pauper families including children should be the basic unit for emigration, while his rival supported the idea of restricting emigration to young couples.[2]

These differences, important as they undoubtedly were, were not altogether irreconcilable, as, indeed Horton himself pointed out in his *Causes and Remedies of Pauperism* (fourth series, 1830). They would hardly have justified Charles Tennant's contention on behalf of Wakefield that the Society's conflict with Horton was 'one, not of detail, but of main principles': 'We agree in nothing but the expediency of colonization as a measure for the cure and prevention of pauperism'.[3] Hence there must have been some more fundamental conflicts between the two groups which made reconciliation impossible.

The real difference between Wakefield and Horton certainly lay in their basic approach to the technique of colonization. It was Wakefield's idea to introduce the British type of large-scale farming into the colonies. His model was unmistakably a large farm worked by hired labourers under the direction of capitalist-farmers. With this end in view, he proposed restrictions on the appropriation of colonial lands so as to prevent labourers from becoming landowners too soon. From

[1] See, for instance, E. G. Jones, op. cit., pp. 308–9.
[2] On all this see Charles Tennant, *Letters forming part of a Correspondence with Nassau Williams Senior, concerning Systematic Colonization, etc.*, 1831.
[3] Ibid., p. 41.

the beginning, however, Horton was opposed to this idea. It was his idea to create a body of independent thriving peasant-proprietors from the pauper-emigrants to Canada. It was his belief, although he might not have expressed it clearly, that the motive which inspired paupers to undertake a risky voyage to an alien land was largely the desire to improve their condition by becoming part of a landowning class. He was apprehensive that by requiring 'a sufficient price' for land, this opportunity would be denied to them so that they would probably be condemned to the status of wage-labourers.[1]

There were also other differences of some importance. Wakefield refused to believe that there could be an excess supply of labour in the colonies for any reasonable length of time. It was his main argument that the lack of an adequate supply of labour had always contributed to the failure of the previous experiments in colonization. On the other hand, Horton insisted that there was a constant and real danger that the supply of labour could exceed the demand for it in the colonies. Indeed, he pointed out that such an excess supply of labour had already once occurred in Canada. Whenever such a situation was likely to recur, he proposed that 'the evil should be prevented, by *funding* what would otherwise constitute the supply of labour, in location and settlement on unappropriated lands'.[2] By the adoption of his principle of colonization, he thought that it would be possible to colonize to an indefinite extent – 'the only limit . . . will be the extent and the fertility of the unoccupied soil'.[3] But he warned that if any attempt was made to increase the supply of labour without regard to its demand, the results would be 'the most calamitous'. He accepted, however, that 'if care be taken to keep the supply adjusted to the demand, and to transfer to the class of settlers that portion of labour which would otherwise be redundant, the results will be alike advantageous to the individual emigrant and to the colony at large'.[4]

[1] For a similar view of McCulloch's, see his edition of the *Wealth of Nations*, 1850, *Supplemental Notes*, XXIII, p. 612.

[2] *Lectures . . .*, 1831, Lecture VIII, p. 7.

[3] *Ireland and Canada*, 1839, p. vii.

[4] *Lectures . . .*, 1831, Lecture VIII, p. 21.

Another important source of disagreement was the rôle of the state. Notwithstanding his theory of 'a sufficient price' on free land in the colonies – a theory which James Mill interpreted to mean a challenge to the traditional doctrine of *laissez-faire* – Wakefield was a genuine advocate of individual liberty and freedom of enterprise. In fact, it would otherwise have been extremely difficult for him to have secured J. S. Mill's support for his colonization schemes. He always insisted on the desirability of leaving the general process of colonial development to the forces of free enterprise. Horton did not share this view. In his *Letters on Colonial Policy* (1839) he made it quite clear that in a backward region such as a colony certain investments had to be made deliberately by public authority to provide the initial stimulus to economic development. As he put it: 'Tanks, water-courses, and roads are the sort of "capital" which, *in the first instance* is most required. These can only be created under the direction of the Government; these improvements being made, the opportunity of employing private capital commences: without them, the limitation to that employment must be early and conclusive.'[1] In a colony a large volume of initial 'public expenditure must precede private expenditure'. This view, compared with that of Wakefield, demanded a much more dynamic rôle for the state in the process of colonial development.

III

When his controversy with Wakefield began, Horton approached contemporary economists to win them over to his side. He was able to get James Mill and Malthus to express criticism of the Wakefield Plan. These comments he intended to publish in the fifth series of his *Causes and Remedies of Pauperism*, the first four of which, together with an introductory volume, had appeared in 1829–30. But he was probably not able to carry out this intention.[2] However, the manuscript letters of James Mill and Malthus are preserved in the

[1] *Letters (of Philalethes) Containing Observations on Colonial Policy*, 1839, pp. 19–20.
[2] See, for instance, Lionel Robbins, *Robert Torrens and the Evolution of Classical Economics*, 1958, p. 168 n.

Horton Papers at the Central County Library, Derby. On the basis of these letters it is possible to assess their contribution in the Horton–Wakefield controversy.

James Mill's attitude to the Wakefield System was positively unfavourable. He opposed the principle of the artificial concentration of population in the new colonies by restrictions on the freedom of the colonists to appropriate land. He also criticized the idea of making the colonists pay the cost of emigration from the mother country by the establishment of an emigration-fund from the sale of colonial land. In a letter, dated 11 January 1831 he expressed his opinions thus:

> First, if the question were unincumbered with that of the removal of paupers from the mother country, and related only to what was best for independent settlers who had resorted to the colony with their own means, I should say that the rule of freedom, which is best for other people, would be best also for them, they should be allowed to bestow their capital and industry wherever they found it most advantageous. The advantages of concentration are so obvious, that contiguous land would be always cultivated, when the inferiority of soil was not more than a counter-balance. The government should exact no price for the land, and for a certain number of years, no rent. After these years, it should be let on lease, for a convenient number of years and the rent determined by public auction. If the colony flourished the rent thus accruing would soon exceed the expences of the government; but the rent of the land should always be considered as the fund from which the whole of the expences of the State should be defrayed. Secondly, I see no advantage in loading the colony with the expence of removing a redundant population from the mother country.[1]

Malthus's views on the Wakefield System were more ambiguous. He was not against Wakefield's idea of creating an emigration-fund by the sale of colonial land at a sufficient price. Nor was he opposed to the idea of selective emigration of young couples from the mother country. But he felt that

---

[1] Horton Papers: Letters from James Mill, 1829–33.

the emigration-fund would not work satisfactorily 'to furnish adequate funds for the purpose intended', that is to effect the emigration of a sufficient number of able-bodied paupers from the home country. In a letter dated 25 August 1830 he also expressed doubts about the practicability of the principle of selective emigration of young couples:

> I should not think that the emigration of a large pro-portion of young men just arrived at the age of puberty, who cannot certainly be considered as the most distressed part of the community, would either be generally popular, or be looked upon with a favourable eye by the Govern-ment, with a view to the recruiting service and the military strength of the country.[1]

Finally, Malthus was definitely critical of Wakefield's plan of securing an 'artificial concentration' of population in the new colony by restricting the facility of owning lands. His argu-ments are worth quoting at length:

> Anything like a persevering attempt at concentration round a single town would soon lower wages, and destroy the true principle of colonization. In colonizing a large country many centres of concentration are necessary, and villages in various situations must be established, which are to grow into towns, and afford new markets for produce. Many of these will naturally be fixed at a considerable dis-tance from the metropolis, determined by fertility of soil, vicinity of rivers, and other circumstances.[2]

IV

McCulloch, who never supported Horton openly, also was critical of the Wakefield System. He argued that neither capital-ists nor paupers had 'the stamina of modern emigrants', but that the majority of voluntary emigrants were small farmers, tradesmen, and others, who had a moderate capital, ranging up

[1] Horton Papers: Letters from Malthus.
[2] Horton Papers: Letters from Malthus. For a detailed account of Malthus's views on emigration and colonization, see my previously-cited article in *Econo-mica*, Vol. XXX (1963).

to £1,000. Their main motive to migrate was the desire of 'acquiring the property of a less or greater piece of land, the culture of which is to be carried on wholly or almost wholly by themselves and their families'.[1]

McCulloch's position was different from Horton's in two respects: (i) his support of voluntary emigration, that is, emigration carried out without any state assistance; and (ii) his idea that small capitalists, not paupers, constituted the majority of emigrants. At the same time his support of peasant-proprietorship in the colonies was distinctly Hortonian. He argued, like Horton, that a price on land might encourage settlers in Canada to migrate to the United States, and that in fact 'for the last eight or ten years (1840–50), nine-tenths of the most valuable emigrants from this country, that is, of industrious individuals, possessed of capital, have established themselves in some part of the Union'.[2]

Robert Torrens's attitude to Horton's plan was initially also distinctly favourable. His private correspondence with Horton began as early as 1826, about three years before the Wakefield System made its appearance.[3] In a letter dated 1 April 1827 he supported the most controversial aspect of Horton's plan of state-aided emigration, namely the mortgaging of the poor-rates for raising an emigration-loan and its slow repayment by the parishes in annual instalments. He asked Horton: 'In what manner can superfluous numbers be removed, without occasioning an increase in the public expenditure?' And then he proceeded to answer this question himself: 'It appears to me that to this difficult, I might almost say momentous problem, your plan of long and short annuities furnishes a perfect solution. You remove superfluous numbers, and you do not increase public expenditure. The plan so works as exactly to meet the appropriate difficulties of the case.'[4] Four years later, in a letter dated 16 June 1830, Torrens wrote to Horton

---

[1] See Note XXIII by McCulloch in his edition of the *Wealth of Nations*, 1850.

[2] Ibid., Note XXIII, p. 612.

[3] One file entitled *Originals – Letters from Torrens to Horton*, containing 17 letters from Torrens is in the Derby collection of Horton Papers. The first letter in the file is dated 23 March 1826.

[4] Horton Papers: Letters from Torrens.

expressing his full approval for the latter's plan of colonization: 'I have no hesitation in expressing my entire conviction that your proposed measure of an extended and regulated system of colonization . . . is the appropriate remedy for pauperism; and that it is calculated, if judiciously and perseveringly acted upon, to relieve the landed interest of this country from the growing and almost intolerable pressure of the poor rates.'[1]

Later Torrens and Horton entered into a *Written Controversy* with the other members of the National Colonization Society. They argued that the attempt to create a concentration of population by imposing a price on colonial lands was undesirable because of its tendency to force into cultivation poor qualities of soil while fertile lands were still uncultivated.[2] Shortly afterwards, however, Torrens made his intellectual surrender to Wakefield.[3]

Nassau William Senior was another notable economist involved in the Horton–Wakefield controversy. Horton seems to have drawn Senior's attention to the subject of colonization. Horton was busy during the years 1828 to 1830 in an attempt to secure the approval of Parliament for his ambitious Emigration Bill, which contained a plan for the emigration of 95,000 people from Britain with an advance of about a million pounds from the government. By dint of extensive propaganda he secured public support, and gradually he was able to obtain the approval of many politicians and practical men for his proposed Bill. But he was somehow led to believe that Parliament would never sanction his scheme of colonization on an extended scale for the relief of pauperism 'unless the principles on which that measure was founded had received the sanction of scientific men'. He therefore approached Senior, who as Henry Drummond Professor of Political Economy at Oxford had established his reputation as an economist. The two men

[1] Horton Papers: Letters from Torrens.

[2] See Charles Tennant, *A Letter to the Right Honourable Sir George Murray, on Systematic Colonization: also Containing the Written Controversy between the Right Hon. Robert Wilmot Horton and Colonel Torrens, and the Other Members of the Committee of the National Colonization Society*, 1830.

[3] The process of Torrens's intellectual conversion is discussed in Robbins, op. cit., pp. 167–9.

entered into correspondence probably in the beginning of 1829. Their correspondence covered a wide range of interesting topics such as the law of population and the definition of capital; but they were always more specifically concerned with the analysis of the merits of the scheme of state-aided emigration of which Horton was an uncompromising champion.[1]

One common objection to Horton's scheme was that the vacuum created by the emigration of paupers would soon be filled by a fresh increase of population, and that the initial favourable effects of emigration would be neutralized before long. Senior did not approve this line of criticism. He was ready to accept Horton's view that an improvement in the circumstances of the people brought about by a well-regulated system of emigration might improve their foresight and check any excessive growth of population. He was not in sympathy with the pessimistic Malthusian view that any attempt to improve the conditions of the working class would be frustrated by the inevitable tendency of population to increase faster than the supply of food. In a letter dated 4 February 1830, he wrote to Horton that the improvement in the means of subsistence of the people brought about initially by a carefully devised plan of emigration, 'though likely to be followed by a *positive* increase of population, are not likely to be followed by a *proportionate* one: that the progress of improvement resembles the childish puzzle of the snail that every day crawled up the wall four feet and fell back three, and that on no other supposition can the increased comfort of the inhabitants of every well governed country be accounted for'.[2]

There were, of course, other objections to Horton's proposed Emigration Bill. It was said that it would involve unnecessary jobbing and intervention by the parishes, and that the expenses of implementing the scheme would be exorbitant. On all these points Horton addressed a series of 52 questions to Senior, and he received the latter's reply in a letter dated 5 May 1830. He published it in the fourth series of his *Causes and Remedies of Pauperism*. From what Senior wrote it was

[1] A file containing some letters from Senior to Horton is preserved in the Horton Papers.   [2] Horton Papers: Letters from Senior.

obvious that he was generally in agreement with Horton, and that his approach to the Emigration Bill was largely favourable. He observed: 'As far as external colonization is concerned, I see no objection to your proposed Bill, strong enough to balance its advantages. The dangers of profusion and jobbing on the part of the parish are avoided, by investing Government with the whole execution of the measure; and the publication of detailed accounts might perhaps be a sufficient check on the conduct of Government.'[1]

It appears that for some time Senior continued to support Horton. With James Stephen he circulated privately in 1831 a small pamphlet called *Remarks on Emigration with a Draft of a Bill*, in which, as Lord Robbins has pointed out, he 'definitely relied on the Hortonian principles'.[2] In his private correspondence also he continued his support. Thus, for instance, after reading Horton's *Lectures on Statistics and Political Economy* (1831), in which an attempt was made to build up a strong economic case for the colonization of paupers, he sent the following comment to the author: 'It looks as if I generally differed from you, whereas I generally agree, but where I agree I have been silent; where I differ I have expressed it.'[3] In another letter, dated 15 April 1831, the expression of his approval was even more explicit: 'I agree with the main doctrines of the emigration report, and certainly am quite ready to be represented in any way as doing so.'[4]

But Senior's optimistic approval of the doctrine of state-aided emigration did not endure. By about 1836 he must have been seriously assailed by doubts about the ultimate utility to the mother country of any large-scale scheme of emigration. In that year he published *An Outline of the Science of Political Economy*; and although in it he paid a tribute to Horton,[5] he

---

[1] *Causes and Remedies of Pauperism*, fourth series, 1830, p. 92.

[2] Robbins, op. cit., p. 155 n.

[3] Horton Papers: Letters from Senior.

[4] Horton Papers: Letters from Senior.

[5] He said: 'Sir Robert Wilmot Horton's plans for effecting Emigration on an extended scale, and as a national undertaking, have not received the attention which the magnitude of the probable advantage, and the unwearied diligence and public spirit of its proposer, deserved.' (*An Outline of the Science of Political Economy*, p. 224 of the 1938 edition.)

clearly pointed out the inadequacy of emigration as a measure 'to keep down the population of any large, well peopled, and tolerably civilized country . . .'.[1] It is important to remember, however, that the argument in *An Outline* was not against Horton in particular but against any scheme of emigration as such. Moreover, during his second term of the Drummond Professorship at Oxford he delivered lectures (1847–52), in which he made a departure from the basic argument of *An Outline*.[2] He was now prepared to grant the effectiveness of emigration to keep down the pressure of population in the mother country.[3] But whereas he formerly had been an active supporter of Horton's scheme of state-aided emigration, his approach now was definitely critical. After pointing out the great expense of the two schemes of emigration to Canada which were inspired and planned by Horton and carried out by one Peter Robinson in 1823 and 1825 – the actual expenses of the experiment of 1823 were £22 per head, and those of 1825 £21 per head – he completely withdrew his earlier support of Horton's plan. Referring to these experiments, he observed that 'emigration in terms so costly as these could not be defrayed to any great extent either by private beneficence or at the cost of the public'.[4]

V

Horton's death in 1841 put an end to his cause. In his lifetime he had a considerable reputation among his fellow economists. Senior never challenged him openly. James Mill's attitude on

---

[1] *An Outline of the Science of Political Economy*, p. 42.

[2] These lectures were compiled and edited by S. Leon Levy from the original manuscripts, and published in 1928 in two volumes under the title *Industrial Efficiency and Social Economy*.

[3] *Industrial Efficiency and Social Economy*, Vol. I, p. 340, where Senior described emigration as 'the remedial check' for over-population.

[4] Ibid., Vol. I, p. 342. At about this time Senior made his intellectual surrender to Wakefield. 'It is a remarkable instance of the slowness with which political knowledge advances, that though colonization has been vigorously carried on for above 3,000 years by the nations which during that long period have from time to time been the most civilized, the mode of effecting it in the manner most beneficial both to the mother country and to the colony was discovered only about twenty-five years ago. The discoverer was Edward Gibbon Wakefield.' (Ibid., Vol. I, pp. 351–2.)

the whole was favourable. Malthus's sympathy was with him and his principles. With certain reservations, McCulloch was also willing to support him. Torrens alone had deserted him to join Wakefield's camp.

Horton's plan of state-aided emigration did not compare unfavourably with Wakefield's 'systematic colonization'. The plan to create a body of peasant-proprietors was at least as plausible as the plan to establish capitalist farmers in the colonies. The idea of mortgaging the poor-rates to raise emigration-loans from the government was not altogether impracticable. Nor was the scheme of state-aided emigration more expensive than the alternative plan. The claim that the Wakefield System meant colonization at no cost to the mother country was certainly false. Under either scheme capital for colonization was to come from the metropolis. The difference between the two plans lay in this: while Horton wanted to carry out emigration at the public's expense, Wakefield proposed to throw the burden on private capitalists. But if colonization was claimed to be a national project to relieve the mother country of economic distress, there was no reason why the state should not pay its cost.

Yet despite all the favourable factors, it was clear long before his death that Horton was losing in the struggle with his rivals. His failure is not difficult to explain. His political opportunism in 1828 alienated Wellington and Peel and ruined his cause in Parliament. Wakefield's scheme, on the other hand, received the powerful support of the small group of philosophical radicals.[1] Horton did not have any public press or forum to carry on his propaganda, while Wakefield was lucky

[1] The story of Horton's political blunder is well known. In the early days of his campaign for state-aided emigration he received much support from Tory leaders like Wellington and Peel. But when in April 1827 Wellington's ministry collapsed and Canning came to power, Horton made a serious mistake in not resigning with his Tory friends; instead, he deserted them and associated himself with the Canningites. He was naturally not forgiven for this political opportunism. When the Tories regained power in January 1828 he faced stiff opposition from his old friends. For a full account of Horton's failure on this score, see William Forbes Adams, *Ireland and Irish Emigration to the New World from 1815 to the Famine*, 1932, pp. 275–96. See also R. D. Collison Black, *Economic Thought and the Irish Question, 1817–1870*, 1960, Chapter VII.

to have the consistent support of the *Spectator* in the early years of his career, and later also that of the *Colonial Gazette* and the *Weekly Chronicle*. Finally, Horton made the mistake of leaving Britain in 1831 to be Governor of Ceylon for seven years, while his controversy with Wakefield was still open. Wakefield did not fail to make use of this opportunity to advance the cause of 'systematic colonization'. It was during these years that the fateful South Australian Colonization Act was passed, which led to the colonization of South Australia on Wakefield's principles.

In reviewing the unfortunate controversy between Horton and the Wakefield group, it is impossible not to apportion some blame to both sides. But while Horton was prepared to allow a certain degree of flexibility in his scheme to accommodate his rival, Wakefield with his oversanguine temperament refused to make any concession. On Wakefield's own admission – through Charles Tennant – Horton was not opposed to the Wakefield experiment being carried out in South Africa and Australia, although he felt that his own scheme of emigration was more suitable for Canada.[1] But Wakefield laughed at the suggestion, and claimed a scientific universality for his principles.[2] It would also appear that in the controversy Wakefield was perhaps a little less generous and a little more relentless in his criticism of his opponent. There was almost a touch of personal vindictiveness when on Horton's appointment as Governor of Ceylon he said: 'Another important step, perhaps, towards the adoption of such a measure,[3] is the appointment of Mr. Horton to the Governorship of Ceylon; for, until that zealous and persevering, but ignorant and meddling pretender in political economy, shall cease to torment the public and the colonial office with his "preparations to show", there will be difficulty in establishing rational views on this deeply interesting subject.'[4]

---

[1] See Charles Tennant, *Letters forming part of a Correspondence with N. W. Senior*, 1831, p. 43.

[2] Ibid., pp. 42–3.

[3] This refers to the plan of 'systematic colonization'.

[4] *Spectator*, Vol. IV, 26 February 1831, p. 207.

Horton is reported once to have said that there was a 'spell and curse' on his career. This appears to be true. Indeed, it is difficult to believe that a man whom James Stephen had described as 'the pleasantest of companions and the most restless of politicians', and who fought almost single-handedly for roughly a decade to make the subject of emigration worthy of public attention, should have been forgotten so quickly, at a time when the emigration movement was actually gaining momentum. His is a forlorn figure in that age of intense campaigning to promote emigration.

6 The Application and Significance of Theories of the Effect of Economic Progress on the Rate of Profit, 1800–1850

G. S. L. TUCKER

[This article is edited from G. S. L. Tucker, *Progress and Profit in British Economic Thought*, *1650–1850*, Chapter 8, Cambridge University Press, 1960.]

In the decades following the close of the Napoleonic wars, the question of the effect of economic progress on the rate of profit attained a position of primary importance in English political economy. It stood out as a central theme in the *Principles* of both Ricardo and Malthus, two outstanding writers of the period; and while it is true that John Stuart Mill's *Principles* was a far less specialized work, the problem of 'the tendency of profits to a minimum' frequently came to his notice, obliging him to anticipate his conclusions on the subject many times before he came to its formal development in his later chapters. Of the lesser figures, references can be derived from the work of almost every writer who sought to provide a general and systematic treatment of political economy, and the problem was considered in numbers of essays and reviews.

*　　*　　*

If British profits were relatively low, as many thought, it seemed equally true that the nation's stock of capital was relatively large. There was now an increasing tendency on the part of economists to emphasize the abundance of capital, and a greater willingness to tolerate its dissipation by individuals or governments. This is an outstanding characteristic of economic writing in the early nineteenth century.

*   *   *

E. G. Wakefield claimed that 'Abundance of *capital* invested, and ready to be invested, is the most marked, nay the peculiar, characteristic of England'.[1] John Stuart Mill tended to adopt a similar point of view. . . . In 1848 Mill seems to have been greatly impressed by the prospect of England's overflowing capital and the lowness of the rate of profit. This, he argued, must reduce 'the immense importance which used to be attached by political economists to the effects which an event or a measure of government might have in adding to or subtracting from the capital of the country'. British capital was already so abundant that it was being exported to other countries or wasted by speculators in a search for higher profits. A sudden addition to capital would tend to force profits even lower and hence to create even greater drains of this kind; a sudden subtraction from capital would have opposite effects, and the gap in the nation's stock would be filled almost at once by new savings or by capital which would otherwise have been exported or wasted.[2]

*   *   *

Ricardo, McCulloch, and Torrens threatened that British capital might soon begin to leave the country in search of higher profits and interest; this they seem to have regarded as their most effective argument against the Corn Laws and high taxation. By means of foreign investment English capitalists could escape the peculiar disabilities that had been imposed on them by a government of landlords. But in doing so, they would promote the economic growth of other countries at England's expense, and add to the distress of English labourers, who would then be separated from a portion of the capital which should have employed them.

The first serious modification of this attitude towards overseas investment by a member of the Ricardian group is to be found in the work of William Ellis. It has already been noted that in the *Westminster Review* of January 1826 Ellis stressed the

[1] *England and America*, Vol. I, pp. 12–13. See also G. P. Scrope, *Principles of Political Economy*, p. 389.

[2] *Principles*, pp. 740–1.

buoyancy of English capital, its pressure on all existing outlets for profitable investment, and its ability to increase quickly and bountifully in response to any extension of those outlets. He was primarily concerned to show that the apprehensions sometimes expressed regarding the effects of machinery on the demand for labour were without foundation. It will be convenient to digress for a moment to summarize his argument on this point, before going on to the question of the exportation of capital.

All writers agreed that improvements in technique, by raising the productive powers of labour, tended to increase the rate of profit. There were some, however, who objected to the introduction of new kinds of machinery on the ground that it might diminish the demand for labour and so lead to a fall of wages. Such fears were needless, Ellis claimed, for even on the most unfavourable assumptions consistent with common sense, wages could not possibly suffer a more than temporary reduction. The demand for labour might be reduced for a short period if the introduction of machinery caused a sudden absorption of capital which would otherwise have been used for the payment of wages. But meanwhile the rate of profit would have risen, giving a new stimulus to saving and investment. Accumulation would proceed rapidly until the enlarged investment opportunities had been fully exploited and the rate of profit had fallen back to its former level. Thus even if the immediate effect of machinery was to divert capital from the wages-fund, the demand for labour would be restored very quickly, and almost certainly increased, by the new capital called into existence by higher profits. It was even likely that wages would remain steady throughout, avoiding even a temporary reduction, for in most cases the capital absorbed in the form of machinery was not abstracted from the wages-fund – it was supplied from new savings made expressly in anticipation of a more attractive rate of profit, or from existing money savings hitherto idle for want of a satisfactory outlet.[1]

Ellis then applied his theory to the effects of the exportation of capital, concluding once again that 'the fear of any evil

[1] 'Employment of Machinery', *Westminster Review*, Vol. V, 112–23.

to the labouring classes from this source is utterly groundless'.[1]
England had accumulated a very large stock of capital in relation to her limited area of fertile land; therefore profits at home
tended to be lower than those in other countries and English
capitalists might be tempted to invest a part of their savings
abroad. But these, Ellis urged, would be fresh savings, induced by the prospect of a profitable investment opportunity;
they would not reduce the amount of capital invested in England, for this had already filled every employment that offered
the minimum rate of return necessary to compensate capitalists for the risks of business adventure.[2] On the contrary, 'the
act of exporting capital would be the means of increasing the
capital of the country from which it was exported'.[3] If English
savings were invested in countries where wheat and other
necessaries could be produced at a lower cost, the supply of
these cheap commodities offered in exchange for English manufactures would be extended; this would tend to raise and
maintain the rate of profit at home, so enlarging the field of
employment for capital.

These conclusions were repeated later by J. S. Mill in his
Principles. First, with regard to machinery, Mill allowed that
if new techniques employing large amounts of fixed capital
were introduced suddenly, it was possible that they might have
to be financed out of capital formerly devoted to the payment
of wages. In this case the interests of labourers would be
temporarily injured. 'But in a country of great annual savings
and low profits, no such effects need be apprehended.' The gap
in the wages-fund would be filled immediately by capital which
would otherwise have been exported or wasted in fruitless
speculative ventures; further, innovations must raise profits
and promote new savings and investment – they must help to
defer the approach of the stationary state. 'It is this which is
the conclusive answer to the objections against machinery.'[4]

Secondly, Mill argued that the constant overflow of British

[1] Ibid., p. 128.
[2] It will be noticed that Ellis, unlike Ricardo, ignored the question of the
Corn Laws, thus giving a new turn to the discussion.
[3] 'Employment of Machinery', p. 129.
[4] *Principles*, pp. 94–9, 742–5.

capital into the colonies and foreign countries, where it was invested mainly in agriculture, had been for some time one of the most important factors counteracting the tendency of profits to a minimum.

> It is to the emigration of English capital, that we have chiefly to look for keeping up a supply of cheap food and cheap materials of clothing, proportional to the increase of our population; thus enabling an increasing capital to find employment in the country, without reduction of profit, in producing manufactured articles with which to pay for this supply of raw produce. Thus, the exportation of capital is an agent of great efficacy in extending the field of employment for that which remains: and it may be said truly that, up to a certain point, the more capital we send away, the more we shall possess and be able to retain at home.[1]

Thus J. S. Mill, like William Ellis, believed the exportation of capital to be not only harmless, but positively beneficial.

These arguments in favour of overseas investment put forward by some of the younger followers of Ricardo can be traced, partly at least, to their belief in the abundance of English capital, and the ready response shown by saving to a small rise in the rate of profit. It will be noticed, however, that their conclusions also depended on an assumption that a liberal commercial policy would not in itself be sufficient to prevent a fairly rapid decline of profits. For Ricardo, abolition of the Corn Laws was a primary consideration; and supposing this could be secured, he did not question the ability of less advanced countries to provide a supply of cheap corn proportional to England's increasing needs. If England could draw freely on the raw produce of the whole commercial world, the obstacles to economic growth arising from a low and falling rate of profit would scarcely be felt, at least until some distant future time. J. S. Mill, writing after the repeal of the Corn Laws, was less confident. It was true that the cost of wage-goods and raw materials in England now depended, not on the productivity of her soil, but on that of the soil of the whole

[1] *Principles*, p. 739.

world. 'It remains to consider,' he added, 'how far this resource can be counted upon, for making head during a very long period against the tendency of profits to decline as capital increases.'

If England's population happened in future to grow at a slower rate than her capital, wages would rise and profits would fall in spite of the cheapness of corn and other necessaries. On the other hand, if population grew in the same proportion as capital, there would be no scarcity of labourers, but the nation would require rapidly increasing supplies of raw produce from overseas. The ability of exporting countries to meet this demand would depend both on technical progress and an extension of investment in agriculture. In Europe, however, producers were slow to introduce improved methods; while in the United States and the British colonies the best techniques known to farmers had already been adopted, leaving little scope for improvement unless new discoveries should be made. Thus England would probably be forced to rely mainly on new investment in agricultural nations. In both Europe and America, Mill believed, the native capital available to produce surpluses of food and materials was unlikely to increase as rapidly as England's demand. It followed that an adequate supply of cheap corn could be ensured only by England's exporting the capital necessary for its production.[1]

There can be little doubt that J. S. Mill's attitude towards overseas investment was greatly influenced by the work of E. G. Wakefield, who, at the end of the 1820s, played a dominant part in creating 'the new science of systematic colonization'. Wakefield's ideas were developed originally in his *Letter from Sydney*, which was published anonymously in 1829.[2] His influence on English economic thought depended chiefly, however, on *England and America* (1833).[3] In this work Wakefield

[1] *Principles*, pp. 737–8.

[2] [E. G. Wakefield], *A Letter from Sydney, the Principal Town of Australasia.* Edited by Robert Gouger. Together with *The Outline of a System of Colonization* (1829).

[3] Many of the arguments contained in *England and America* were repeated in Wakefield's notes to his edition of *The Wealth of Nations*. Vols. III and IV, however, which should have included his comments on colonization, were published without notes.

based his arguments in favour of colonization, or the transfer of capital and labour to new unoccupied lands, on the familiar contrast between the levels of profits and wages in England and America. In America all social classes were prosperous, while in England capitalists and labourers were experiencing distress – this demonstrated the importance of 'the field of production', the area of land from which a society derived its food.[1] In England the field of production was limited naturally by the country's small resources of fertile land, and artificially by the Corn Laws; therefore the rapid growth of capital and population since 1815 had forced down profits and wages, whereas in America they had been maintained as a result of the overflow of capital on to good unoccupied land. All English trades were overcrowded, for as cultivation was extended to successively less fertile soils, the produce obtained by equal additions to capital had declined, so reducing the amount available for distribution between profits and wages.[2]

It followed that the prosperity typical of America could be achieved in England by the repeal of the Corn Laws and the adoption of a policy of colonial development. The emigration of English capital and labour to the colonies would reduce competition for employment at home and raise the productivity of industry; it would create new markets for the sale of English manufactures, and it would ensure a steady supply of cheap corn which could be increased at will in response to England's growing demand.[3] Wakefield believed that capital was already flowing out of the country in considerable quantities; the only problem was to attract it to colonial areas by the provision of an abundant supply of labour. He argued that free grants of colonial land should end, and that it should not be sold at less than a certain minimum price. This policy would serve two purposes: it would restrict the ability of labourers to

[1] For this definition of 'the field of production', see *England and America*, Vol. I, p. 126. In some places the term was used more loosely to refer simply to the scope for employment of capital and labour.

[2] Ibid., Vol. I, pp. 120–6, 129–30. For Wakefield's views on the question of the Corn Laws see Note VI, 'Free Trade in Corn, as a Means of Enlarging the Field of Employment for English Capital and Labour', ibid., Vol. I, 209–44.

[3] Ibid., Vol. II, Note XII, 'The Art of Colonization', especially pp. 83–111.

acquire land and thus become independent, and it would provide a fund with which to finance a stream of assisted emigration from England. The details of this scheme are well known and need not be repeated here.

It is a peculiar feature of Wakefield's writing that he regarded his analysis of the causes of the low rate of profit in England as a direct contradiction of the theories of Ricardo, James Mill, and McCulloch.[1] For this confusion James Mill may have been partly to blame: in writing *England and America* Wakefield seems to have relied chiefly on James Mill's *Elements of Political Economy* as a source of Ricardian ideas, and it happens that Mill's only clear explanation of the effects on profits of diminishing marginal returns in agriculture is compressed into a few paragraphs at the end of a chapter.[2] This short discussion could easily have escaped the notice of a careless reader, and certain of Wakefield's references suggest that he must in fact have overlooked it.[3] Subsequently, however, in his edition of *The Wealth of Nations* (1835), Wakefield quoted from one of McCulloch's very satisfactory expositions of Ricardo's theory of profits.[4] How then are we to explain his continued assertions that 'the modern worshippers of capital' did not appreciate the importance of 'the field of production' or the supply of fertile land available to provide a nation's food? It is difficult to resist the conclusion that Wakefield simply did not understand the theories that he criticized so confidently.

On questions of economic policy (as opposed to pure theory) there were of course real and important differences between Wakefield and the older members of the Ricardian group. James Mill, in an article in the *Supplement to the Encyclopaedia Britannica* (1824), had denied almost every argument which could conceivably have been advanced in favour of colonies. In particular, he had questioned the utility of emigration as a means of relieving distress – allowing for the costs of

[1] J. S. Mill, on the contrary, argued that Wakefield's doctrines were in fact developments or corollaries of 'the principles of the best school of preceding political economists'. *Principles*, p. 728; *Westminster Rev.*, XLIII (June 1845), p. 320.
[2] *Elements*, pp. 61–2.
[3] See, for example, *England and America*, Vol. I, pp. 107–8, 115–16.
[4] Vol. I, pp. 243–5.

transportation there was a danger that 'the population which remains behind in the mother country, may suffer more by the loss of capital, than it gains by the diminution of numbers'.[1] James Mill's views subsequently became a standard point of departure in discussions of the advantages and disadvantages of colonies.

Wakefield himself quickly obtained the support of a number of English economists. In 1834 John Stuart Mill wrote in favour of the project for the establishment of a new colony in South Australia on Wakefield's principles.[2] This plan would help to raise wages and profits in England, Mill argued, and in general its advantages were so great that some of its former opponents could now be named as active supporters: among these were G. P. Scrope and Robert Torrens.[3] Shortly afterwards Torrens made an effective contribution to the new cause in his *Colonization of South Australia* (1835).

Like J. S. Mill, Torrens realized that the case for colonization depended on an assumption that the abolition of restrictions on the importation of corn and raw materials would not by itself be sufficient to ensure a long era of high profits in England. With some show of originality, he put forward an argument which in fact had already been employed by Malthus, though admittedly in a different context. This concerned the effects on England's terms of international trade that would be produced by a rapid increase in the amount of capital invested in manufacturing industry. Malthus had concluded that in a commercial and manufacturing nation such as England, the rate of profit would fall if the home demand for foreign corn grew more rapidly than the overseas demand for manufactured goods. The prices of English exports were determined in foreign markets by supply and demand, not cost of production, and it might become necessary to exchange

[1] *Supplement to the Encyclopaedia Britannica* (1824), Vol. III, p. 262. For Wakefield's references to this article, see *England and America*, Vol. II, pp. 62, 97–102.

[2] 'The New Colony', *The Examiner*, 29 June 1834; 'The New Colony', ibid. 6 July 1834; review of *The New British Province of South Australia* (London, C. Knight, 1834), ibid. 20 July 1834; 'New Australian Colony', *Morning Chronicle*, 23 October 1834.

[3] Scrope added little to Wakefield's doctrines: see *Principles of Political Economy*, pp. 375–83.

manufactures for corn on increasingly unfavourable terms. The rate of profit would then be reduced by the fall in the prices of exported manufactures in relation to their costs of production.[1] In his work of 1835 Torrens developed this idea at length.[2] If a liberal commercial policy was adopted, England would come to depend more and more on imported foodstuffs and raw materials; but the prices of these commodities would probably rise in relation to the prices of English exports, thereby depressing profits in the country's staple manufacturing industries. Such a change in the terms of trade could be caused by the high rate of capital accumulation and rapid increase of production in English manufactures, which was likely to exceed that in foreign agriculture, or by the policies of other nations to protect their own nascent manufacturing industries by means of tariffs. The decline of profits could not be averted by shifting capital from one English manufacture to another, or by transferring it to domestic agriculture, which was in any case subject to rapidly diminishing returns. The only solution was to export capital and labour to the colonies, where they would produce the food and raw materials that England required, and at the same time create new and growing markets for her export industries. England would no longer depend so heavily on foreign markets and foreign tariff policies; by regulating the outflow of capital and labour, and by setting up 'a colonial Zollverein', she could control her own economic destiny. To Torrens it must have seemed that the threat of a falling rate of profit, and a slackening in the rate of economic growth, had finally been surmounted.

[1] *Principles*, pp. 329–30. In his *Notes on Malthus* Ricardo admitted this possibility and claimed that it was quite consistent with his own theory of profits. For the deterioration in England's terms of international trade would be equivalent to an increase in the labour cost of a given quantity of corn. 'Profits in all countries must mainly depend upon the quantity of labour given for corn, either when grown on their own land, or embodied in manufactures and with them bought from other countries' (pp. 288–91).

[2] *Colonization of South Australia*, pp. 231–70. See also *The Budget. On Commercial and Colonial Policy* . . . (1844), Letter IV, pp. 79–102. The substance of Torrens's argument was reproduced by Herman Merivale in *Lectures on Colonization and Colonies* (1841), Vol. I, Lecture VI, pp. 162–81. Merivale, however, was much more guarded than Torrens in his references to the benefits of colonies.

7 The Imperialism of Free Trade

JOHN GALLAGHER AND RONALD ROBINSON

[This article was first published in the *Economic History Review*, 2nd series, Vol. VI, No. I (1953).]

I

It ought to be a commonplace that Great Britain during the nineteenth century expanded overseas by means of 'informal empire'[1] as much as by acquiring dominion in the strict constitutional sense. For purposes of economic analysis it would clearly be unreal to define imperial history exclusively as the history of those colonies coloured red on the map. Nevertheless, almost all imperial history has been written on the assumption that the empire of formal dominion is historically comprehensible in itself and can be cut out of its context in British expansion and world politics. The conventional interpretation of the nineteenth-century empire continues to rest upon study of the formal empire alone, which is rather like judging the size and character of icebergs solely from the parts above the water-line.

The imperial historian, in fact, is very much at the mercy of his own particular concept of empire. By that, he decides what facts are of 'imperial' significance; his data are limited in the same way as his concept, and his final interpretation itself depends largely upon the scope of his hypothesis. Different hypotheses have led to conflicting conclusions. Since imperial historians are writing about different empires and since they are generalizing from eccentric or isolated aspects of them, it is hardly surprising that these historians sometimes contradict each other.

[1] The term has been given authority by Dr C. R. Fay. See *Cambridge History of the British Empire* (Cambridge, 1940), Vol. II, pp. 399.

The orthodox view of nineteenth-century imperial history remains that laid down from the standpoint of the racial and legalistic concept which inspired the Imperial Federation movement. Historians such as Seeley and Egerton looked on events in the formal empire as the only test of imperial activity; and they regarded the empire of kinship and constitutional dependence as an organism with its own laws of growth. In this way the nineteenth century was divided into periods of imperialism and anti-imperialism, according to the extension or contraction of the formal empire and the degree of belief in the value of British rule overseas.

Ironically enough, the alternative interpretation of 'imperialism', which began as part of the radical polemic against the Federationists, has in effect only confirmed their analysis. Those who have seen imperialism as the high stage of capitalism and the inevitable result of foreign investment agree that it applied historically only to the period after 1880. As a result they have been led into a similar preoccupation with formal manifestations of imperialism because the late-Victorian age was one of spectacular extension of British rule. Consequently, Hobson and Lenin, Professor Moon and Mr Woolf[1] have confirmed from the opposite point of view their opponents' contention that late-Victorian imperialism was a qualitative change in the nature of British expansion and a sharp deviation from the innocent and static liberalism of the middle of the century. This alleged change, welcomed by one school, condemned by the other, was accepted by both.

For all their disagreement these two doctrines pointed to one interpretation; that mid-Victorian 'indifference' and late-Victorian 'enthusiasm' for empire were directly related to the rise and decline in free-trade beliefs. Thus Lenin wrote: 'When free competition in Great Britain was at its height, i.e. between 1840 and 1860, the leading British bourgeois politicans were ... of the opinion that the liberation of the colonies and their complete separation from Great Britain was inevitable and

---

[1] J. A. Hobson, *Imperialism* (1902); V. I. Lenin, *Imperialism, the Highest Stage of Capitalism* (Selected Works, (n.d.), v); P. T. Moon, *Imperialism and World Politics* (New York, 1926); L. Woolf, *Empire and Commerce in Africa* (n.d.).

desirable.'[1] Professor Schuyler extends this to the decade from 1861 to 1870: '. . . for it was during those years that tendencies toward the disruption of the empire reached their climax. The doctrines of the Manchester school were at the height of their influence.'[2]

In the last quarter of the century, Professor Langer finds that 'there was an obvious danger that the British [export] market would be steadily restricted. Hence the emergence and sudden flowering of the movement for expansion. . . . Manchester doctrine had been belied by the facts. It was an outworn theory to be thrown into the discard.'[3] Their argument may be summarized in this way: the mid-Victorian formal empire did not expand, indeed it seemed to be disintegrating, therefore the period was anti-imperialist; the later-Victorian formal empire expanded rapidly, therefore this was an era of imperialism; the change was caused by the obsolescence of free trade.

The trouble with this argument is that it leaves out too many of the facts which it claims to explain. Consider the results of a decade of 'indifference' to empire. Between 1841 and 1851 Great Britain occupied or annexed New Zealand, the Gold Coast, Labuan, Natal, the Punjab, Sind, and Hong Kong. In the next twenty years British control was asserted over Berar, Oudh, Lower Burma, and Kowloon, over Lagos and the neighbourhood of Sierra Leone, over Basutoland, Griqualand, and the Transvaal; and new colonies were established in Queensland and British Columbia. Unless this expansion can be explained by 'fits of absence of mind', we are faced with the paradox that it occurred despite the determination of the imperial authorities to avoid extending their rule.

This contradiction arises even if we confine our attention to the formal empire, as the orthodox viewpoint would force us to do. But if we look beyond into the regions of informal empire, then the difficulties become overwhelming. The normal account of South African policy in the middle of the century

---

[1] Lenin, op. cit., Vol. V, p. 71.

[2] R. L. Schuyler, *The Fall of the Old Colonial System* (New York, 1935), p. 45.

[3] W. L. Langer, *The Diplomacy of Imperialism, 1890–1902* (New York 1935), Vol I, pp. 75–6.

is that Britain abandoned any idea of controlling the interior. But in fact what looked like withdrawal from the Orange River Sovereignty and the Transvaal was based not on any *a priori* theories about the inconveniences of colonies but upon hard facts of strategy and commerce in a wider field. Great Britain was in South Africa primarily to safeguard the routes to the East, by preventing foreign powers from acquiring bases on the flank of those routes. In one way or another this imperial interest demanded some kind of hold upon Africa south of the Limpopo River, and although between 1852 and 1877 the Boer Republics were not controlled formally for this purpose by Britain, they were effectually dominated by informal paramountcy and by their dependence on British ports. If we refuse to narrow our view to that of formal empire, we can see how steadily and successfully the main imperial interest was pursued by maintaining supremacy over the whole region, and that it was pursued as steadily throughout the so-called anti-imperialist era as in the late-Victorian period. But it was done by shutting in the Boer Republics from the Indian Ocean: by the annexation of Natal in 1843, by keeping the Boers out of Delagoa Bay in 1860 and 1868, out of St Lucia Bay in 1861 and 1866, and by British intervention to block the union of the two republics under Pretorius in 1860.[1] Strangely enough it was the first Gladstone Government which Schuyler regards as the climax of anti-imperialism, which annexed Basutoland in 1868 and Griqualand West in 1871 in order to ensure 'the safety of our South African Possessions'.[2] By informal means if possible, or by formal annexations when necessary, British paramountcy was steadily upheld.

Are these the actions of ministers anxious to preside over the liquidation of the British Empire? Do they look like 'indifference' to an empire rendered superfluous by free trade? On the contrary, here is a continuity of policy which the conventional interpretation misses because it takes account only of formal methods of control. It also misses the continuous grasp

[1] C. J. Uys, *In the Era of Shepstone* (Lovedale, Cape Province, 1933); and C. W. de Kiewiet, *British Colonial Policy and the South African Republics* (1929), *passim*.
[2] De Kiewiet, op. cit., p. 224.

of the West African coast and of the South Pacific which British sea-power was able to maintain. Refusals to annex are no proof of reluctance to control. As Lord Aberdeen put it in 1845: '. . . it is unnecessary to add that Her Majesty's Government will not view with indifference the assumption by another Power of a Protectorate which they, with due regard for the true interests of those [Pacific] islands, have refused.'[1]

Nor can the obvious continuity of imperial constitutional policy throughout the mid- and late-Victorian years be explained on the orthodox hypothesis. If the granting of responsible government to colonies was due to the mid-Victorian 'indifference' to empire and even a desire to be rid of it, then why was this policy continued in the late-Victorian period when Britain was interested above all in preserving imperial unity? The common assumption that British governments in the free-trade era considered empire superfluous arises from over-estimating the significance of changes in legalistic forms. In fact, throughout the Victorian period responsible government was withheld from colonies if it involved sacrificing or endangering British paramountcy or interests. Wherever there was fear of a foreign challenge to British supremacy in the continent or sub-continent concerned, wherever the colony could not provide financially for its own internal security, the imperial authorities retained full responsibility, or, if they had already devolved it, intervened directly to secure their interests once more. In other words, responsible government, far from being a separatist device, was simply a change from direct to indirect methods of maintaining British interests. By slackening the formal political bond at the appropriate time, it was possible to rely on economic dependence and mutual good-feeling to keep the colonies bound to Britain while still using them as agents for further British expansion.

The inconsistency between fact and the orthodox interpretation arises in yet another way. For all the extensive anthologies of opinion supposedly hostile to colonies, how many

[1] Quoted in J. M. Ward, *British Policy in the South Pacific, 1786–1893* (Sydney 1948), p. 138.

colonies were actually abandoned? For instance, the West Africa Committee of 1865 made a strong and much quoted case for giving up all but one of the West African settlements, but even as they sat these settlements were being extended. The Indian empire, however, is the most glaring gap in the traditional explanation. Its history in the 'period of indifference' is filled with wars and annexations.

Moreover, in this supposedly *laissez-faire* period India, far from being evacuated, was subjected to intensive development as an economic colony along the best mercantilist lines. In India it was possible, throughout most of the period of the British Raj, to use the governing power to extort in the form of taxes and monopolies such valuable primary products as opium and salt. Furthermore, the characteristics of so-called imperialist expansion at the end of the nineteenth century developed in India long before the date (1880) when Lenin believed the age of economic imperialism opened. Direct governmental promotion of products required by British industry, government manipulation of tariffs to help British exports, railway construction at high and guaranteed rates of interest to open the continental interior – all of these techniques of direct political control were employed in ways which seem alien to the so-called age of *laissez-faire*. Moreover, they had little to do, particularly in railway finance, with the folk-lore of rugged individualism. 'All the money came from the English capitalist' as a British official wrote, 'and, so long as he was guaranteed five per cent on the revenues of India, it was immaterial to him whether the funds which he lent were thrown into the Hooghly or converted into bricks and mortar.'[1]

To sum up: the conventional view of Victorian imperial history leaves us with a series of awkward questions. In the age of 'anti-imperialism' why were all colonies retained? Why were so many more obtained? Why were so many new spheres of influence set up? Or again, in the age of 'imperialism', as we shall see later, why was there such reluctance to annex further territory? Why did decentralization, begun under the

[1] Quoted in L. H. Jenks, *The Migration of British Capital to 1875* (1938), pp. 221–2.

impetus of anti-imperialism, continue? In the age of *laissez-faire* why was the Indian economy developed by the state?

These paradoxes are too radical to explain as merely exceptions which prove the rule or by concluding that imperial policy was largely irrational and inconsistent, the product of a series of accidents and chances. The contradictions, it may be suspected, arise not from the historical reality but from the historians' approach to it. A hypothesis which fits more of the facts might be that of a fundamental continuity in British expansion throughout the nineteenth century.

II

The hypothesis which is needed must include informal as well as formal expansion, and must allow for the continuity of the process. The most striking fact about British history in the nineteenth century, as Seeley pointed out, is that it is the history of an expanding society. The exports of capital and manufactures, the migration of citizens, the dissemination of the English language, ideas, and constitutional forms, were all of them radiations of the social energies of the British peoples. Between 1812 and 1914 over twenty million persons emigrated from the British Isles, and nearly 70 per cent of them went outside the Empire.[1] Between 1815 and 1880, it is estimated, £1,187 million in credit had accumulated abroad, but no more than one-sixth was placed in the formal empire. Even by 1913, something less than half of the £3,975 million of foreign investment lay inside the Empire.[2] Similarly, in no year of the century did the Empire buy much more than one-third of Britain's exports. The basic fact is that British industrialization caused an ever-extending and intensifying development of overseas regions. Whether they were formally British or not, was a secondary consideration.

Imperialism, perhaps, may be defined as a sufficient political function of this process of integrating new regions into the

---

[1] Sir W. K. Hancock, *Survey of British Commonwealth Affairs* (1940), Vol. II, Pt. 1, 28.

[2] A. H. Imlah, 'British Balance of Payments and Export of Capital, 1816-1913' *Econ. Hist. Rev.* 2nd ser. v (1952), pp. 237, 239; Hancock, op. cit., p. 27.

expanding economy; its character is largely decided by the various and changing relationships between the political and economic elements of expansion in any particular region and time. Two qualifications must be made. First, imperialism may be only indirectly connected with economic integration in that it sometimes extends beyond areas of economic development, but acts for their strategic protection. Secondly, although imperialism is a function of economic expansion, it is not a necessary function. Whether imperialist phenomena show themselves or not is determined not only by the factors of economic expansion, but equally by the political and social organization of the regions brought into the orbit of the expansive society, and also by the world situation in general.

It is only when the politics of these new regions fail to provide satisfactory conditions for commercial or strategic integration and when their relative weakness allows, that power is used imperialistically to adjust those conditions. Economic expansion, it is true, will tend to flow into the regions of maximum opportunity, but maximum opportunity depends as much upon political considerations of security as upon questions of profit. Consequently, in any particular region, if economic opportunity seems large but political security small, then full absorption into the extending economy tends to be frustrated until power is exerted upon the state in question. Conversely, in proportion as satisfactory political frameworks are brought into being in this way, the frequency of imperialist intervention lessens and imperialist control is correspondingly relaxed. It may be suggested that this willingness to limit the use of paramount power to establishing security for trade is the distinctive feature of the British imperialism of free trade in the nineteenth century, in contrast to the mercantilist use of power to obtain commercial supremacy and monopoly through political possession.

On this hypothesis the phasing of British expansion or imperialism is not likely to be chronological. Not all regions will reach the same level of economic integration at any one time; neither will all regions need the same type of political control at any one time. As the British industrial revolution

F

grew, so new markets and sources of supply were linked to it at different times, and the degree of imperialist action accompanying that process varied accordingly. Thus mercantilist techniques of formal empire were being employed to develop India in the mid-Victorian age at the same time as informal techniques of free trade were being used in Latin America for the same purpose. It is for this reason that attempts to make phases of imperialism correspond directly to phases in the economic growth of the metropolitan economy are likely to prove in vain. The fundamental continuity of British expansion is only obscured by arguing that changes in the terms of trade or in the character of British exports necessitated a sharp change in the process.

From this vantage point the many-sided expansion of British industrial society can be viewed as a whole of which both the formal and informal empires are only parts. Both of them then appear as variable political functions of the extending pattern of overseas trade, investment, migration, and culture. If this is accepted, it follows that formal and informal empire are essentially interconnected and to some extent interchangeable. Then not only is the old, legalistic, narrow idea of empire unsatisfactory, but so is the old idea of informal empire as a separate, non-political category of expansion. A concept of informal empire which fails to bring out the underlying unity between it and the formal empire is sterile. Only within the total framework of expansion is nineteenth-century empire intelligible. So we are faced with the task of re-fashioning the interpretations resulting from defective concepts of organic constitutional empire on the one hand and Hobsonian 'imperialism' on the other.

The economic importance – even the pre-eminence – of informal empire in this period has been stressed often enough. What was overlooked was the inter-relation of its economic and political arms; how political action aided the growth of commercial supremacy, and how this supremacy in turn strengthened political influence. In other words, it is the politics as well as the economics of the informal empire which we have to include in the account. Historically, the relationship between these two factors has been both subtle and complex. It has been by no means a simple case of the use of gunboats to demolish a recalcitrant state in the cause of British trade. The type of political line between the expanding economy and its formal or informal dependencies, as might be expected, has been flexible. In practice it has tended to vary with the economic value of the territory, the strength of its political structure, the readiness of its rulers to collaborate with British commercial or strategic purposes, the ability of the native society to undergo economic change without external control, the extent to which domestic and foreign political situations permitted British intervention, and, finally, how far European rivals allowed British policy a free hand.

Accordingly, the political lien has ranged from a vague, informal paramountcy to outright political possession; and, consequently, some of these dependent territories have been formal colonies whereas others have not. The difference between formal and informal empire has not been one of fundamental nature but of degree. The ease with which a region has slipped from one status to the other helps to confirm this. Within the last two hundred years, for example, India has passed from informal to formal association with the United Kingdom and, since the Second World War, back to an informal connection. Similarly, British West Africa has passed through the first two stages and seems today likely to follow India into the third.

III

Let us now attempt, tentatively, to use the concept of the totality of British expansion described above to restate the main themes of the history of modern British expansion. We have seen that interpretations of this process fall into contradictions when based upon formal political criteria alone. If expansion both formal and informal is examined as a single process, will these contradictions disappear?

The growth of British industry made new demands upon British policy. It necessitated linking undeveloped areas with British foreign trade and, in so doing, moved the political arm to force an entry into markets closed by the power of foreign monopolies.

British policy, as Professor Harlow has shown,[1] was active in this way before the American colonies had been lost, but its greatest opportunities came during the Napoleonic wars. The seizure of the French and Spanish West Indies, the fili-bustering expedition to Buenos Aires in 1806, the taking of Java in 1811, were all efforts to break into new regions and to tap new resources by means of political action. But the policy went further than simple house-breaking, for once the door was opened and British imports with their political implica-tions were pouring in, they might stop the door from being shut again. Raffles, for example, temporarily broke the Dutch monopoly of the spice trade in Java and opened the island to free trade. Later, he began the informal British paramountcy over the Malacca trade routes and the Malay peninsula by founding Singapore. In South America, at the same time, British policy was aiming at indirect political hegemony over new regions for the purposes of trade. The British navy car-ried the Portuguese royal family to Brazil after the breach with Napoleon, and the British representative there extorted from his grateful clients the trade treaty of 1810 which left British imports paying a lower tariff than the goods of the mother country. The thoughtful stipulation was added 'that the Present Treaty shall be unlimited in point of duration, and that the obligations and conditions expressed or implied in it shall be perpetual and immutable'.[2]

From 1810 onwards this policy had even better chances in Latin America, and they were taken. British governments sought to exploit the colonial revolutions to shatter the Span-ish trade monopoly, and to gain informal supremacy and the good will which would all favour British commercial penetra-tion. As Canning put it in 1824, when he had clinched the policy of recognition: 'Spanish America is free and if we do

[1] V. T. Harlow, *The Founding of the Second British Empire, 1763–1793* (1952) pp. 62–145.

[2] Quoted in A. K. Manchester, *British Pre-eminence in Brazil* (Chapel Hill, 1933), p. 90.

not mis-manage our affairs sadly she is *English*.[1] Canning's underlying object was to clear the way for a prodigious British expansion by creating a new and informal empire, not only to redress the Old World balance of power but to restore British influence in the New. He wrote triumphantly: 'The thing is done . . . the Yankees will shout in triumph: but it is they who lose most by our decision . . . the United States have gotten the start of us in vain; and we link once more America to Europe.'[2] It would be hard to imagine a more spectacular example of a policy of commercial hegemony in the interests of high politics, or of the use of informal political supremacy in the interests of commercial enterprise. Characteristically, the British recognition of Buenos Aires, Mexico, and Colombia, took the form of signing commercial treaties with them.

In both the formal and informal dependencies in the mid-Victorian age there was much effort to open the continental interiors and to extend the British influence inland from the ports and to develop the hinterlands. The general strategy of this development was to convert these areas into complementary satellite economies, which would provide raw materials and food for Great Britain, and also provide widening markets for its manufactures. This was the period, the orthodox interpretations would have us believe, in which the political arm of expansion was dormant or even withered. In fact, that alleged inactivity is seen to be a delusion if we take into account the development in the informal aspect. Once entry had been forced into Latin America, China, and the Balkans, the task was to encourage stable governments as good investment risks, just as in weaker or unsatisfactory states it was considered necessary to coerce them into more co-operative attitudes.

In Latin America, however, there were several false starts. The impact of British expansion in Argentina helped to wreck the constitution and throw the people into civil war, since

---

[1] Quoted in W. W. Kaufmann, *British Policy and the Independence of Latin America, 1804–1828* (New Haven, 1951), p. 178.

[2] Quoted in J. F. Rippy, *Historical Evolution of Hispanic America* (Oxford, 1946), p. 374.

British trade caused the sea-board to prosper while the back lands were exploited and lagged behind. The investment crash of 1827 and the successful revolt of the pampas people against Buenos Aires[1] blocked further British expansion, and the rise to power of General Rosas ruined the institutional framework which Canning's strategy had so brilliantly set up. The new regime was unco-operative and its designs on Montevideo caused chaos around the Rio de la Plata, which led to that great commercial artery being closed to enterprise. All this provoked a series of direct British interventions during the 1840s in efforts to get trade moving again on the river, but in fact it was the attractive force of British trade itself, more than the informal imperialist action of British governments, which in this case restored the situation by removing Rosas from power.

British policy in Brazil ran into peculiar troubles through its tactless attempt to browbeat the government of Rio de Janeiro into abolishing slavery. British political effectiveness was weakened, in spite of economic predominance, by the interference of humanitarian pressure groups in England. Yet the economic control over Brazil was strengthened after 1856 by the building of the railways; these – begun, financed, and operated by British companies – were encouraged by generous concessions from the government of Brazil.

With the development of railways and steamships, the economies of the leading Latin American states were at last geared successfully to the world economy. Once their exports had begun to climb and foreign investment had been attracted, a rapid rate of economic growth was feasible. Even in the 1880s Argentina could double her exports and increase seven-fold her foreign indebtedness while the world price of meat and wheat was falling.[2] By 1913, in Latin America as a whole, informal imperialism had become so important

---

[1] M. Burgin, *Economic Aspects of Argentine Federation* (Cambridge, Mass., 1946) pp. 55, 76–111.

[2] J. H. Williams, *Argentine International Trade under Inconvertible Paper Money, 1880–1900* (Cambridge, Mass., 1920), pp. 43, 103, 183. Cf. W. W. Rostow, *The Process of Economic Growth* (Oxford, 1953), p. 104.

for the British economy that £999 million, over a quarter of the total investment abroad, was invested in that region.[1]

But this investment, as was natural, was concentrated in such countries as Argentina and Brazil whose governments (even after the Argentine default of 1891) had collaborated in the general task of British expansion. For this reason there was no need for brusque or peremptory interventions on behalf of British interests. For once their economies had become sufficiently dependent on foreign trade the classes whose prosperity was drawn from that trade normally worked themselves in local politics to preserve the local political conditions needed for it. British intervention, in any case, became more difficult once the United States could make other powers take the Monroe doctrine seriously. The slackening in active intervention in the affairs of the most reliable members of the commercial empire was matched by the abandonment of direct political control over those regions of formal empire which were successful enough to receive self-government. But in Latin America, British governments still intervened, when necessary, to protect British interests in the more backward states; there was intervention on behalf of the bond holders in Guatemala and Colombia in the seventies, as in Mexico and Honduras between 1910 and 1914.

The types of informal empire and the situations it attempted to exploit were as various as the success which it achieved. Although commercial and capital penetration tended to lead to political co-operation and hegemony, there are striking exceptions. In the United States, for example, British business turned the cotton South into a colonial economy, and the British investor hoped to do the same with the Mid-West. But the political strength of the country stood in his way. It was impossible to stop American industrialization, and the industrialized sections successfully campaigned for tariffs, despite the opposition of those sections which depended on the British trade connection. In the same way, American political strength

[1] J. F. Rippy, 'British Investments in Latin America, end of 1913', *Inter-American Economic Affairs* (1951), v, 91.

thwarted British attempts to establish Texas, Mexico, and Central America as informal dependencies.

Conversely, British expansion sometimes failed, if it gained political supremacy without effecting a successful commercial penetration. There were spectacular exertions of British policy in China, but they did little to produce new customers. Britain's political hold upon China failed to break down Chinese economic self-sufficiency. The Opium War of 1840, the renewal of war in 1857, widened the inlets for British trade but they did not get Chinese exports moving. Their main effect was an unfortunate one from the British point of view, for such foreign pressures put Chinese society under great strains as the Taiping Rebellion unmistakably showed.[1] It is important to note that this weakness was regarded in London as an embarrassment, and not as a lever for extracting further concessions. In fact, the British worked to prop up the tottering Pekin regime, for as Lord Clarendon put it in 1870, 'British interests in China are strictly commercial, or at all events only so far political as they may be for the protection of commerce'.[2] The value of this self-denial became clear in the following decades when the Pekin Government, threatened with a scramble for China, leaned more and more on the diplomatic support of the honest British broker.

The simple recital of these cases of economic expansion, aided and abetted by political action in one form or other, is enough to expose the inadequacy of the conventional theory that free trade could dispense with empire. We have seen that it did not do so. Economic expansion in the mid-Victorian age was matched by a corresponding political expansion which has been overlooked because it could not be seen by that study of maps which, it has been said, drives sane men mad. It is absurd to deduce from the harmony between London and the colonies of white settlement in the mid-Victorian age any British reluctance to intervene in the fields of British interests.

[1] J. Chesnaux, 'La Révolution Taiping d'après quelques travaux récents', *Revue Historique*, CCIX (1953), 39–40.

[2] Quoted in N. A. Pelcovits, *Old China Hands and the Foreign Office* (New York, 1948), p. 85.

The warships at Canton are as much a part of the period as responsible government for Canada; the battlefields of the Punjab are as real as the abolition of suttee.

Far from being an era of 'indifference', the mid-Victorian years were the decisive stage in the history of British expansion overseas, in that the combination of commercial penetration and political influence allowed the United Kingdom to command those economies which could be made to fit best into her own. A variety of techniques adapted to diverse conditions and beginning at different dates were employed to effect this domination. A paramountcy was set up in Malaya centred on Singapore; a suzerainty over much of West Africa reached out from the port of Lagos and was backed up by the African squadron. On the east coast of Africa British influence at Zanzibar, dominant thanks to the exertions of Consul Kirk, placed the heritage of Arab command on the mainland at British disposal.

But perhaps the most common political technique of British expansion was the treaty of free trade and friendship made with or imposed upon a weaker state. The treaties with Persia of 1836 and 1857, the Turkish treaties of 1838 and 1861, the Japanese treaty of 1858, the favours extracted from Zanzibar, Siam, and Morocco, the hundreds of anti-slavery treaties signed with crosses by African chiefs – all these treaties enabled the British Government to carry forward trade with these regions.

Even a valuable trade with one region might give place to a similar trade with another which could be more easily coerced politically. The Russian grain trade, for example, was extremely useful to Great Britain. But the Russians' refusal to hear of free trade, and the British inability to force them into it, caused efforts to develop the grain of the Ottoman empire instead, since British pressure at Constantinople had been able to hustle the Turk into a liberal trade policy.[1] The dependence of the commercial thrust upon the political arm resulted in a general tendency for British trade to follow the invisible flag of informal empire.

[1] V. J. Puryear, *International Economics and Diplomacy in the Near East* (1935), pp. 216–17, 222–3.

Since the mid-Victorian age now appears as a time of large-scale expansion, it is necessary to revise our estimate of the so-called 'imperialist' era as well. Those who accept the concept of 'economic imperialism' would have us believe that the annexations at the end of the century represented a sharp break in policy, due to the decline of free trade, the need to protect foreign investment, and the conversion of statesmen to the need for unlimited land-grabbing. All these explanations are questionable. In the first place, the tariff policy of Great Britain did not change. Again, British foreign investment was no new thing and most of it was still flowing into regions outside the formal empire. Finally the statesmens' conversion to the policy of extensive annexation was partial, to say the most of it. Until 1887, and only occasionally after that date, party leaders showed little more enthusiasm for extending British rule than the mid-Victorians. Salisbury was infuriated by the 'superficial philanthropy' and 'roguery' of the 'fanatics' who advocated expansion.[1] When pressed to aid the missions in Nyasaland in 1888, he retorted: 'It is not our duty to do it. We should be risking tremendous sacrifices for a very doubtful gain.'[2] After 1888, Salisbury, Rosebery, and Chamberlain accepted the scramble for Africa as a painful but unavoidable necessity which arose from a threat of foreign expansion and the irrepressible tendency of trade to overflow the bounds of empire, dragging the government into new and irksome commitments. But it was not until 1898 that they were sufficiently confident to undertake the reconquest of so vital a region as the Sudan.

Faced with the prospect of foreign acquisitions of tropical territory hitherto opened to British merchants, the men in London resorted to one expedient after another to evade the need of formal expansion and still uphold British paramountcy in those regions. British policy in the late, as in the mid-Victorian period preferred informal means of extending imperial supremacy rather than direct rule. Throughout the two alleged periods the extension of British rule was a last

---

[1] Quoted in Cromer, *Modern Egypt* (1908), Vol. I, p. 388.
[2] *Hansard*, 3rd Series, CCCXXVIII, Col. 550, 6 July 1888.

resort – and it is this preference which has given rise to the many 'anti-expansionist' remarks made by Victorian ministers. What these much quoted expressions obscure, is that in practice mid-Victorian as well as late-Victorian policy makers did not refuse to extend the protection of formal rule over British interests when informal methods had failed to give security. The fact that informal techniques were more often sufficient for this purpose in the circumstances of the mid-century than in the later period when the foreign challenge to British supremacy intensified, should not be allowed to disguise the basic continuity of policy. Throughout, British governments worked to establish and maintain British paramountcy by whatever means best suited the circumstances of their diverse regions of interest. The aims of the mid-Victorians were no more 'anti-imperialist' than their successors', though they were more often able to achieve them informally; and the late-Victorians were no more 'imperialist' than their predecessors, even though they were driven to annex more often. British policy followed the principle of extending control informally if possible and formally if necessary. To label the one method 'anti-imperialist' and the other 'imperialist', is to ignore the fact that whatever the method British interests were steadily safeguarded and extended. The usual summing up of the policy of the free-trade empire as 'trade not rule' should read 'trade with informal control if possible; trade with rule when necessary'. This statement of the continuity of policy disposes of the over-simplified explanation of involuntary expansion inherent in the orthodox interpretation based on the discontinuity between the two periods.

Thus Salisbury as well as Gladstone, Knutsford as well as Derby and Ripon, in the so-called age of 'imperialism', exhausted all informal expedients to secure regions of British trade in Africa before admitting that further annexations were unavoidable. One device was to obtain guarantees of free trade and access as a reward for recognizing foreign territorial claims, a device which had the advantage of saddling foreign governments with the liability of rule while allowing Britons the commercial advantage. This was done in the Anglo-Portuguese

Treaty of 1884, the Congo Arrangement of 1885, and the Anglo-German Agreement over East Africa in 1886. Another device for evading the extension of rule was the exclusive sphere of influence or protectorate recognized by foreign powers. Although originally these imposed no liability for pacifying or administering such regions, with changes in international law they did so after 1885. The granting of charters to private companies between 1881 and 1889, authorizing them to administer and finance new regions under imperial licence, marked the transition from informal to formal methods of backing British commercial expansion. Despite these attempts at 'imperialism on the cheap', the foreign challenge to British paramountcy in tropical Africa and the comparative absence there of large-scale, strong, indigenous political organizations which had served informal expansion so well elsewhere, eventually dictated the switch to formal rule.

One principle then emerges plainly: it is only when and where informal political means failed to provide the framework of security for British enterprise (whether commercial or philanthropic or simply strategic) that the question of establishing formal empire arose. In satellite regions peopled by European stock, in Latin America or Canada, for instance, strong governmental structures grew up; in totally non-European areas, on the other hand, expansion unleashed such disruptive forces upon the indigenous structures that they tended to wear out and even collapse with use. This tendency in many cases accounts for the extension of informal British responsibility and eventually for the change from indirect to direct control.

It was in Africa that this process of transition manifested itself most strikingly during the period after 1880. Foreign loans and predatory bankers by the 1870s had wrecked Egyptian finances and were tearing holes in the Egyptian political fabric. The Anglo-French dual financial control, designed to safeguard the foreign bondholders and to restore Egypt as a good risk, provoked anti-European feeling. With the revolt of Arabi Pasha in 1881, the Khedive's government could serve no longer to secure either the all-important Canal or the foreign investors' pound of flesh.

The motives for the British occupation of 1882 were confused and varied: the desire, evident long before Disraeli's purchase of shares, to dominate the Canal; the interests of the bondholders; and the over-anxiety to forestall any foreign power, especially France, from taking advantage of the prevailing anarchy in Egypt to interpose its power across the British road to India. Nearly all Gladstone's Cabinet admitted the necessity of British intervention, although for different reasons, and, in order to hold together his distracted ministry, the Prime Minister agreed.

The British expedition was intended to restore a stable Egyptian government under the ostensible rule of the Khedive and inside the orbit of informal British influence. When this was achieved, the army, it was intended, should be withdrawn. But the expedition had so crushed the structure of Egyptian rule that no power short of direct British force could make it a viable and trustworthy instrument of informal hegemony and development. Thus the Liberal Government following its plan, which had been hastily evolved out of little more than ministerial disagreements, drifted into the prolonged occupation of Egypt it was intent on avoiding. In fact, the occupying power became directly responsible for the defence, the debts, and development of the country. The perverse effect of British policy was gloomily summed up by Gladstone: 'We have done our Egyptian business and we are an Egyptian government.'[1] Egypt, then, is a striking example of an informal strategy misfiring due to the undermining of the satellite state by investment and by pseudo-nationalist reaction against foreign influence.

The Egyptian question, in so far as it was closely bound with the routes to India and the defence of the Indian empire itself, was given the highest priority by British policy in the eighties and nineties. In order to defend the spinal cord of British trade and empire, tropical African and Pacific claims

[1] Quoted in S. Gwynn and G. M. Tuckwell, *Life of Sir Charles Wentworth Dilke* (1917), Vol. II, p. 46.

were repeatedly sacrificed as pawns in the higher game. In 1884, for example, the Foreign Office decided that British vulnerability in Egypt made it unwise to compete with foreign powers in the opening scramble for West Africa; and it was therefore proposed '. . . to confine ourselves to securing the utmost possible freedom of trade on that [west] coast, yielding to others the territorial responsibilities . . . and seeking compensation on the east coast . . . where the political future of the country is of real importance to Indian and imperial interests.'[1] British policy was not one of indiscriminate land-grabbing. And, indeed, the British penetration into Uganda and their securing of the rest of the Nile Valley was a highly selective programme, in so far as it surrendered some British West African claims to France and transferred part of East Africa to Germany.

IV

Thus the mid-Victorian period now appears as an era of large-scale expansion, and the late-Victorian age does not seem to introduce any significant novelty into that process of expansion. The annexations of vast undeveloped territories, which have been taken as proof that this period alone was the great age of expansion, now pale in significance, at least if our analysis is anywhere near the truth. That the area of direct imperial rule was extended is true, but it is the most important or characteristic development of expansion during this period? The simple historical fact that Africa was the last field of European penetration is not to say that it was the most important; this would be a truism were it not that the main case of the Hobson school is founded on African examples. On the other hand, it is our main contention that the process of expansion had reached its most valuable targets long before the exploitation of so peripheral and marginal a field as tropical Africa. Consequently arguments, founded on the technique adopted in scrambling for Africa, would seem to be of secondary importance.

[1] F.O. Confidential Print (East Africa), 5037.

Therefore, the historian who is seeking to find the deepest meaning of the expansion at the end of the nineteenth century should look not at the mere pegging out of claims in African jungles and bush, but at the successful exploitation of the empire, both formal and informal, which was then coming to fruition in India, in Latin America, in Canada and elsewhere. The main work of imperialism in the so-called expansionist era was in the more intensive development of areas already linked with the world economy, rather than in the extensive annexations of the remaining marginal regions of Africa. The best finds and prizes had already been made; in tropical Africa the imperialists were merely scraping the bottom of the barrel.

8 The Anti-Imperialism of Free Trade

OLIVER MACDONAGH

[This article was first published in the *Economic History Review*, 2nd series, Vol. XIV (1962).]

I

In their article 'The Imperialism of Free Trade'[1] Mr Gallagher and Dr Robinson have argued that the British empire of the nineteenth century should be interpreted, not so much in terms of political or constitutional status, as in terms of 'overseas trade, investment, migration and culture', and especially of the first two. Where, and in so far as it was avoidable, Great Britain did not bring the areas which 'received' this expansion under direct rule. 'The usual summing up of the policy of the free trade empire as "trade not rule" should read "trade with informal control if possible; trade with rule where necessary".' But whether or not Great Britain was forced to pass from indirect to direct rule was merely a matter of expedience. There was no difference in kind between 'formal' and 'informal' sway, only a difference of tactics. This economic aggression was the steadfast imperial policy of the nineteenth century, no matter what persons or parties were in office; and the whole process, so far as the middle decades of the nineteenth century at least are concerned, should be named 'The Imperialism of Free Trade'. Such is the argument in substance.

All this is a most useful corrective to excessive formalism and constitutionality in imperial studies. But (the present paper

[1] J. Gallagher and R. Robinson, 'The Imperialism of Free Trade', *Econ. Hist. Rev.* 2nd ser. VI, (1953), 1–15. This article was written before the publication of *Africa and the Victorians*, by R. E. Robinson, J. Gallagher, and A. Denny, and is therefore related only to their earlier work.

argues) it carries us too far in the opposite direction. The assertion that the formal and informal empires constituted 'but variable political functions' and were 'to some extent, interchangeable'[1] merely replaces the old conceptual difficulties with new.[2] Again, the universality and depersonalization of the thesis is excessive. It did matter from time to time which parties and persons were in power in Britain. The British Government's purchase of Suez canal shares in 1875 is an obvious case in point. 'There is no doubt,' writes Ensor, 'that the decision to purchase was entirely Disraeli's, and that he carried it in the cabinet against strong opposition.'[3] Nor is there any doubt that Disraeli's decision was governed by his own peculiar concept of empire, or that he was, in Jenks's words, making 'foreign investment a veritable weapon of British foreign policy'.[4] But there is also no doubt that had Gladstone been in office in 1875 (as might well have been the case) the Khedive's offer would have been refused. Yet the purchase of these shares was a pre-condition of the whole series of events which issued eventually in Great Britain's becoming 'an

---

[1] The direct quotations used above are taken from Gallagher and Robinson, loc. cit., pp. 6–7, 13.

[2] The Gallagher–Robinson notion of 'informal empire' presents several conceptual difficulties. First, it is not sufficiently exclusive as a definition. By way of *reductio ad absurdum* we might remind ourselves that the U.S.A. was the main recipient of British capital and people during these years (G. Paish, 'Great Britain's Capital Investment in Individual Colonial and Foreign Countries', *Journ. Roy. Stat. Soc.*, LXXIV (1911), 167–87), and it would surely be extravagant to regard her as portion of the 'informal empire'. Again, although our authors deny that there is any essential difference between the two, the criteria of 'informal empire' are hardly applicable to formal. If they were, we might find ourselves constrained to drain Canada of colour while the Balkans were being painted off-red. And there are cases which seem to defy the categories altogether. Is, for example, nineteenth-century Ireland to be regarded as imperializing or imperialized? Ireland was indeed the prime exporter of population from the United Kingdom; but she was also the major exporter of French Revolutionary ideology, Roman Catholic religion, and anti-British sentiment. In fact, 'overseas trade, investment, migration and culture' were not four battalions in the same regiment: they did not even march in the same direction.

[3] R. C. K. Ensor, *England 1870–1914* (Oxford, 1936), p. 38.

[4] L. H. Jenks, *The Migration of British Capital to 1875* (London, 1938), p. 325. On the general subject of nineteenth-century foreign investment as an instrument of foreign policy, see H. Feis, *Europe: The World's Banker* (Yale, 1930).

Egyptian government',[1] and materially influenced the course of the scramble for Africa. Conversely, had Disraeli been in office in 1870 (as might again have been the case) the whole body of the Suez shares, instead of a minority interest, might have fallen into British hands. Finally, while there is much truth in the Gallagher–Robinson view of a stable and aggressive mid-Victorian imperialism, it is also true that this imperialism was continuously – and not altogether unsuccessfully – challenged. Here in fact our authors are misleading. Although they do not define free trade, they certainly leave us to understand that the free traders promoted the growth of empire. It is true that the pre-eminent free traders of the period 1840–70 were well aware of the development of 'informal empire', and discerned many of the features which Mr Gallagher and Dr Robinson have re-discovered. But they also pronounced them to be a sin against free trade, and opposed them with all the resources at their command. This last is the theme which the present paper will attempt to elaborate.

II

Let us begin by attempting to supply the missing definition of free trade in terms, first, of groups, secondly, of beliefs, and finally, of political technique. Since we are concerned with actual historical happenings from first to last, 'free trade' here is not disembodied theory – although the argument would scarcely vary if it were. It must mean doctrine translated into immediate political objects by specific persons and associations. Obviously the Manchester school formed the very centre of political trade in the years 1840 to 1870: to contemporaries and posterity alike political free trade and Manchester were, and are, virtually interchangeable terms. Who is to be added? There was but one body among the traditional political classes whom Bright and Cobden regarded as truly sympathetic, the

[1] 'One day in the autumn of this year [1884], towards the end of the business in the cabinet, a minister asked if there was anything else. "No", said Mr Gladstone with sombre irony as he gathered up his papers, "we have done our Egyptian business, and we are an Egyptian government".' J. Morley, *The Life of William Ewart Gladstone* (1903), Vol. III, p. 119.

Peelites. Cobden was under no illusions about the Whigs. Even at the most auspicious moment of all, in the months between the publication of Russell's Edinburgh letter and the final Corn-Law triumph, Cobden regarded the leading Whigs as either opportunistic and disingenuous, like Palmerston, or honest but incapable of a serious appreciation of economics, like Lord John. 'What a bold farce is it now,' he wrote in February 1846, 'to attempt to parade the Whig party as the Free Traders par excellence! I will be no party to such a fraud.' 'I have far more confidences in Peel than in the Whig leaders,' he wrote a little later. 'He understands politico-economic questions better than Lord John, and attaches far more importance to sound principles in practical legislation.' Or again, 'He [Russell] breathes the atmosphere of a privileged clique. His sympathies are aristocratic. He is sometimes thinking of the House of Russell, while Peel is occupied upon Manchester. They are in a false position; Peel ought to be the leader of the middle class and I am not sure that he is not destined to be so before the end of his career.'[1]

As to the political programme of the Manchester school, the very phrase 'free trade' and the very victory of the Anti-Corn Law League have tended to confuse the issue. Free trade was crucial to the Manchester programme, but it was a part and not the whole. Like the crown in the Elizabethan constitution, it was the symbol and the *primum mobile* of a system, but not the system itself. As Welby says of the system, 'the interests of the individual, the interests of the nation and the interests of all nations are identical; and these several interests are all in entire and necessary concordance with the highest interests of morality. With this belief, an economic truth acquired . . . the dignity and vitality of a moral law.'[2] Free trade, then, had two functions within the whole. First, it was the particular economic manifestation of a general moral and human principle; and secondly, it was (like the less-eligibility principle) one of those

[1] Cobden to J. Parkes, 16 February 1846; Cobden to G. Combe, 7 March 1846; Cobden to T. Hunter, 12 March 1846, quoted in J. Morley, *The Life of Richard Cobden* (one volume edition, 1903), pp. 363, 366, 370.

[2] Lord Welby, *Cobden's Work and Opinions*, p. 18, quoted in J. A. Hobson, *Richard Cobden: The International Man* (1919), p. 20.

simple, yet fundamental and universal mechanisms, immanent
in society and self-adjusting, which were so dear to the minds
of the Victorians. The description 'middle-class radical' is also
revealing here. True, it embraces the species, 'radical imperialist', descending from the Roebucks and Horsmans of the early
Victorian years to the various crusaders of our own. But it
also brings out an element of class antagonism which, however
difficult it proved to tailor, was part of the stuff of mid-
Victorian politics. It was at this point that Manchester hoped
to drive a wedge between Peel and Gladstone and their
acquired environments and associates. After all, Peel's famous
denunciation of the idle and unworthy members of the gentry[1]
in 1846 was matched by Gladstone's exclamation of 1876 that
from the aristocracy 'there has never on any occasion within
my memory proceeded the impulse which has prompted, and
finally achieved, *any* of the great measures which in the last
half century have contributed so much to the fame and happiness of England; all were done by other agencies than theirs,
and despite their opposition'.[2] Whether or not such outbursts
represented more than momentary irritation, Cobden himself
could not have spoken more frankly than when he said in
1845, 'The sooner the power in this country is transferred
from the landed oligarchy, which has so misused it, and is
placed absolutely – mind I say absolutely – in the hands of
the intelligent middle and industrial classes, the better for the
condition and destinies of this country.'[3] For in the eyes of
Bright and Cobden a single line of demarcation ran down
British politics from top to bottom. Avoidable government
activity; avoidable truck with other governments; avoidable
state expenditure; avoidable public servants; the aristocracy;

[1] '. . . men who have not access to your knowledge, and could not profit by it
if they had, who spend their time in eating and drinking, hunting and shooting,
gambling, horse racing, and so forth. . . .' C. S. Parker, *Sir Robert Peel from his
papers* (1899), Vol. III, pp. 473–4.

[2] Morley, *Gladstone*, loc. cit., Vol. II, p. 557. See also Gladstone's concluding
speech in the Midlothian campaign, at West Calder on 1 April 1880, which was
still more explicit in asserting the reactionary character of the bulk of the nobility,
gentry, and clergy of the established church, ibid., Vol. II, p. 610.

[3] J. Bright and J. E. Thorold Rogers (eds.), *Cobden's Speeches on Questions of
Public Policy* (Oxford, 1870), Vol. I, p. 256.

the army, the navy; formal imperialism, informal imperialism – all these were not merely ranged upon the same hostile side, but were interacting and interdependent. Both formal and informal imperialism supported the armed forces; the armed forces supported the aristocracy; the aristocracy supported empire, and with it bellicosity, war, waste, outdoor relief for its cadets and clients, and a steadfast opposition to free trade. Conversely, Cobden observed as early as 1842, 'it would be well to engraft our free trade agitation upon the peace movement. They are one and the same cause.'[1] Thus, to understand the anti-imperialism of free trade we must understand, first, that it was an inextricable portion of a *general* political attitude, and secondly that it wore a positive as well as a negative aspect.

Let us now turn to political technique. Here the essential circumstance is that the Manchester school never exercised, or hoped to exercise, direct political power. Cobden advocated middle-class self-help, arguing that aristocratic influence might be diminished by the conversion of the farmers, the purchase of property and the scrutiny of the rolls. Bright looked to the extension of the franchise to achieve the same end. But these were distant prospects. At no stage did either man believe that a national party to realize their ends was practicable. It was their fundamental assumption throughout that their political objects could be attained only by indirect means. They might (according to their own thinking) exploit registration and mount so formidable an agitation that the ruling politicians would be driven to surrender; or they might infiltrate the enemy position by exercising pressure – private or bureaucratic – upon susceptible statesmen; or they might do both. But this was the limit of their political capacity and although they neither sought office nor constituted a 'responsible' opposition, they were shrewd and calculating politicians. Hence the fact that they tried always to determine upon a

---

[1] Cobden to H. Ashworth, 12 April 1842, quoted in Morley, *Cobden*, loc. cit., pp. 230–1. In the course of this letter Cobden impressed on Ashworth the importance of enlisting the support of the Society of Friends, 'They have a good deal of influence over the City moneyed interest which has the ear of the Government'. On the later, more specific issues of anti-imperialism and pacificism, Cobdenites and Quakers had, of course, much common ground.

single,[1] simple and concrete issue, on which to arouse the public and persuade the amenable. But this strategy, so dazzlingly successful in the early years, failed them in the 1850s. Here, in a nutshell, we have the history of Manchester radicalism in that decade. And if we were required to find a single cause, a single word, to explain that failure, 'imperialism' might serve the best of all.

III

The stage is now set for a consideration of imperialism and free trade in mid-Victorian years, and especially in the 1850s; and we may usefully enter upon the subject at 1846. 1846 marked, among other things, the beginning of the end of British absorption in domestic issues, and Palmerston's return to the Foreign Office. The next three years were ominous to the Cobdenites, as Palmerston gradually revealed his hand. His diplomatic note which promised British pressure upon foreign governments whenever the folly of British investors threatened to prove particularly costly;[2] the dispatch of a fleet 'to protect British interests' in Portugal; the intervention in Borneo; the renewed Kaffir war; and the inevitable demands of this 'forward' policy for increased naval expenditure and a heavier taxation, all showed the writing on the wall. The radicals were not slow to read. Together with Henry Richard,[3] the secretary

[1] Cobden quoted with approval Bacon's aphorism, 'If you have a handful of truths, open but one finger at a time', ibid., p. 203. Bright – and indeed most other mid-nineteenth-century agitators of the constitutional variety – shared his view that each political objective required a distinct and autonomous agitation and organization.

[2] The 1848 note told the foreign governments that although losses might teach the imprudent a salutary lesson, they might also become so great 'it would be too high a price for the nation to pay for such a warning, and in such a state of things it might become the duty of the British government to make these matters the subject of diplomatic negotiations', quoted in Jenks, loc. cit., p. 125.

[3] The Rev. Henry Richard was also editor of the *Herald of Peace*, an editorial writer in the *Star* newspapers, and a contributor to the *Daily News*, and as such plied with anti-imperialist data and propaganda by Cobden. He entered parliament in 1868 for Myrthyr Boroughs, which constituency he was to represent for twenty years. Like Bright and Cobden he introduced motions in favour of international arbitration and gradual disarmament, with some success – so far as the carrying of resolutions means success – in 1873 and 1880. John Morley was the last editor of the *Star*.

of the Peace Society, Cobden launched a series of meetings denouncing the 'loan-mongering and debt-collecting operations in which our Government engaged either as principal or as agent'; and he believed that Rothschild's subsequent repudiation of intervention on behalf of British creditors overseas (a significant if short-lived check on Palmerstonianism)[1] was a direct consequence of this pressure. As to the attempted intimidation of Portugal, Cobden urged Bright and 'our other Free Trade friends' to fight the 'Palmerston system, and try to prevent the Foreign Office from undoing the good which the Board of Trade has done'.[2] It was, however, Borneo which aroused them most. 'Something should be done,' Cobden wrote 'about that horrid and cowardly butchery. . . . What fiendish atrocities may be committed by English arms, without arousing any conscientious resistance at home, provided they be only far off enough, and the victims too feeble to trouble us.'[3] And it may be useful to add here a later comment: 'There are debts and mortgages and pecuniary interests of all sorts impelling certain parties to incessant activity to get the Government to take to Sarawak. . . . All free-traders who really know what their principles mean will sign the Memorial [of protest].'[4] The Free Trade, Financial Reform, Peace, and Aborigines societies and associations all strove to arouse the public against the Borneo intervention of 1849; and Cobden attempted to carry the war into the House of Commons. But before the agitation was effectively concentrated – if it ever could have been – the fatal Don Pacifico debate took place.

Meanwhile in 1849 the free-trade radicals believed that an offensive against Palmerstonianism, in contradistinction to mere denunciation, was still possible. For a time, Cobden held that it might be assailed indirectly by building upon the existing Liverpool movement, headed by Robertson Gladstone

[1] Cobden to H. Richard, 20 April 1850, quoted in Hobson, loc. cit., p. 63.
[2] Cobden to Bright, 24 October 1846, quoted in Morley, *Cobden*, loc. cit., p. 476.
[3] Cobden to H. Richard, 26 December 1849, quoted in Hobson, loc. cit., pp. 58–9.
[4] Cobden to H. Richard, undated, 1852, quoted ibid., p. 59.

(W. E. Gladstone's brother), for Financial Reform.[1] Bright preferred the spearhead of parliamentary reform, other radicals, national education; but Cobden argued that neither issue would provide a sufficient basis for an agitation, and that public expenditure was Palmerston's Achilles heel.

> The people [he wrote] want information and instruction upon armaments, colonies, taxation and so forth. There is a fearful mass of prejudice and ignorance to dispel on these subjects, and whilst these exist, you may get a reform of parliament, but you will not get a reformed policy. I believe there is as much clinging to colonies at the present moment amongst the middle class as among the aristocracy; and the working people are no wiser than the rest. . . . Now all these questions can be discussed most favourably with reference to the expenditure. You may reason ever so logically, but never so convincingly as through the pocket. But it will take time to play off John Bull's acquisitiveness against his combativeness.[2]

He himself proposed that £8½ million be saved upon the armed forces (a cut of 45 per cent) and £1½ million by 'administrative reform', and that a further £1½ million be raised by death duties upon real property; the whole £11½ million to be disposed of by abolishing or reducing the duties upon nine articles of consumption, and removing the window tax and the advertisement duty. This proposal and the preceding discussion indicate very clearly the extent of the free-traders' front, and the interconnection of their anti-imperialism with their economy, pacificism, anti-rentier and anti-aristocratic prejudices, and other parts. The usual tactics of public meetings and resolutions in the House of Commons were employed; and during the 1849 session motions for the reduction of public expenditure by £10 million, and in favour of arbitration as a diplomatic method were proposed. The first was defeated by 197 votes to 78, the second by 176 votes to 79. But Bright

[1] For a detailed analysis of the Financial Reform Association, see W. N. Calkins, 'A Victorian Free Trade Lobby', *Econ. Hist. Rev.*, 2nd ser. XIII, 90–104.

[2] Cobden to Bright, 23 December 1848, quoted in Morley, *Cobden*, loc. cit., pp. 502–3.

and Cobden were not despondent. After all, the first year of
the anti-Corn Law agitation had been less promising; and
although the spread of imperialist sentiments among the manufacturing, commercial and labouring classes was manifest, they
held that since these classes (unlike the aristocracy) had no
true interest in empire or in open or covert force, but very
much the reverse, time would dissipate their bellicosity. Moreover, Peel had seemed increasingly sympathetic to the causes
of reduced armaments and arbitration in 1849; and a succession
of public meetings held in the northern towns in the autumn
of 1849 to promote retrenchment and anti-imperialism had
evoked an encouraging response.

One week's work in 1850 withered these growing hopes.
There can be no doubt that the entire 'Palmerstonian system'
stood on trial in the Don Pacifico debate. Nor can it be
doubted that Palmerston's margin of 46 votes was an inadequate index of his victory. His support in the country at
large was overwhelming. As he himself observed upon the
conclusion of the debate, it had been many a long day since a
foreign minister of Great Britain had been so popular;[1] and it
was to be many a long day – a decade at the least – before the
position which he had won in 1850 was seriously endangered.
To fill the radicals' cup of bitterness, Peel died within forty-
eight hours of his speech in the debate, in which he had
seemed to them to move closer to their position.

> Poor Peel, [Cobden noted]. We do not yet know the full
> extent of our loss . . . I had observed his tendencies most
> attentively during the last few years, and had felt convinced
> that on questions . . . such as the reduction of armaments,
> retrenchment of expenditure, the diffusion of peace prin-
> ciples, etc., he had strong sympathies stronger than he had
> yet expressed – in favour of my views. Read his last speech
> again, and observe what he says about diplomacy, and in
> favour of settling international disputes by reference to
> mediation instead of by ships of war.[2]

[1] E. Ashley, *Life of Viscount Palmerston* (1879), Vol. II, p. 161.
[2] Cobden to G. Hadfield, 5 July 1850, quoted in Morley, *Cobden*, loc. cit.,
pp. 540–1.

Whether or not this view of Peel was justified, it was certainly
true that, so far as the anti-imperialist cause depended upon
influencing men in the first rank of politics, it had now to
await the doubtful and dilatory rise of Gladstone.

Seven lean years followed the Don Pacifico debate, and the
eighth brought the absolute disaster. The various Kaffir,
Bornean, and Burmese wars and the Central American and
Caribbean imbroglios of the early 1850s paved the way for the
final catastrophes in China and India. Like the legendary Gaels,
the free-trade radicals always went forth to battle, and always
fell. Even the sanguine Cobden wrote bitterly after the publication of his pamphlet, *How wars are got up in India*,[1] 'I should
advise no-one who did not wish to reap the disappointment
which Burke so feelingly confesses at the close of his career
to meddle with Indian politics with a view to arresting
our career of spoliation and wrong.'[2] 1857 represented
the nadir of their fortunes. There was perhaps no clearer
case of mid-Victorian imperialism than the Arrow episode
and the Canton bombardment; and no mid-Victorian electorate spoke its will more clearly than that which endorsed
Palmerston at the general election of the same year, and
drove Bright, Cobden, Miall, Milner Gibson, and Fox, the
Manchester radicals, bag and baggage, from the House of
Commons.

Before abandoning the 1850s, I propose to set out Cobden's
reactions to three of the Palmerstonian ventures, so that his
recognition of, and opposition to, contemporary imperialism
may be decisively established. Let us take first his observations
on the second Burmese war:

Never was the military spirit half so rampant in this
country since [1815] as at the present time. Look at the late
news from Rangoon. . . . This makes 5,400 persons killed by
our ships in the East during the last five years, without our

[1] *How Wars are got up in India: The Origin of the Burmese War* (1853). This pamphlet provides the fullest and most consecutive of Cobden's condemnations of
contemporary imperialism, although his very first venture into print, *England,
Ireland and America* (Manchester, 1835), foreshadowed 'the anti-imperialism of
free trade' in many ways.
[2] Cobden to H. Richard, 21 May 1856, quoted in Hobson, loc. cit., p. 144.

having lost one man by the butcheries. Now give me Free
Trade as the recognized policy of all parties in this country,
and I will find the best possible argument against these
marauding atrocities. I will then demonstrate to all by their
own admission that they cannot profit by such proceedings.

'*Esprit de corps*, the spirit of nationality, and the great social
sway of the military class, all tend to sweep us more and more
into the martial vortex.' 'There is always the lurking bribe in
the minds of *all* that the game of spoliation though often foully
played is yet profitable. . . . But the modern application of the
principles of political economy has destroyed the motive of
self interest which tempted us formerly to wars of conquest.
I *could* turn the batteries against the £. *s. d.* argument most
successfully.'[1]

Next let us consider Cobden's view of the Indian possessions
after the mutiny of 1857. It would, he wrote, 'be a happy day
when England has not an acre of territory in Continental
Asia'. The task of governing a hundred million Asiatics
effectively had always been impossible. But even were it not,
what advantage could the enterprise confer? Those who
regarded India as a market which could only be kept open by
force did not 'understand the full meaning of Free Trade principles! If you talk to our Lancashire friends they argue that
unless we occupied India there would be no trade with that
country, or that someone else would monopolize it, forgetting
that this is the old protectionist theory which they used formerly to ridicule.' It was doubtful (Cobden argued) if the
English occupation had added anything to Indian trade, but
certain that that trade would have been larger had occupation
and coercion not been employed: wherever, as in India, the

[1] Cobden to J. Sturge, 11 March 1852, quoted in Morley, *Cobden*, loc. cit.,
pp. 578–9; Cobden to H. Richard, 10 and 24 August and 8 September 1852,
quoted in Hobson, loc. cit., pp. 87–9. Cobden's correspondence with Richard on
the second Burmese campaign includes the following interesting observation.
'It is quite clear that our so-called battles with these people are nothing but
battues. They have no more chance against our 64-pound red-hot shot . . . than
they would in running a race on their roads against our railways. War has become, like manufacturing and industrial rivalry, very much a competition of
capital, skill and chemical and mechanical discovery.'

elements of self-government were destroyed, it was international commerce which ultimately suffered.[1]

Finally, Cobden's reaction to the Chinese interventions of
the late 1850s is instructive. He repeatedly drew attention to the
statistics of Chinese trade since the ending of the Opium War,
when everyone in England was persuaded that there would be
an intoxicating increase in exports to the East. 'Observe,' said
Cobden, 'that we have gained scarcely anything. . . . Indeed
some of the years since the war have been less favourable.'[2]
Such increase as there was had been paid for not by British
manufactures but by opium – 'and it is the opium trade, and
not the exclusive policy of the Chinese, which according to
our best authorities stands in the way of our increasing our
exports'. The Chinese was, next to the British, the least protectionist government in the world. All that those who wished
for a permanent trade with China could desire 'is that the duties
shall be moderate, the trade regular and that facilities shall be
afforded at the ports of entry for the quick dispatch of business.
All these conditions exist in China to as great an extent as in
any other considerable maritime state.' It was the interest of
Great Britain to preserve these conditions, but her activity was
fast destroying them. 'It is very like attempting to enter a house
in the rear of a burglar and offering to transact business whilst

[1] Cobden to H. Richard, 16 July 1857, quoted in Hobson, loc. cit., pp. 233–4;
Cobden to Bright, 22 September 1857; Cobden to Col. Fitzmayer, 18 October
1857; Cobden to G. Combe, 16 May 1858, quoted in Morley, *Cobden*, loc. cit.,
pp. 677–80. Bright differed from Cobden on the Indian issue, not on the un-
wisdom and immortality of what had been done, but on what was practicable
for the future. 'However deplorable,' Bright argued, 'the possession of India is a
fact. There we are; we do not know how to leave it. . . .' When the inevitable
day arrived when British power should be withdrawn, five or six compact self-
governing states should be already in existence. Immediate withdrawal would
mean that the 'whole country, in all probability, [would] lapse into chaos and
anarchy and into sanguinary and interminable warfare', G. M. Trevelyan, *The
Life of John Bright* (1913), pp. 262, 265–6. Cobden, however, never directly
advocated 'doing a Congo' over India: he was more concerned with the avoid-
ance of the Indian 'errors' elsewhere, and with the establishment of some type of
Esterling system for British merchants in China and Japan. Hobson, loc. cit.,
pp. 315–16.

[2] In the years 1869–73 China still had a favourable annual trade balance with
Great Britain, though a larger deficit with India. S. B. Saul, 'Britain and World
Trade, 1870–1914', *Econ. Hist. Rev.*, 2nd ser. VII, 50.

some of its inmates are still weltering in their blood and others still struggling with their assailants.' But it was the long-term consequences which disturbed Cobden most. He believed that Palmerstonian interventions were eating away the authority and prestige of the central government: and if pursued for sufficient time and with sufficient force, they would surely lead to the *summum malum* (not least from the standpoint of British merchants and manufacturers), anarchy. Ultimately, 'there may be no government with which to treat – who knows but we may be step by step drawn into participation in the civil broils of the vast empire'.[1]

Cobden's analyses speak for themselves. Moral judgements apart, the economic purposes of 'contemporary' imperialism, and the inter-relationship of formal and informal empire, are here laid bare. To those who argued for the forcible 'opening up' of markets (even if they were ready to open them to the world at large), Cobden replied that not merely did coercion contradict free trade, which was essentially 'natural' and pacific, but also that empire *per se* supported that aristocratic caste which was the implacable enemy of economic virtue; that it fostered wars and hatreds; that it led to the squandering of resources which might otherwise fructify; and that so far from increasing commerce and creating lasting markets, it reduced them – even absolutely upon occasions. In short, Cobden was both sensitive and opposed to imperial growths and exercises *because* of his adherence to free trade. It may be objected, of course, that Cobden's 'free trade' was merely theoretical and unrepresentative.[2] But such an objection misconceives the

[1] Cobden to W. Gregson, 14 January 1857; Cobden to H. Richard, 18 January and 20 June 1857, quoted in Hobson, loc. cit., pp. 197–9, 222; Cobden to W. Hargreaves, undated, 1861, quoted in Morley, *Cobden*, p. 846. Gregson was chairman of the East India and China Association and doctrinaire free trader. George Thompson, M.P. for Aberdeen down to 1857, was another East India and China merchant of Cobdenite sympathies.

[2] In a loose and non-commital sense of the words, Palmerston might have claimed to have been the oldest free trader of them all. He had sat under Dugald Stewart at Edinburgh University at the turn of the eighteenth century. But Smith's doctrine and its underlying metaphysics sat very lightly, if at all, on Palmerston, who was the very antithesis of the doctrinaire. Even on such an issue as Corn Law Repeal, and even as late as 1852, he confessed that he opposed

doctrine and the situation. Free trade was presented to the world not as a mild opinion but as a scientific certitude; and the cause and justification of Cobden's pre-eminence lay quite as much in his grasp of theory and powers of apologetic as in his capacity as an agitator. None seriously attempted to wrestle with Cobden in terms of free-trade doctrine; no school of free-trade imperialists, claiming a purer descent from Adam Smith, set up. Sinners abounded, but schisms failed to emerge. Objections to Cobden's 'arid dogmatism' were at bottom, objections to the logical deductions from a doctrine grounded in 'natural harmony'. Correspondingly, Cobden articulated and attempted to rationalize antipathies lying deep in nineteenth-century English society. W. E. Forster dismissed the Manchester school in 1863 with 'Cobden and Bright are impracticable and un-English, and there are hardly any hopeful radicals'.[1] The truth is that Cobden and Bright spoke for and helped to shape considerable forces of opinion which were to express themselves in later rather than contemporary electorates and parties. Their type of class-conscious and pacifist anti-imperialism was probably at its most powerful in politics in the first decade of the present century. It found a lodgment in the ideology and literature of an important section of the post-Gladstonian liberals, partly by means of the 'lives' and collected writings of the Schoolmen, partly by surviving associations, clubs, and direct disciples, such as Richard, Edmund Muspratt,[2] or John Morley. It coloured most of the early forms of modern Socialism in the United Kingdom. At certain junctures it dominated the purposes of the Independent Labour

---

'not the principle, but . . . the expediency, of the imposition of any duty . . . upon foreign corn' (P. Guedella, *Palmerston* (1926), p. 336). As for imperialism, Palmerston neither considered nor cared what free-trade doctrine might have to say upon the subject.

[1] Sir W. Reid, *The Life of W. E. Forster* (1888), Vol. I, p. 362.

[2] Edmund K. Muspratt (1833–1923), chemical manufacturer and director and subsequently president of the United Alkali Company, was president of the Financial Reform Association and an ardent Cobdenite. The heavy chemical manufacturers were, as a group, free-trade Liberals, and in many cases contested parliamentary elections in the Liberal interest. D. W. F. Hardie, *A History of the Chemical Industry in Widnes* (Birmingham, 1950), pp. 124–5.

Party, or at least its leadership.[1] More perhaps than any other single factor, it helped to create some semblance of a common front of radical, chapel, labour, and Irish interests in the years 1900 to 1914. Cobden's analyses of mid-Victorian empire fully anticipated Hobson's theory of imperialism, and may even have contributed to Lenin's. Naturally, something of an opposite line of succession was maintained. As Bright noted while Chamberlain still spoke from the ministerial benches as a Liberal, 'the whole tone and argument of his speech are exactly of the stuff on which the foreign policy of Lord Palmerston, and I may almost say of Lord Beaconsfield, was defended'.[2]

Meanwhile, in the course of Palmerston's second administration, the cause of Manchester radicalism revived. The fundamental and interconnected reasons for the revival were, first, the re-emergence of economic and financial issues which appealed to long 'subservient' elements in the electorate, and secondly, Gladstone's long spell as chancellor of the exchequer – and virtual leader of the opposition to his own prime minister. Military and naval expenditure was the main ground of battle. Palmerston began with an expenditure of £28 million and desired an expenditure of £36 million. But the utmost he secured was £26 million, and he was forced back to £24 million before his death. These figures provide some index of Gladstone's success within the cabinet. They also provide a measure of the fortunes of the anti-imperialist cause, for this was inevitably involved in the conflict over expenditure. 'As to the amount of the final demand [for the China war],' Gladstone told Argyll, 'what it really demonstrates is *one* among the follies and dangers of our high-handed policy.'[3] For despite material

---

[1] E.g. The report of the Council of the I.L.P. to the Annual Conference, 1901, which includes this passage: 'The terrible expenditure of blood and treasures which the [Boer] war has entailed is the least of the price which our country will have to pay. The war has already cost us our good name amongst freedom-loving peoples in all lands . . . and increased our military expenditure to such a degree as to overburden the trade and commerce of the nation.' The report went on to say that – 'as every one is now aware' – the war had been undertaken on behalf of 'a gang of international speculators'. The whole is strongly reminiscent of Cobden's broadsides of the 1850s.

[2] Bright to G. Dixon, 1 December 1882, quoted in Trevelyan, loc. cit., p. 435.

[3] Morley, *Gladstone*, loc. cit., Vol. II, p. 637.

differences in attitude – especially in his desire to revive and extend a form of the Congress system[1] – Gladstone was commonly in sympathy with the anti-imperialists and even echoed them on some issues. From the outset of Palmerston's second government, Bright and Cobden, following the classic strategy of Manchester, set out 'to disturb Gladstone's tranquillity' by ceaseless pressure and appeals to conscience; and when on 1 January 1861 Bright wrote to Gladstone, 'Depend upon it, peace must ever be insecure so long as you have armed ships and armed men, prowling about parts of the globe many thousands of miles away from the immediate control of the Government, and from those who pay taxes to support them', Gladstone hastened to fulfil 'the duty of thanking you for being disposed to believe that I desire the adoption of a policy of which the temper shall not be likely to produce more wars in China'.[2] Even the exacting Cobden acknowledged Gladstone's truth as a free trader, and begged Bright to make allowances for the fact that as a responsible minister and cabinet member he was constrained by circumstances and colleagues in a way that independent members were not. Gladstone, Cobden told his fellow radical in 1860, 'has a strong aversion to the waste of money on our armaments. He has no class feeling about the Services. He has much more of our sympathies. . . . He has more in common with you and me than any other man of his power in Britain.'[3] In fact, Palmerstonianism in general was on the wane by 1862. 'The tide is turned,' Gladstone noted in the middle of that year, 'Lord Palmerston is now "the stronger swimmer in his agony"';[4]

[1] 'Men like Gladstone, representing the revival of the vast force of emotion in international politics, broke it [the Concert of Europe] by attempting to place upon it, in the shape of the internal administration of Egypt and the reform or dissolution of the Ottoman Empire, burdens which it was not designed to bear – by attempting in fact to convert it back to a Congress system.' F. H. Hinsley, 'The Development of the European States System since the Eighteenth Century', *Trans. Roy. Hist. Soc.* 5th ser., xi, 78. The Bright–Gladstone split of 1882 derived from just this divergence.

[2] Bright to Gladstone, date as above; Gladstone to Bright, 3 January 1861, quoted in W. E. Williams, *The Rise of Gladstone to the Leadership of the Liberal Party, 1859–68* (Cambridge, 1934), pp. 47–50.

[3] Morley, *Cobden*, loc. cit., p. 772.

[4] Morley, *Gladstone*, loc. cit., Vol. II, p. 50.

and if a counterpart to the Don Pacifico debate be needed we might perhaps take the Kagosima affair of 1863 to mark the close of this particular phase of imperial expansion. When Asiatic governments had 13-inch mortars at their own command, the days of cheap glory in the East were numbered.

IV

To sum up, what is the bearing of the present paper upon the Gallagher–Robinson thesis? This involves three consequential propositions. The first is that the concept of 'the imperialism of free trade' should be modified. Concepts do signify: and this phrase suggests the opposite of the truth. The doctrinaire free traders were both anti-imperialist, whatever the form of empire, and quick to discover and denounce all types of informality. They hunted down confusions of 'free trade' with mere increases of commerce or with the forcible 'opening up' of markets; and they predicted with no little accuracy the consequences of casual interventions. The second proposition is this. It was the achievement of Mr Gallagher and Dr Robinson to establish the essentially imperialist character of British policy and public sentiment in the years 1845 to 1860, and to dissipate the contrary myth. But when they step out farther and ignore the existence of an implacable opposition to imperialism, and deny variety to British imperial policy in the Victorian age, they mislead us dangerously. In fact, Victorian imperialism and anti-imperialism were locked in unending if intermittent combat. In no other decade, perhaps, did fortune favour the imperialists so markedly as in the 1850s. And the greatest victory of substantial Cobdenism – *eo vel alio nomine* – at the polls occurred not in the nineteenth, but in the twentieth century. The sweeping Liberal–Labour Representation Committee victory of 1906 was not, as is sometimes supposed, the victory of social reform, still less of socialism.[1] It was the victory of free trade, of anti-imperialism, of the opposition to coolie labour – for it was these constituents of the old Manchester creed which formed the burning issues of the day – and

[1] F. Bealey and H. Pelling, *Labour and Politics 1900–1906: A history of the Labour Representation Committee* (1958), p. 265.

it was the common radical tradition and programme of the respective leaders which made possible the fateful Gladstone–MacDonald collaboration, from which the parliamentary Labour Party ultimately derived. Nor must we forget our first lesson in the dialectic. Not only forces in history, but also the collisions between forces signify. Much of the history of imperial policy is the history of such collisions.

The third proposition both qualifies and amplifies the second. The simple theme of a conflict of imperialist and anti-imperialist forces must be balanced by an appreciation of complications and ambivalence which were also involved. The first complication is that imperial issues were never really separable from the great nexus of domestic concerns and prejudice. Secondly, there were significant differences of view within each of the great alignments. Palmerston might not have reacted as Disraeli did to the offer of the Khedive's shares. Bright resigned from Gladstone's cabinet in 1882 because of the bombardment of Alexandria. No doubt, the stabilizing influence of the permanent officials of the Foreign Office was great; but it was not irresistible. And the Gallagher–Robinson assumption that in the history of nineteenth-century empire, the relationship of the economic and political arms was one of master and servant, oversimplifies. Lastly, we might perhaps usefully apply R. Pares's observation that even eighteenth-century politicians entered parliament for fun. The Victorian attitude towards empire was compounded of more elements than self-interest. Trade was certainly a consideration. But missionary Christianity and plain jingoism were also influences of importance – not least among the radical imperialists. 'There's a little fellow', said Bright of Kinnaird, 'who will vote for any amount of slaughter on Evangelical principles.' 'Mr Roebuck', wrote Cobden, 'is all for force, for cannon and squadrons, and regiments and fleets.' And there was another element, drama and vicarious excitement, which Cobden described harshly in these words:

Like the Romans at the Amphitheatre, or the French populace in the first Revolution, we acquire a habit of enjoying scenes of carnage, the only difference being that we look at them through the columns of the newspaper. And hence 'our own correspondent' is sent to the seat of war to deck out in pictorial phrase, for the amusement of the reader, the scenes of slaughter and wounds and agony which we peruse with precisely the same zest as if we were witnessing a mimic battlefield at Astley's.[1] Observe the eager levity with which *The Times* correspondent at Hong Kong is urging on the fray, calling for 'the opening of the ball', and threatening Lord Elgin with recall if he does not execute his behests.[2]

While few might accept such a sinister interpretation, no student of the mid-Victorian press would deny the existence of this phenomenon. It is one type of complication that opinion upon imperial issues was compounded of such various and volatile materials. It is another that imperialists and anti-imperialists alike often used identical grounds of appeal: economic interest, Christian principle, national honour.

[1] Astley's *Royal Amphitheatre*, founded in 1798 by Philip Astley (1742–1842).
[2] Cobden to H. Richard, 14 January 1858, quoted in Hobson, loc. cit., p. 237.

9 Imperialism and Free Trade Policy in India, 1853–1854

R. J. MOORE

[This article is edited from the *Economic History Review*, 2nd series, Vol. XVII (1964).]

In his recent article, 'The Anti-Imperialism of Free Trade',[1] Professor O. MacDonagh set out to break the connection which Gallagher and Robinson had drawn between British overseas expansion and free-trade policy during the mid-Victorian period.[2] MacDonagh sought 'a definition of free trade in terms, first, of groups, secondly, of beliefs, and finally, of political technique'. He accepted the Manchester school as the essential free-trade group. In terms of their beliefs, free trade was a 'portion of a *general* political attitude', a political morality which included 'economy, pacifism, anti-rentier and anti-aristocratic prejudices'. Their political technique was not to seek office, but to 'infiltrate the enemy position by exercising pressure . . . upon susceptible statesmen'. MacDonagh then proceeded to question the relationship between 'free trade' and imperialism, 'especially in the 1850s', through a study of Cobden's thought. After establishing that 'Cobden was both sensitive and opposed to imperial growths and exercises *because* of his adherence to free trade', he concluded that 'free-trade' policy represented an 'implacable opposition to imperialism'.[3]

[1] *Economic History Review*, 2nd ser. XIV (1961–2), 489–501.

[2] J. Gallagher and R. Robinson, 'The Imperialism of Free Trade', *Econ. Hist. Rev.*, 2nd ser. VI (1953), 1–15.

[3] C. A. Bodelsen, long ago, described 'the Manchester School' as 'the centre of Separatism' during the mid-Victorian period, *Studies in Mid-Victorian Imperialism* [Copenhagen, 1924] (1960 edition), pp. 32–6. Unlike MacDonagh, however, he was little concerned with Manchester's Indian policy during the fifties.

Manchester's policy towards India is a prominent theme in MacDonagh's analysis. He believed that the pamphlet, *How Wars are got up in India* (1853), provides 'the fullest and most consecutive of Cobden's condemnations of contemporary imperialism'. Without question, Manchester deplored Dalhousie's wars, and generally his annexations. To the evidence of Cobden's pamphlet might be added the many questions and speeches on extensions to British India which the Mancunians put before the House of Commons. However, it would be wrong to suppose that Manchester's Indian policy was merely negative. MacDonagh's concentration upon Cobden's conviction of the worthlessness and futility of British rule in India obscures their pressure for positive reform. They propounded, in fact, a policy of internal development through the promotion of communications and public works. There is good reason to suggest that this policy was inspired by the motive of obtaining Indian cotton, and that the espousal of it involved condoning improvements being effected by private capital upon which the returns were secured against the public revenue of India. That is to say, in anti-imperialist terms, the Manchester school were associated with the 'exploitation' of India as a source of raw material, and as a field for the guaranteed investment of 'finance capital'.[1] If these contentions are justified, MacDonagh's case for 'the anti-imperialism of free trade' would require modification.

I

Occasion for the full expression of Manchester's Indian policy was provided in 1853 by the imminent expiry of the East India

[1] Much has been written of the exploitation of India as a market for Manchester's cotton goods, e.g. A. Redford, Chapter III, 'Manchester and India . . .', in his *Manchester Merchants and Foreign Trade* (Manchester, 1934-56), Vol. II, pp. 21-31; P. Harnetty, 'The Indian Cotton Duties Controversy, 1894-1896', *English Historical Review*, LXXVII (1962), 684-702. H. Furber recently endorsed the view which Ottavio Barié had expressed (*Idee e dottrine imperialistische nell' Inghilterra Vittoriana* (Bari, 1953), pp. 18 *et seq.*) of 'the failure of the "Manchester school" to grapple with the problem posed by the economic importance to the Midlands of the possession of India' ('The Theme of Imperialism . . . in Modern Historical Writing on India', *Historians of India, Pakistan and Ceylon*, ed. C. H. Philips (1961), p. 338).

Company's charter. On 11 March, in the Commons, Bright questioned Russell on the Whig–Peelite ministry's intentions for 'the future government of India'.[1] Bright stressed his position as a representative of 'that constituency which . . . is probably the most deeply interested in . . . the question', and as one who, in 1848, had 'obtained and presided over a Committee to enquire into the obstacles which existed to the cultivation and growth of cotton in India'. He announced that he would oppose a renewal of the Company's charter, chiefly because of the past neglect of 'material improvements'. On the evidence of petitions recently sent Home, he believed that there were 'virtually no roads in the country', and that railroad construction was 'proceeding with a dilatoriness . . . and inefficiency of management and hopelessness of results'. He complained of the 'impossibility of introducing articles from abroad into the interior, or of conveying the products of the interior to the ports', and deplored the want of irrigation and the disrepair of canals and reservoirs. From the evidence of the 1848 committee, he had concluded that the reason for the Indians' failure to grow more cotton was their 'degraded condition', for which he blamed the government's 'unaccountable neglect' of public works. The Company had, therefore, made a 'scandalous sacrifice of the interests of the district of this country with which I am connected'.[2]

Bright urged that permanent legislation for the government of India should await the completion of inquiries which were then being made by parliamentary committees on Indian affairs. He expected that the evidence presented to them would confirm his view of the need for a large reform of the governing authorities. He was supported in the Commons by J. G. Phillimore, who referred to the 'neglect of internal communication' and the reluctance 'to spend money on public works',

---

[1] *Hansard*, 3rd ser. cxxv (1853), 37–47.

[2] For the agitation of Bright and the Manchester Chamber of Commerce, between the 'cotton famine' of 1846 and 1850, to have India's potentiality as a source of raw cotton investigated and developed, see A. Redford, op. cit., Vol. I, pp. 223–5; D. Thorner, *Investment in Empire, British Railways and Steam Shipping Enterprise in India, 1825–1849* (Philadelphia, 1950), pp. 112–14, 117–18 n. 24, 145–59.

J. F. Blackett, Danby Seymour, and Cobden.[1] However, Russell left no doubt of the ministry's intention to legislate during the current session, and this made a large reform in the governing powers unlikely.[2] His announcement drew a quick response from Manchester. On 13 March, two days after the debate, Bright helped to form the Indian Reform Society. He was joined on its committee by Phillimore and Blackett, while Danby Seymour became its first president.[3]

In the following weeks Bright prepared for an attack upon the government's proposals. At this period 'the subject [of India] was hardly a day out of his thoughts and his reading was almost confined to it'. About a week after the debate, he addressed a 'commercial meeting in Manchester on Indian affairs and complained that neither its resolutions nor its petition to Parliament were "earnest enough"'. On 18 March he advised Russell 'not to go wrong by hasty legislation', and four days later talked with Robert Lowe, Secretary to the Board of Control for India, 'on Indian affairs'. On 25 March he 'spoke of India' with Sir William Molesworth, then a member of the Cabinet, who 'said he should convey my ideas on the subject to his colleagues'.[4] On 15 April he moved for a return detailing expenditure on public works in recent years.[5] The same day, he noted in his diary: 'Had some talk with Wood [President of the Board of Control for India] . . . on the position of the Govt. and our section, and told him plainly that a large party could not be kept together without some respect being shown to every influential section of it.'[6] In May he

---

[1] *Hansard*, op. cit., 55, 57–8, 63.

[2] Ibid., 55

[3] R. P. Masani, *Dadabhai Naoroji: The Grand Old Man of India* (1939), p. 59; *The Diaries of John Bright*, ed. R. A. J. Walling (1930), p. 145 n. 1; *The Times*, 10 May 1853.

[4] *Bright's Diaries*, op. cit., pp. 138–41, 145 n. 1. The meeting which Bright addressed was probably that which the mayor of Manchester called 'to consider the better development of the resources of British India, and the consequent amelioration of the condition of the people [*sic*]' (*The Times*, 17 March). For a petition, dated 25 April, from the 'City of Manchester', see *Select Committee on Indian Affairs*, Parl. Papers (H.C.) 1852–3, XXVII, App. 7, p. 251.

[5] P.P. (H.C.) 1852–3, LXXIV.

[6] *Bright's Diaries*, op. cit., p. 141.

spoke on India at Bristol, and, on 1 June, at Birmingham.[1] When Sir Charles Wood introduced his Bill on 3 June he knew that its provisions would be opposed by the 'Indian Reform Association'.[2]

During the Commons debate on Wood's Bill, the members of the Indian Reform Society 'clustered . . . closely below the gangway' of the House.[3] They held a meeting on the day following the first night's debate,[4] which had been wholly taken up by Wood's introductory speech of five hours and by Bright's virulent two-hour reply to it. Later in the debate, the group were referred to as 'Young India'.[5] They were, it was said, 'better known as the Manchester school'.[6]

In his second reading speech,[7] Bright reiterated his views of 11 March, confident that 'he was . . . speaking almost the unanimous sentiments of the merchants and manufacturers of Manchester'. This was no glib boast. Earlier in the debate, Wood had alluded to representations which the cotton interest had 'earnestly pressed' upon him.[8] Again, Milner Gibson had presented a petition from the Manchester Chamber of Commerce and Manufactures which they had drawn up on 22 June, after Bright had impressed upon them the connection between the 'Government of India question' and 'the permanence and

[1] Ibid., p. 145 n.1.

[2] *Hansard*, 3rd ser. cxxvii, 1097–8.

[3] Ibid. cxxviii, 77, 1010; see also [E. M. Whitty], *History of the Session 1852–3* . . . (1854), p. 176. Whitty wrote, with something of the satirist's exaggeration, of the alignment over the Bill as being 'Sir Charles and Mr Lowe against the Indian Reform Society – these being the only two parties . . . taking the slightest notice of the legislation' (p. 194).

[4] *Bright's Diaries*, op. cit., p. 146.

[5] R. D. Mangles (*Hansard*, op. cit., 776), Cumming Bruce (ibid., 990) and Digby Seymour (ibid., 1010) used the expression. It also occurs in letters from Wood to Dalhousie, e.g. 4, 8, 24 June, 8 July, 8 August 1853, Wood Papers (subsequently referred to as W.P.), India Office Library. All references to the Wood–Dalhousie correspondence relate to letters in this collection.

[6] Cumming Bruce, op. cit. Sir Robert Inglis also spoke of the 'Manchester school' during the debate (op. cit., 656). W. H. Sykes, a director of the Company, associated 'the Manchester school' with the case for increasing India's cotton production. On 31 May he sent to the *Morning Chronicle* a copy of a letter published in Bombay, which he believed to be a 'reply' to them (P.R.O. 30/29/21).

[7] *Hansard*, op. cit., 877–80.

[8] Ibid., cxxvii, 1111.

stability of the supply of cotton'.[1] Bright now attacked the Company's failure to build roads for 'agricultural, commercial and economical purposes', and contrasted such niggardliness with the liberality of 'the people of Manchester [who] had expended more for their internal improvement than the East India Company with their vast empire'.

Bright's colleagues echoed his sentiments. Phillimore described the Company's public works policy as 'disastrous'.[2] Danby Seymour called for such a government as would encourage the investment of English capital in India, in consequence of which 'the aspect of Hindoostan would be changed enormously before ten years had passed'.[3] Digby Seymour, who acknowledged his attachment to the 'Young India' group, revealed that India's consumption of British goods was low compared with South America's, and that while England's imports of American cotton had climbed steadily, the quantities drawn from India had remained constant.[4] 'How', he asked, 'was that to be accounted for? America had 11,000 miles of railway; but in India . . . the expenditure for railways had not been more than sufficient to place 100 miles in course of construction.' He condemned the existing form of government because he believed that it inhibited internal development: 'What were the tests they ought to take in order to try the merits of the system? He would ask whether by the present system peace was encouraged – whether the works of peace, such as canals and roads, the means of transit and internal traffic flourished . . . ; instead of peace, the system had been the instigation and the cause of war. . . .' Cobden, who 'saw no benefit which could arise to the mass of the English people from their connection with India, except that which might arise from honest trade', drew the same antithesis between the

---

[1] *The Times* 22 and 24 June 1853. For this and similar Manchester petitions, see *S.C. on Indian Affairs*, P.P. (H.C.) 1852–3, Vol. XXVIII, Appendix 2, pp. 241–2, 252. On 9 August, after the Commons had passed the Bill, Wood received a memorial from the Manchester Commercial Association expressing their concern over the 'extension and improvement of cotton cultivation' in India (W.P. 1).

[2] *Hansard*, op. cit., 1238.

[3] Ibid., 1339–40.

[4] Ibid., cxxviii, 1009–1016.

G

existing system as productive of wars, and reformed government as the basis of development.[1]

II

Manchester's arguments did not deflect the Aberdeen ministry from its purpose of renewing, with modification, the Company's charter. However, in Sir Charles Wood the Manchester school found a 'susceptible statesman', and their subjection of him to their techniques of 'exercising pressure' contributed to the impressively energetic prosecution of public works and railways during his Presidency of the Board of Control. Wood was apprehensive of the effect of the Reformers' opposition to the uneasy coalition government in what he described as a 'very uncertain' House of Commons.[2] On 8 March he remarked upon Disraeli's 'disposition to join the Radicals in opposing any [Indian] legislation',[3] and after the debate of 11 March, he predicted 'a nasty storm about India'.[4] On 24 March he wrote to Dalhousie: 'The Manchester people want to pull down the Directors [of the East India Company] because they don't grow cotton; . . . Disraeli and Derby are ready to join in any opposition to us. . . .' On 24 May he elaborated upon 'the Manchester school's' dissent from his plan for the future government of India.[5] During the same period, he gave particular attention to railways and public works.

On 8 March Wood pressed Dalhousie, 'with some anxiety', for a report on the best means of providing India with a system of railways. 'Our Manchester people,' he commented, '. . . look, and naturally, with great interest to opening the cotton growing districts.' He wrote at length on this, and associated questions, in the next mail: '. . . I hope that you will have reported on railroads before I have to bring in my Bill. I am very anxious to push the railroad from Bombay into the Cotton Districts if I knew which is really the best line. The

---

[1] Ibid., 822–3, 831.

[2] Wood to Dalhousie, 8 June 1853.

[3] Letter to Dalhousie.

[4] Wood to 3rd Earl Grey, 14 March 1853, in Howick Collection, The Prior's Kitchen, The College, Durham.

[5] Letter to Dalhousie.

other points are to do in the Madras and other districts what
has been done in the North West Provinces; improve the
irrigation, and open roads for conveying the cotton down. . . .
This is in truth the only thing that the Manchester people care
for, and if I can satisfy them that these points will not be
neglected, I hope to keep them all in good humour. They are
however a powerful body in the House of Commons, and
besides this I think they are right in their object; it would be
a great point to render ourselves somewhat independent of
United States cotton.'[1] Wood's next letter to Dalhousie
repeated that he was 'anxious to push forward the railroads
and irrigation'. An increased import of Indian cotton 'would be
a great national object, besides satisfying a large and powerful
party in this country'.[2] On 8 May he was, like Manchester, 'very
anxious to see a period of peace and internal improvement',
and favoured 'spending any surplus [revenue] in Public Works'.[3]

In his speech of 3 June Wood acknowledged the importance
of railways and public works to the British cotton interest.[4] He
promised that upon receiving Dalhousie's proposals 'no time
shall be lost in carrying the railroads through . . . and no
expense shall be spared to effect that object'. As for other
works, he alluded to the results of the inquiries into the
superintendence and execution of public works which the Company had commissioned in 1850.[5] Dalhousie's recommenda-
tions for a new department of public works in Bengal had been
approved, and similar organizational improvement would be
introduced in the other presidencies. He also referred to a
recent dispatch to India, providing for the reform of the system
of estimating public works requirements and costs in each

[1] Wood to Dalhousie, 24 March 1853.

[2] 8 April 1853.

[3] Letter to Dalhousie.

[4] Wood had been briefed by memoranda on public works by his secretary,
T. G. Baring ('Public Works, Bengal', n.d.), and by 'Mr [Edward] Thornton'
(31 May 1853) from the 'Examiner's Office', East India House (W.P. 36). For
the public works section of his speech, see op. cit., 1111–18.

[5] Dispatch from Court of Directors to Governor-General, 30 January 1850, in
'Board's Collections', No. 149,783, India Office Records. The reports of the
Commissioners, and the documents reflecting the action which arose from them,
appear in P.P. (H.C.) 1852–3, LXXIV, and 1854, XLVIII.

presidency, and thereby facilitating the control of the governor-general and the Home government over the execution of improvements. It also provided for 'a considerable portion of the revenue' to be spent annually on public works. Wood had had a large hand in shaping this dispatch.[1]

The first outcome of Wood's promise to hasten works of improvement was his ready approval of Dalhousie's proposals for India's great trunk railroads.[2] He had, in January, noted his inclination to have the main lines constructed by 'private Companies under Government control'.[3] Now, in July, with Dalhousie's scheme before him, he recorded that the government's guarantee of interest on the private capital invested in 'the construction of the main trunk lines . . . may properly be given'.[4] He wrote of the 'objects' of railways policy as 'the general & public advantages of the government & people of India generally, and also the commercial advantage of carrying produce to & from the coast'. He again expressed his concern to open 'the great cotton districts of Berar to the Western coast'. For these purposes, then, he agreed to the government's guarantee of 5 per cent per annum interest for ninety-nine years, on the capital invested by shareholders in the companies engaged upon constructing the authorized lines.[5] In so doing he was employing the method of financing and constructing Indian railways upon which Manchester had, four years earlier, placed its imprimatur. For in 1849 Bright and Cobden, to-

[1] Dispatch of 24 May (No. 32) 1853. The Court's copy of the document shows Wood's alterations in red ink ('India and Bengal Despatches', 81). They are also acknowledged in Stark to Melvill, 20 May 1853, in 'Letters from the Board to the Court', 17. Wood intended the dispatch to carry to India the form of the Parliamentary Ordnance Estimates which he had settled as Chancellor of the Exchequer, 1846–52 (Wood to Lieut.-Gen. G. Anson, 25 November 1854, W.P.).

[2] Wood to Dalhousie, 19 August 1853.

[3] Wood to Dalhousie, 22 January 1853.

[4] 'Memorandum on Indian Railroads', 30 July 1853, W.P. 27.

[5] A few months later, Wood was obliged to go further, and to guarantee principal as well as interest on £1 million worth of debentures in the East Indian Railway Company. He did so to avert a stoppage in construction when a gap in the cash flow was occasioned by the Company's inability to float its shares, guaranteed as to interest, on the capital-cautious money market of early 1854 (J. C. Melvill, *ex-officio* director of E.I.R. Company, to Wood, 9 June 1854, Hickleton papers; mem., W. P., 27; Wood to Dalhousie, 24 March, 8 April, 24 May, 24 June, 24 July 1854).

gether with other members of parliament for the Midlands
and representatives of Manchester commercial interests, had
attended at the Board of Control to press for the adoption of
the guarantee system.[1]

*   *   *

III

On 8 August Wood presented to the House of Commons his
first annual statement on the finances and the general progress
of the affairs of India.[2] He gave prominence to his efforts to
encourage the cultivation of cotton. He mentioned the recent
'lapse' of the cotton-growing state of Nagpur, which even
Manchester had not questioned in the House,[3] and spoke of
the surveys of the Godavery River which he had authorized.
If it proved navigable, the Godavery might 'open up one of
the greatest cotton districts in India, and bring down that
valuable product at a much cheaper rate than any . . . railway,
to the great advantage of the people of this country'. He told
of the progress which had been made in railway construction,
and of the large increase of funds which he had made available
for public works. Having at last learned that Dalhousie was
making good progress with the new public works departments,[4] he was able to report with satisfaction upon the
question of reorganization.

In a thin House, Wood's account of his efforts to promote
public works won the plaudits of Manchester. Though Bright
himself was absent, Sir T. E. Perry, who acclaimed 'the
soundness of his views' and argued that his speeches on Wood's
Bill in 1853 had revealed his 'statesmanlike mind', praised
Wood for giving 'to public works in India a stimulus such as
those enterprises had never before received'.[5] Danby Seymour

[1] Thorner, op. cit., pp. 158–9.

[2] *Hansard*, op. cit., 1450, 1452–7.

[3] Wood to Dalhousie, 8 March 1854. Dalhousie stressed the bearing of the
acquisition of Nagpur and Berar upon 'the supply of raw cotton' (4 March 1854).

[4] Dalhousie to Wood, 29 June 1854.

[5] Op. cit., 1464–6. Perry had retired from the post of chief justice of Bombay in
1852. In 1853 he had written a number of letters to *The Times* under the pseudo-
nym of 'Hadjee', opposing the renewal of the Company's charter (e.g. 7, 14
March). He was returned an M.P. in May 1854, and became a vocal opponent of

'admitted great improvement . . . had been made during the last twelve months in the government of India, which in great measure was due to the influence and exertions of [Wood] . . .'.[1] J. G. Phillimore 'fully concurred in the panegyrics which had been pronounced on the speech'.[2] He 'took great interest [in] . . . the navigation of the Godavery . . . [which] would do more for India than any other step that could be taken, and . . . enable us to grow cotton at a much cheaper cost than could be done by America itself'.

The Manchester school was clearly more sympathetic towards Wood's statement of August 1854 than it had been towards his Bill in 1853. There seems no doubt that the change of attitude arose from his attentiveness to the cotton question and from his vigorous prosecution of railways and public works. It seems reasonable to claim that the Manchester school underwrote the government's heavy investment of borrowed funds in public works,[3] and its pledge of the security of the returns on the capital invested in private railways.[4] Such

---

annexation (*D.N.B.*; R. P. Masani, op. cit., *passim*). Bright noted on 25 February 1855 that Seymour and Perry had 'called': 'Long conversation with . . . Perry [who] compliments me; . . . wishes me when war is over to lead the independent party in the House. . . . I spoke of my Sect and principles as great obstacles to any official career, which he and Seymour would not admit' (*Diaries*, op. cit., p. 191).

[1] *Hansard*, op. cit., 1474.

[2] Ibid., 1475.

[3] In his 'final minute', Dalhousie referred to the government's 'enormous expenditure . . . annually . . . upon public works', and attributed the financial deficiencies of the years 1853–6 to it. In 1853–4, £2½ million was so spent, in 1854–5 £3 million. While of these sums 'a very large proportion [was] expended on new works', in 1855–6 the estimated charge for what Wood had termed 'important' works was £2½ million. (*Dalhousie to Court, 28 February 1856*, P.P. (H.C.) 1856, xLv).

[4] Early in 1855, arrangements had already been made for railway companies to construct lines which would cost an estimated £22½ million to complete, on the understanding that the interest on the sums raised from time to time would be guaranteed at 5 per cent for ninety-nine years (*Select Committee on East India Railways*, P.P. (H.C.) 1857–8, xIv, see paras, indexed under 'Guarantee'; *Railways in India*, (1855), pp. 41–3). L. H. Jenks estimated that by summer 1857 the returns on £14 million had been so secured (*The Migration of British Capital to 1875* (1938), p. 213). J. N. Sahni (*Indian Railways . . . 1853 to 1953* (New Delhi, 1953), p. 187) and N. Sanyal (*Development of Indian Railways* (Calcutta, 1930), graph facing p. 1) agree with this estimate. From Sahni's data it appears that the rate of 'net earnings' on 'capital at charge' in 1855 was 0.7 per cent, in 1857, 1.25 per cent.

policies were consistent with those which Manchester espoused both before and after the period under review. In the late forties, 'manufacturers and Members of Parliament from Manchester . . . were among the leading advocates of governmental intervention to underwrite railways for India'.[1] And early in the sixties, the Chamber of Commerce 'called for a loan [of some £30 million or £40 million], backed if necessary by an imperial guarantee, to finance public works, in India'.[2]

Just as the costs of the earlier wars and annexations were met from the revenues of India, so now the interest charges which arose from the application of the Reformers' policy of internal development increased the dependency's financial burden. Ironically, in this instance Manchester's technique of 'exercising pressure . . . upon susceptible statesmen' contributed to the existence of a class of investors with a fixed interest in the permanence of the imperial connection. Manchester's Indian policy helped to create a class of rentiers or finance capitalists which Hobson later described as the 'taproot of Imperialism'.[3] Yet MacDonagh averred that 'anti-rentier' prejudice was endemic to 'free trade', and that Cobden 'fully anticipated Hobson's theory of imperialism'.

IV

In his analysis of the relationship between 'free trade' and imperialism in the 1850s, MacDonagh erred in concentrating almost exclusively upon Cobden's thought. He insisted that 'free trade' 'must mean doctrine translated into immediate political objects by specific persons and associations'. He ought therefore, in his consideration of 'free-trade' policy as regards India, to have looked beyond Cobden, who appreciated that

[1] Thorner, op. cit., p. 178.

[2] Redford, op. cit., II, 13.

[3] J. A. Hobson, *Imperialism. A Study* [1902] (1948 edition), pp. 81-2, 85. Jenks, pitching his emphasis somewhat later than the period under review, discerned a link between public works investment and imperialism: 'From 1857 to 1865 the major movement of British capital was towards India, to transform the land with public works. . . . And the effort that was made brought home with the dividends a spirit ripe for imperialism. . . .' (Op. cit., p. 207. See pp. 213-32 for Jenks's development of the argument that Indian railways investment played a central rôle in Britain's later extension of her empire.)

on this question he held 'opinions of a somewhat abstract kind and not adapted for the practical work of the day'.[1] At the time of the Mutiny, in the context of a discussion of Britain's government of India, he wrote: 'For a politician of my principles there is really no standing ground.'[2] He recognized as 'abstractions' the 'free-trade' principles which led him to denounce British rule in India as 'protectionist'.[3] By following Cobden's thought too exclusively, MacDonagh exaggerates 'the anti-imperialism of free trade' at the level of practical politics. In relation to India during the 1853–4 period, his 'free-trade' group employed its characteristic political technique to press a positive policy of economic development. It is necessary to recognize that as 'Reformers' they contributed to the strength and endurance of Britain's imperial connection with India.

[1] Cobden to Mr Ashworth, 16 October 1857, quoted in J. Morley, *The Life of Richard Cobden* (1903 edition), p. 671.
[2] Cobden to Col. Fitzmayer, 18 October 1857, ibid., p. 678.
[3] Ibid.

10 Wakefield and Marx

H. O. PAPPÉ

[This article was first published in the *Economic History Review*, 2nd series, Vol. IV (1951).]

I

Edward Gibbon Wakefield's rôle as an empire builder is today beyond dispute. He played an active part in the process of empire-building by persistently drawing attention to the possibilities of settlement in undeveloped areas of Australia and in New Zealand. However, his part in laying the foundation for a Commonwealth in the future was even more important. His share in the Durham report began, in J. S. Mill's words, 'a new era'. His never-ceasing interest in, and his fight for colonial responsible self-government have brought Graham Wallas to his opinion that 'there are few political inventors to whom historians would ascribe so large a measure of political success'.

When Wakefield took the political stage, emigrants were largely adventurers or fugitives. The adventurers went out to prepare themselves for a future in the home country, to which they were to return prosperous. The colonies were to them a means and not an end. The fugitives were partly compulsory emigrants, such as the convicts who provided largely the first two generations of the Australian settlement. Those who went out without legal compulsion were fugitives too. They were not – like the pilgrim fathers – bent on establishing a new country in which they would be able to worship God to their own private pattern. They had to escape the bleak age of a contorted society. To all those Wakefield held out the promise of a dignified life without the risks of a departure into the uncharted seas of a new lawless world.

He believed that it was possible to transplant the vital elements and the effective order of the mother country to the new world. It is this that has made his memory precious to those who approved the order which he helped to spread over the globe. His name, for this reason, carried more weight with those who contemplate 'Oceana' from the centre than with many living at the periphery. It is felt widely among the latter that the particular measures of Wakefield's systematic colonization soon came to grief. There were obviously innate economic and psychological weaknesses in the system arising from difficulty in arriving at a just price for the land, especially in areas that were surrounded by land free from Wakefield's restrictive policy and open to the speculative enterprise of the squatter. It is these technical failures which appear to condemn Wakefield in the eyes of some historians in Australia and New Zealand.

But it is another line of thought that has led to a much more pungent criticism in recent years. It is conceived from the viewpoint of the men of 1848 who feel that Wakefield's planning in terms of old-world society has spoilt the free development of a brave new world. This sceptical attitude is at the back of J. C. Beaglehole's description of Wakefield's work, and the same attitude has determined Fitzpatrick's bitter strictures.[1] The most outspoken condemnation of Wakefield's part in founding an inequitable society has been offered by W. B. Sutch.[2] He cannot see 'why Wakefield's name still receives honour in New Zealand school books'. He thinks that New Zealand had to develop a system of Social Security because its society, largely under Wakefield's influence, was based on a system of insecurity; an insecurity inevitably suffered by the less privileged in a class-ruled country. New Zealand thus differed considerably from other colonial societies, in particular the North American, where social services were felt a necessity only at a later stage. The basic make-up of the

---

[1] J. C. Beaglehole, *New Zealand. A Short History* (London, 1936). Brian Fitzpatrick, *The British Empire in Australia: An economic history, 1834–1939* (Melbourne, 1941), p. 40 et seq.

[2] *The Quest for Security in New Zealand* (Penguin Special, 1942).

early New Zealand colony was closely related to the *mentalité hiérarchique* and the economic system of the mother country, while the older colonies had pursued their own ways and had worked out their own social constitutions. 'That is why Edward Gibbon Wakefield's ideas are so important to the story of the quest of security, for whether he was responsible or not, it was the economic relationships advocated by him which produced conditions needing social services to alleviate them.'[1]

The general omission of Marx's name in this discussion[2] is curious, as Marx decidedly took sides in the debate on colonization; the more curious as it was Wakefield's writings on colonization which made him take up the challenge. For Marx, his views on colonization were considerably more than a contribution to contemporary controversy; they were to be the crowning confirmation of his economic theory.

II

'Modern Theory of Colonization' is the heading of the last chapter of Book 1 of *Capital*. It is entirely in the form of a controversy with E. G. Wakefield's *England and America* which had been published in 1833. It was not only in this context that Marx dealt with Wakefield, whom he considered as the most notable political economist of the thirties. There is a significant affinity between the two thinkers. Wakefield's idea of making the labourers, as potential purchasers of land in the colonies, pay for the immigration of future workers appears to be a striking illustration of Marx's surplus value theory. The statement that 'labour creates capital before capital employs labour'[3] seemed to anticipate Marx's famous version: 'By its surplus labour this year, the working class creates the capital that will next year employ additional labour.'[4]

A similar degree of agreement covers their factual approach

---

[1] Sutch, op. cit., p. iv.
[2] This applies also to such outstanding works as Dr Farnett's and Prof. Mills's. Of Wakefield's biographers only Dr Harrop mentions Marx, in passing.
[3] E. G. Wakefield, *England and America* (1833), Vol. II, p. 110.
[4] Marx, *Capital*, Vol. II, p. 640 (Everyman's edition).

to the question of the accumulation of capital. Marx distinguished between two types of private property, one of which is based upon the producer's own labour, while the other is based upon the labour of others. Current economic thinking lumped both kinds of property together under the term capital. Marx claimed that only the latter was capital, and that capital could grow only upon the tomb of the former or, in other words, upon the expropriation and exploitation of the small producers. This process of primary accumulation, i.e. of appropriation of the means of production by a minority, was more or less completed in the European scene. 'It is otherwise in the colonies. There the capitalist regime encounters on all hands the resistance of producers who own the means of production with which they work and who can gain wealth for themselves by their own labour instead of working to enrich a capitalist.'[1]

In the virgin conditions of new settlements it seemed to become obvious that capital was not more than a social relation between persons, rather than a stock of goods at a given moment.[2] This was illustrated in the case of Mr Peel who went to Western Australia with means of subsistence and of production to the value of £50,000, as well as with 300[3] persons; men, women, and children, of the working class. These, on arrival at Swan River, dispersed to take up land as independent owners, and Mr Peel was 'left without a servant to make his bed or fetch him water from the river'.[4] As long as it was possible to take up land and produce peacefully, anyone could accumulate on his own account. Capitalist accumulation was impossible under such conditions.

'Where land is very cheap and all men are free, where every one who so pleases can easily obtain a piece of land for himself, not only is labour very dear, as respects the labourers' share of the produce, but the difficulty is to obtain combined

[1] Ibid., p. 848.

[2] Ibid., p. 849.

[3] Marx mistakenly thought they had been 3000. Also elsewhere he is not completely reliable in his quotations from Wakefield.

[4] E. G. Wakefield, *England and America*, Vol. II, p. 33.

labour at any price.'[1] Under such conditions, hired workers soon 'would have ceased to be labourers for hire; they would have become independent landowners, if not competitors with their former masters in the market of labour'.[2] This is what happened in the North American colonies up to the time of the Civil War, where the progressive population of the frontier was not to be counted upon as hired labourers.

To Wakefield this development appeared to be an unnatural state of affairs. He considered the division of labour and the accumulation of capital as part of the social contract. The development leading to the division of the people into owners of capital and owners of labour rested, like every step in civilization, 'on concert or combination amongst all the members of society';[3] and it was in order to prevent what he considered a dispersion of national wealth and to further 'primary accumulation' that Wakefield advocated 'systematic colonization'. His intention was to transfer the stratified society of England to the colonies by means of a strictly enforced social constitution.

Marx, on the other hand, though he agreed about the facts, concluded that the passion for owning land was a natural and justified claim of the individual. He urged that capitalists had been created artificially in the mother country. In the colonies, he said, Wakefield's systematic colonization was called upon to produce wage-earners. This development was far from being natural, as Wakefield had claimed. In fact, Marx commented, if there were such a natural law, then 'the mass of mankind (would have) expropriated itself, in honour of the accumulation of capital. One would suppose, then, that this instinct for self-denying fanaticism would, above all, have free play in the colonies; for there only do men and things exist under conditions which might make it possible to translate a social contract from dreamland into the world of reality. Were things thus, why should systematic colonization be called upon to replace the spontaneous colonization which is its opposite?'

[1] Ibid., Vol. I, p. 247.
[2] Ibid., Vol. II, p. 5.
[3] Ibid., Vol. I, p. 17.

Such, in a simplifying rearrangement, is the gist of the Wakefield–Marx controversy.

III

Habent fata sua libelli. Wakefield's thought suffered an eclipse in the nineteenth century. Marx's theory of colonization gave rise to that controversy on imperialism to which Hobson, Rosa Luxemburg, Lenin, Hilferding, Schumpeter, and Hancock have contributed. The discussion has narrowed down to the question of colonies ruled by the mother country. It has, at the same time, widened out into an analysis of the causes of imperialist wars and of the final fate of capitalism. However, there is sufficient substance in its original form to justify its rescue from oblivion.

One point of striking interest emerges at a first glance. It is that Wakefield and Marx should travel such a distance together. We have got used to the spectacle of capitalists and socialists differing deeply in their fundamental approach to social economic questions. We are apt to forget that their starting-point was the same and their methods were originally alike. When Marx attacked the Wakefield scheme as the prototype of the villainous capitalist system, he did not mean to whitewash other contemporary methods by contrast. He intended this as little as he meant to single out England when he exposed labour conditions there. He was aware of the fact that these conditions were much worse on the continent: *De te fabula narratur*, he assured his German reader. He realized that Wakefield's scheme was not the alternative to an equalitarian development. He was much more critical of the virtual monopolies granted by contemporary colonial practice in America and Australia. The appeal of 'systematic colonization' to an exemplary stock of settlers was too obvious to be overlooked. Marx wanted to expose the Wakefield scheme as the best that capitalism could produce in the circumstances, and he wanted to show that the best was not good enough. But he was not intent on condemning individuals, whom he held to be unconscious tools of a development they were not able to grasp. 'I should be the last to hold the individual responsible for conditions whose creature he himself is, socially considered, however much he may raise himself above them subjectively.'

Marx was steeped deeply in classical economic thought. He accepted the analysis of classical economics but he differed in the conclusions which he derived from the liberal premises. If liberals saw in the colonies only useless ornaments of governments, Marx saw in them the last straw to which capitalism in its decay could cling. Wakefield, though liberal, was (in common with other utilitarians) nearer to Marx in this respect than to Adam Smith. He accepted Malthus's pessimistic view and is likely to have based his ideas upon Ricardo's opinion that 'with a population pressing against the means of subsistence, the only remedies are either a reduction of people or a more rapid accumulation of capital. In rich countries, where all the fertile land is already cultivated, the latter remedy is neither very practicable nor very desirable, because its effect would be, if pushed very far, to render all classes equally poor.'[1] According to Wakefield, there were three reasons which made colonization desirable and necessary. All three were connected with the pressure of population upon the means of subsistence.

(1) *The extension of markets* for manufactured goods, so as to provide England with cheap corn not available elsewhere.

(2) *Enlargement of the field for employing capital,* offering possibilities of investment better than those at home. There was a definite limit to the 'field of employment' of capital, as Wakefield never tired of emphasizing. 'It does not follow that, because labour is employed by capital, capital always finds a field in which to employ labour.' Wakefield developed this thought in his commentary on the *Wealth of Nations* and thought he had discovered a new principle. What was new, however, was only the emphasis on a maxim which, in J. S. Mill's words. was actually a corollary of the principles of classical economy. It has, indeed, become one of the major tenets of Marxian theory which, in different form, holds that there is a definite and self-destructive limit to the accumulation of capital. Because of this, capitalism, it is held, must branch out into the temporary relief offered by Imperialism, i.e. by additional (and

[1] *Principles*, Chapter V, On Wages.

equally exhaustible) fields of employment in the colonies. Yet little credit has been given to Wakefield by those who share his attitude. There seems to be no mention of Wakefield's name, for instance, in Maurice Dobb's *Political Economy and Capitalism*, a book in which the concept of the field of employment of capital looms large.

(3) *Relief from excessive numbers:* This, in retrospect, seems to be an obvious enough remedy for the impasse of the Bleak Age. But Wakefield's agreement with socialists was only superficial on this point. Like them he saw an impasse, but unlike them he did not want to change the system. He wanted to relieve pressure and restore the old balance of order. He developed this thought as an alternative to the original proposal by philosophical radicalism of securing full employment at high wages on the whole labouring population through a voluntary restriction of their numbers.

There was, of course, widespread opposition to colonization from those desiring a plentiful supply of cheap labour. But excess of numbers and low wages lost their attraction with the growing discontent and revolutionary spirit of the industrial revolution. High wages became a necessity in order to preserve security for property. The class struggle was looming large

in a country situated like England, in which the ruling and the subject orders are no longer separated by a middle class, and in which the subject order, composing the bulk of the people, are in a state of gloomy discontent arising from excessive numbers; for such a country, one chief end of colonization is to prevent tumults, to keep the peace, to maintain order, to uphold confidence in the security of property, to hinder interruptions of the regular course of industry and trade, to avert the terrible evils which, in a country like England, could not but follow any serious political convulsion.[1]

This, one thinks, could have been written by Marx; and, though they differed in their choice of remedies, Wakefield and Marx were largely agreed in stressing the importance of labour

[1] E. G. Wakefield, *England and America*, Vol. II, p. 105.

in the process of creating wealth against 'those political economists who worship capital'.[1]

IV

So much for the ends of colonization as regards the mother country. Actually it is rather their attitude towards the ends of colonization as respects the colony that provides an insight into Wakefield's and Marx's innermost minds. It will be helpful to contrast their views with those of Adam Smith.

Both Marx and Adam Smith were agreed that the conditions of virgin countries, such as America, were ideal for the development of free societies. For Smith the following elements: free, educated, and disciplined colonists, plentiful and cheap land, and high wages were bound to lead to a rise in population, health, wealth, and greatness.

This was in direct contrast to Wakefield who, indeed, had attacked Smith's ideas on colonization as early as in *A Letter from Sydney*. For Wakefield, America was not a Jeffersonian paradise but a Hamiltonian world in the making. He maintained that no progress was attainable but by the method of inequality and compulsion which had developed the European scene. The natural dependence, in ancient civilized countries, of the labourer on the capitalists had to be created in the colonies by artificial means. It was just the newness of the territory with its vast opportunities that blocked the road to progress. It was the government's duty to interfere with colonial development and to establish and maintain the most desirable proportion between people and territory, thus guaranteeing an ample supply of labourers for hire.

> According to Dr Smith, therefore, the [Americans] ought by this time to have rivalled at least, if not to have surpassed, their parent state in wealth and greatness. Yet look at their condition. Their metropolis is not to be compared to many of the mere pleasure-towns of England. Want of capital prevented the State of New York from commencing its great Canal from Lake Erie until long after the profit of that

[1] Ibid., Vol. II, p. 96.

undertaking had been demonstrated; and other States are now attempting to raise money in London for great works, which cannot be undertaken unless capital be obtained from the parent country. In the useful arts, excepting only perhaps that of steam-navigation, they are far behind the parent country. Their manufactures, miserable at best, exist only through restrictive laws. Thus the doctrine of Adam Smith concerning the effect of cheap land and dear labour, in producing national wealth and greatness, has been refuted by the safest of all arguments – an ample experiment.'[1]

Marx and Smith equally looked with favour at the young emerging economy of the colonies. Yet both Marx and Wakefield differed from Adam Smith in picturing the particular state of affairs in the New World not as something *sui generis*, but as a transitory stage of development. This would lead inevitably to old-world conditions once the possibilities of the frontier with their boundless extent of fertile land were exhausted. For Marx this was a process of regression to an inferior order of society. It proved to him that inequality with regard to the possession of productive means, including the land, was at the root of the evil embodied in capitalist society. For Wakefield it was only at this stage, i.e. when labour had become plentiful and cheap, that the disadvantages of a new society would give way to the cultural advantages of an old nation. Society would become firmly established in a definite order and be assured of workers to carry out profitable schemes of development. If the American solution through slavery and the Australian method of using convict labour were no longer morally acceptable, then it was desirable to create a decent menial class by law.

If Adam Smith was a humanitarian optimist, both Wakefield and Marx appear as pessimists regarding human propensities. Marx obviously fears the depraving influence of trade and industry; he can imagine benefits to be derived from the division of labour only if a radically changed human nature is made sociable through the agency of a new economic system.

[1] E. G. Wakefield, *A Letter from Sydney* (Everyman's edition), p. 74.

Wakefield's pleading is in favour of interference by the superior knowledge of tradition and learning as a safeguard against the pernicious trends of undirected development.

Both then may be regarded as planners in the modern sense of the word. However, Wakefield was an outstanding representative of liberal economic thought. And equally in Marx's case there are elements that allow for a different interpretation. In his writings on colonization and the more distant past he extols the free, self-dependent, pre-capitalist farmers (in contrast to the European peasants, those 'troglodytes of civilization'). The flourishing state of fifteenth-century England appealed to him as well as the picture of the unlimited freedom of the colonies. He was not wedded to the Stakhanovite ideal as his epigones contend. On the contrary, he was desperately opposed to the idea of specialization and the principle of the division of labour. Just as Hobbes had attacked Aristotle on this score, so Marx maintained that 'Plato's Republic, in so far as it discusses the division of labour as the formative principle of the State, is nothing but an Athenian idealization of the Egyptian caste system'.[1] His ideal was the rounded personality who can do everything that others do.

This romantic view places Marx well within the company of colonial radicalism. There the advances of technology (and, for that, of European preponderance) were viewed with dismay. Jefferson, despite his great learning, was deeply distrustful of Pandora's gifts. 'In Europe', he said, 'the lands are either cultivated, or locked up against the cultivator. Manufacture must therefore be resorted to of necessity, not of choice, to support the surplus of their people. But we have an immensity of land courting the industry of the husband-man. . . . Those with labour in the earth are the chosen people of God. . . . Dependence (upon customers) begets subservience and venality, suffocates the germ of virtue, and prepares fit tools for the design of ambition.'[2]

Marx then, appears as less doctrinaire than Marxists would often make one believe. On the other hand, he does not appear

[1] *Capital*, p. 388.
[2] *The Living thought of Jefferson* (ed. Dewey), pp. 70, 74.

as a liberal. Though he was so sharply opposed to Wakefield's systematic colonization, he was himself a planner.

V

Wakefield's planning seems to have been concerned only with means. His aim was not to design a new society, but to transplant the conditions for organic growth of the old world to the new. It may be helpful to consider first his place within colonial thought.

Marx we found to be akin to the spirit of the colonial population of the frontier. Though Wakefield played an outstanding rôle in the fight for colonial self-determination and self-government, it may well be said that he viewed colonization through the eyes of the mother country. What he wanted to preserve was the civilization that had grown up in the old world. A system of 'shovelling out paupers' was bound to turn colonies into prison centres ('The Governor of New South Wales is a jailer'), or else into anarchical settlements of the early whaling or later gold-mining type. With no traditional restraints, freedom of enterprise and license of vice were found to be the same thing in practice. Wakefield's concern (and achievement) was therefore, as John Stuart Mill put it, 'that the flower and not the refuse of the old country should be transferred to the new'.

Wakefield, the professed expert on colonial administration, actually thought of colonies as his future home. The vision that drove him was the picture of his paradise re-gained, a paradise that he had irretrievably lost through his own action. He was as single-minded and strong-willed as Marx. As Marx marked out his road in the *Communist Manifesto*, so Wakefield conjured up his vision in his greatest piece of writing, his first treatment of the colonial problem, *A Letter from Sydney*. It was his way of escape from Newgate prison where he had been sent for his attempt at abducting from a boarding school a young heiress whom he wanted to marry for ambition's sake. The rôle that was denied his ambition and ability on the English scene was yet to be provided where his past would not discount him.

This personal motive explains much of Wakefield's zeal and consistency. The colonies were to be made attractive for his like, i.e. for 'a man of independent fortune who prefers his library, even to the beauties of nature, and to whom intellectual society is necessary for his peace of mind'.[1] A colonial career was to be made honourable and worthy of a gentleman.

This is a far cry from the conventional romantic conception. But, though it was connected with a practically new colonial technique, the attitude was well in the colonial tradition. For centuries it had been the ambition of younger sons, and others without an adequate outlet for their enterprise, to found a new home overseas that was safe for gentlemen. The experience won in Ireland under the Tudor re-conquest had left its mark upon the great colonizers of future times. In the pamphlets of the sixteenth century on colonization the same note is struck as in the nineteenth-century discussion. 'Unemployment and overpopulation, the missionary motive, and a union of profit and fame – experience soon taught the persuasive quality of these arguments.'[2] As far as colonial promoters were concerned, the 'condition of England' motive was no particular feature of the early-Victorian period.

Wakefield's technique, as H. Mumford Jones tells us, was anticipated by Francis Bacon who, in his proposals for a feudal constitution for the Irish settlement, had stressed the necessity of living together in towns in order to reap the benefits of the division of labour.[3] Wakefield meant to use the scientific method of systematic colonization to bring about a conventional result. He wanted to ease the birth pangs of his new society, or more accurately, he wanted it to jump the adolescent stage and start like a homunculus at maturity. It may then well be said that, despite his system, he was eventually not a planner, and that Marx was not right in accusing him of interfering with the free play of natural development.

---

[1] *A Letter from Sydney*, p. 11.

[2] Howard Mumford Jones, *Ideas in America* (Harvard, 1944), p. 57.

[3] Also William Penn planned the Philadelphia settlement as 'a great town', aimed to assure the benefits for society of 'help, trade, education, and government, also roads, travel, entertainment', see Curtis F. Nettels, *The Roots of American Civilisation* (New York, 1938), p. 160.

VI

However, the controversy about planning does not lead us far. Nobody who approaches the world with an ordering mind is free from the taint of planning. The divergence consists in differing opinions regarding the methods that are to bring about the desired social ideal. There is no doubt that Marx and Wakefield stood for different methods. Can it be said that this was because their ultimate social aims were not the same? Marx's ideas on this point were those of the French Revolution, fraternity, liberty, equality. Equality was for him the key to his millennium.

Wakefield cannot be classed as easily as Marx. He was curiously half-way between Carlyle–Disraelian conservatism and Whiggish economics. It would be absurd to class him with those we understand to have been rugged individualists. He had a keen social conscience. He knew as well as William Cobbett about the 'poverty, misery, and pauperism that were becoming so frightful in the country'.[1] He did not approve of self-interest let loose.

Both Marx and Wakefield, it may be said, would have agreed on the issue of liberty. Where they differed, was in their attitudes towards equality. The French Revolution had not succeeded in reconciling the ideal of liberty and the passion for equality, in fact, 'le système de l'égalité chassa celui de la liberté'.[2] The liberal concluded from this that the two concepts were incompatible, and that there was something like a natural hierarchy in society. Marx attributed the failure of the revolution to the abortive attempt at grafting liberal principles on an economic order that, by definition, was based upon inequality. Hence his economic teaching.

However, though we have laid our hands here upon a fundamental difference between Marx and Wakefield, it does not seem to be a necessary condition for their diverging conclusions. There are outstanding believers in *laissez-faire* who

[1] *Rural Rides*, 1 August 1823.
[2] Mallet du Pan, as quoted by A. P. D'Entreves, *Cambridge Journal*, 1, No. 2, p. 104.

share in Marx's ultimate aims. The great divergence, then, is one of methods derived from a different reading of historical experience.

If we want to bring the divergence between Marx and Wakefield to a simple formula, it would boil down to this: while they agreed in their critical attitude towards the society of the old world, Wakefield considered the disease as symptomatic and curable, whereas Marx thought it was constitutional, and that the old society had to die to give place to a new society.

Wakefield as a man need not be defended against backwardness. He did more to create a new world within the limits of the period than Marx. But if Marx erred in the sweeping extent of his condemnation before he had means to substitute a better society, Wakefield was too complacent in his acceptance of this society. He put his finger upon the social sores of his time, but he also would have liked to set the scene for a replica of the order that had caused them. Already Adam Smith had added a note of gloom to his optimistic outlook when he considered 'the enormous debts which at present oppress, and will in the long run probably ruin, all the great nations of Europe'.[1] A reverberation of such thoughts appears in Wakefield's theory of the field of employment of capital. But he brushed the uncomfortable thought aside, though he should have anticipated similar difficulties for a later stage of his colonial dream. He wanted to re-build for his own purposes an extension of Britain overseas with its differences in individual wealth. But he, like Marx, thought that the European world was in danger of foundering on the rocks of economic misery and had to be relieved of its human ballast. He therefore must needs hope for a more balanced order than the one he left. Though in him the vision was less accentuated than it was in Carlyle, Dickens, J. S. Mill, Ruskin, Morris, he had started out with a vision of a better world of healthier and lovelier people and of laws forbidding the existence of want, of an Australia Felix.

However, we must not make too much of this. Wakefield

[1] *Wealth of Nations*, Book V, Chapter III, p. 863.

was fundamentally in accord with the aristocratic order from which he started. This is why his reform proposals were concerned with details only. Unlike Marx, he was not a perfectionist. Or to be correct, the liberal economist in him was, but the member of the ruling class in him was not. If we class him among the rationalists because of his professed belief in *laissez-faire*, we have to do so with a qualification. He was not a liberal of Adam Smith's stamp, whose Scottish origin and commercial interests and eighteenth-century mind emphasized a democratic outlook. Wakefield was not naturally inclined to scrap past experience and to base his economic or social plans upon the abstract power of reasoning. He did not want to cut the ties of tradition, that capital and bank of the ages. He made it clear that by 'a new people' he understood an uncivilized people that had still to acquire the benefits of accumulated age-old wisdom. We recall his unfavourable report upon the American settlements, which contrasted with Marx's more admiring view of the U.S.A. Indeed, the report shed more light upon Wakefield than upon the U.S.A. When he wrote it in Newgate prison, America was as unknown to him as Australasia. His knowledge (so often full of an intuitive grasp) was based upon reading, and among the available reports he was free to pick what suited his pleading. But at the same time Tocqueville, the greatest observer of the American scene, was writing that no people in the world had made such rapid progress in trade and manufactures as the Americans . . . 'despite almost unsurmountable natural impediments. . . . In the United States the greatest undertakings are executed without difficulty, because the whole population is engaged in productive industry, and because the poorest as well as the most opulent members of the commonwealth are ready to combine their efforts for these purposes.'[1] This judgement was, in 1844, fully upheld by John Robert Godley, the founder of the Canterbury settlement, who extolled the superiority of the Americans 'in all the faculties . . . which contribute to produce . . . material civilization'.[2]

[1] Alexis de Tocqueville, *Democracy in America*, Oxford Classics, ed. H. S. Commager, p. 425.
[2] *Letters from America*, Vol. I, p. ix.

Wakefield was blind to the possibilities innate in an equalitarian world. They were unknown, whereas the noble components of the old aristocratic order were known – not less than the drawbacks.

The pitfalls of both the aristocratic and egalitarian attitudes should be obvious. Both contain the germ of oppression if not watched. The one offers the high standard developed by and within an aristocratic class, the other that regard for man without which any order is bound to end in oppression and revolt. 'Both are imperfect, both are useful in their way, and therefore both are best together, to correct or to confirm one another.'[1] Both Wakefield and Marx have something to teach us.

[1] William Hazlitt, *Table Talk*, On Genius and Common Sense (Collins ed.), p. 45.

Select Bibliography

The works listed below are intended only to start students and teachers on their own investigations. The list is therefore selective. It does not include the articles in this volume, but mentions the most important of the publications cited in the footnotes to the Introduction.

1. *General Works on Imperialism*

FIELDHOUSE, D. K. '"Imperialism": an Historiographical Revision', *Economic History Review*, 2nd series, XIV (1961).

FIELDHOUSE, D. K. *The Theory of Capitalist Imperialism* (London, 1967 – Problems and Perspectives in History series).

HOBSON, J. A. *Imperialism, a Study* (3rd edn., rev., 1938).

JENKS, L. H. *The Migration of British Capital to 1875* (London, 1963).

KOEBNER, R. and SCHMIDT, H. D. *Imperialism: The Story and Significance of a Political Word 1840–1960* (Cambridge, 1964).

SCHUMPETER, J. A. (ed. P. M. Sweezy) *Imperialism and Social Classes* (Oxford, 1951).

SHAW, A. G. L. 'A Revision of the Meaning of Imperialism', *Australian Journal of Politics and History*, Vol. VII (1961).

WINSLOW, E. M. *The Pattern of Imperialism* (Columbia Univ. Press, 1948).

WINSLOW, E. M. 'Marxian, Liberal and Social Theories of Imperialism', *Journal of Political Economy*, XXXIX (1931).

2. *British Attitudes to the Empire*

BELL, K. N. and MORRELL, W. P. (ed.) *Select Documents on British Colonial Policy, 1830–1860* (Oxford, 1928).

BENNETT, GEORGE *The Concept of Empire* (London, 1953).

BURROUGHS, P. 'Parliamentary Radicals and the Reduction of Imperial Expenditure in British North America, 1827–1834', *Historical Journal*, XI (1968).
Cambridge History of the British Empire, Vol. II (1940).

COWAN, HELEN *British Emigration to North America* (Toronto, 1961).

HARLOW, V., and MADDEN, F. (ed.) *British Colonial Developments, 1774–1834* (Oxford, 1953).

KNAPLUND, P. *James Stephen and the British Colonial System* (Madison, 1953).

KNORR, K. E. *British Colonial Theories, 1570–1850* (Toronto, 1944).

MELLOR, G. R. *British Imperial Trusteeship, 1783–1850* (London, 1951).

MORRELL, W. P. *British Colonial Policy in the Age of Peel and Russell* (Oxford, 1930).

SCHUYLER, R. L. *The Fall of the Old Colonial System: a Study in British Empire Free Trade, 1770–1870* (O.U.P., 1945).

SHAW, A. G. L. 'British Attitudes to the Colonies, ca. 1820–1850', *Journal of British Studies*, IX (1969).

3. *The Classical Economists and 'Imperialism'*.

BLACK, R. D. C. *Economic Thought and the Irish Question, 1817–1870* (Cambridge, 1960).

CORRY, B. A. *Money, Savings and Investment in English Economics, 1800–1850* (London, 1962).

MERIVALE, H. *Lectures on Colonies and Colonization* (London, 1841).

MILL, JOHN STUART *Principles of Political Economy* (1848. 7th edn. 1871 – ed., W. J. Ashley, London, 1909).

ROBBINS, L. *The Theory of Economic Policy in English Classical Political Economy* (London, 1952).

ROBBINS, L. *Robert Torrens and the Evolution of Classical Economics* (London, 1958).

TUCKER, G. S. L. *Progress and Profits in British Economic Thought, 1650–1850* (C.U.P., 1960).

WAKEFIELD, E. G. *A View of the Art of Colonization 1849*. (Oxford, 1913).

WINCH, D. *Classical Political Economy and Colonies* (London, 1965).

4. *The Imperialism of Free Trade*

FERNS, H. S. 'Britain's Informal Empire in Argentina, 1806–1914', *Past and Present*, Vol. IV (1953).

FERNS, H. S. *Britain and Argentina in the Nineteenth Century* (Oxford, 1960).

HARNETTY, P. 'The Imperialism of Free Trade: Lancashire and the Indian Cotton Duties, 1859–1862', *Economic History Review*, 2nd ser., XVIII (1968).

HOPKINS, A. G. 'Economic Imperialism in West Africa–Lagos, 1880–92', *Economic History Review*, 2nd ser., XXI (1968).

MATHEW, W. M. 'The Imperialism of Free Trade: Peru, 1820–70'. *Economic History Review*, 2nd ser., XXI (1968).

PLATT, D. C. M. *Finance, Trade and Politics in British Foreign Policy, 1815–1914* (O.U.P., 1968).

PLATT, D. C. M. 'The Imperialism of Free Trade – some reservations', *Economic History Review*, 2nd ser., XXI (1968).